westermann

EinFach
Englisch

LITERATURE

Series Editor:
Iris Edelbrock

John Lanchester

The Wall

Edited by
Iris Edelbrock

Sprachliche Betreuung: John Poziemski

westermann GRUPPE

John Lanchester: The Wall, Faber & Faber Limited, London
© by Orlando Books Limited, 2019

© 2020 Westermann Bildungsmedien Verlag GmbH, Braunschweig, www.westermann.de

Druck A[1] / Jahr 2020
Alle Drucke der Serie A sind im Unterricht parallel verwendbar.

Redaktion: Marion Kramer
Umschlaggestaltung: LIO Design, Braunschweig; Foto: alamy images/David Colbran
Druck und Bindung: Westermann Druck GmbH, Braunschweig

ISBN 978-3-14-**127390**-8

Contents

John Lanchester
The Wall

Additional material

Additional texts

Skills & vocabulary

In memory of Peggie Geraghty

I
THE WALL

1

It's cold on the Wall. That's the first thing everybody tells you, and the first thing you notice when you're sent there, and it's the thing you think about all the time you're on it, and it's the thing you remember when you're not there any more. It's cold on the
5 Wall.

You look for metaphors. It's cold as slate, as diamond, as the moon. Cold as charity – that's a good one. But you soon realise that the thing about the cold is that it isn't a metaphor. It isn't like anything else. It's nothing but a physical fact. This kind of cold,
10 anyway. Cold is cold is cold.

So that's the first thing that hits you. It isn't like other cold. This is a cold that is all about the place, like a permanent physical at-tribute of the location. The cold is one of its fundamental proper-ties; it's intrinsic. So it hits you as a package, the first time you go
15 to the Wall, on the first day of your tour. You know that you are there for two years. You know that it's basically the same every-where, as far as the geography goes, but that everything depends on what the people you will be serving with are like. You know that there's nothing you can do about that. It is frightening but
20 also in its way a little bit freeing. No choice – everything about the Wall means you have no choice.

You get a little training but not much. Six weeks. Mainly it's about how to hold, clean, look after and fire your weapon. In that order. Some fitness training, but not much; a lot of training in midnight
25 awakening, sleep disruption, sudden panics, sudden changes of or-der, small-hours tests of discipline. They drum that into you: disci-pline trumps courage. In a fight, the people who win are the ones who do what they're told. It's not like it is in films. Don't be brave, just do what you're told. That's pretty much it. The rest of the train-
30 ing happens on the Wall. You get it from the Defenders who've been there longer than you. Then in your turn you give it to the Defenders who come after. So that's what you arrive able to do: get up in the middle of the night, and look after your weapon.

You usually arrive after dark. I don't know why but that's just
35 how they do it. Already you had a long day to get there: walk, bus, train, second train, lorry. The lorry drops you off. You and your rucksack are left standing there in the cold and the blackness. There is the Wall in front of you, a long low concrete monster. It stretches into the distance. Although the Wall is completely verti-
40 cal, when you stand underneath it, it feels as if it overhangs. As if it could topple over onto you. You feel leant on.

slate *Schiefer*

intrinsic being an important and basic characteristic of sb./sth.

disruption *Unterbrechung, Störung*
small hours early morning hours starting after midnight
to trump *trumpfen*

lorry truck

to topple over to lose balance and fall down

moisture *Feuchtigkeit*

The air is full of moisture, even when it isn't actually wet, which it often is, either with rain or with sea-spray splashing over the top. It isn't usually windy, immediately behind the Wall, but it sometimes is. In the dark and the damp, the Wall looks black. The only path or sign or hint for what you should do or where you ⁵ should go is a flight of concrete steps – they always drop you near

flight a set of steps, usually between two floors of a building

the steps. There's a small light at the top, in the guard house, but you don't yet know that's what you're looking at. Instead what you mainly think is that the Wall is taller than you expected. Of course you've seen it before, in real life, and in pictures, maybe ¹⁰ even in your dreams. (That's one of the things you learn on the Wall: that lots of people dream about it, long before they're sent there.) But when you're standing at the bottom looking up, and you know you're going to be there for two years, and that the best thing that can happen to you in those two years is that you sur- ¹⁵ vive and get off the Wall and never have to spend another day of your life anywhere near it – then it looks different. It looks very

exposed having no protection from bad weather
steep *steil*
trapped caught

tall and very straight and very dark. (It is.) The exposed concrete stairs look steep and slippery. (They are.) It looks like a cold, hard, unforgiving, desperate place. (It is.) You feel trapped. (You are.) ²⁰ You are longing for this to be over; longing to be somewhere else; you would give anything not to be here. Maybe, even if you're not religious, you say a prayer, out loud or under your breath, it

under your breath quietly, so that other people cannot hear (exactly) what you are saying

doesn't matter, because it doesn't change anything, because your prayer says, please please please let me get off the Wall, and yet ²⁵ there you are, on the Wall. You start up the steps. You've begun your life on the Wall.

I was shaking as I went up the stairs; I'd like to think it was from the cold but it was probably half that and half fear. There was no

guard rail *Geländer*
damp slightly wet, esp. in an unpleasant way

guard rail and the concrete was more and more damp as I climbed. ³⁰ I've never been good with heights, even quite low ones. It crossed my mind that I might slip and fall off and that thought grew as I got higher up. I'm going to fall off and split my head open and die, and my time on the Wall will be over before it's even begun, I

punchline *Pointe*

thought. I'll be a punchline. Remember that idiot who …? But if ³⁵ that happens, at least I'll be off the Wall.

At the top I got to the guard house. Light was coming through a frosted window. I couldn't see in. I didn't know where to go or what to do, but there were no other options, so I knocked. There was no reply. I knocked again and heard a noise and took that as ⁴⁰ a sign to go in.

I stepped in and a wave of warmth flooded over me. My glasses immediately fogged up so I couldn't see. I heard somebody laugh and somebody else say something under their breath. I took my

to squint to look with almost closed eyes

glasses off and squinted around. The room was an undecorated ⁴⁵

concrete box. The walls were covered in maps. Two people sat in the opposite corners, one of them an imposing black man with scarred cheeks wearing an olive-green cabled uniform sweater. This was the Captain, though I didn't know that yet. He was the
5 only person on the Wall I ever saw wearing uniform. For the rest of us it simply wasn't warm enough. He looked at me unsmiling. Behind him there were three computer monitors with a green-screen radar display.

"A Defender who can't see," he said. "Great."
10 The other person snorted. This was a heavy-set white man wearing a red knitted cap: the Sergeant, though I didn't know that yet either.

"I'm Kavanagh," I eventually said. "I'm new." It seems idiotic now and it seemed idiotic then, but I had no idea what else to say. The
15 two of them didn't even laugh. They just looked at me. The man in uniform got up and walked over to me and looked me up and down. He was tall, at least half a head taller than me.

"I'm the Captain," he said. "This is the Sergeant. Do everything we tell you to without questioning why. It takes about four
20 months before you know what you're doing. I have complete power to extend your stay here, without appeal. I don't have to give a reason. The only way you get off the Wall is that two years go past, and I decide to let you go. If they didn't make that clear in training, I'm making it clear now. Is it clear?"
25 It was. I said so.

"Take him to the barracks," he said to the Sergeant. "I'm going out on the Wall."

He left. The Sergeant's demeanour changed a little when he was on his own.
30 "Right," he said. "There are two sergeants, one for each shift. I'm yours. The other one is on the Wall. I should be in bed but I stayed up to meet you because I'm a fucking saint. Ask anyone. You'll meet the rest of your shift in the morning. I'll give you a quick version of the tour. The rest you can fill in tomorrow. Like the
35 Captain said, it takes a while for it all to sink in, and the best way is through repetition. You can ask questions at the beginning but everyone gets sick of that pretty quickly, so I'd advise you to think if there's an obvious answer to whatever it is you're asking before you open your gob."
40 He showed me around the mess hall, which was a bare concrete box with tables and chairs, the rec room, which was a bare concrete box with a huge television and badly battered sofas, the armoury, which was locked, and the infirmary, which was a bare concrete box with four steel-framed beds and no medical staff.
45 Then he led me down two flights of stairs to the barracks, which

imposing *achtunggebietend*

scarred *vernarbt*
cabled *im Zopfmuster*

to snort *schnauben*
heavy-set *having a large, wide, strong body*

eventually *schließlich, letztendlich*

demeanour [dɪˈmiːnər] *a way of looking and behaving*

shift *shift*

gob (*BE, sl.*) *mouth*
mess hall *Kantine*
bare *empty, without any decoration*
rec room *short for recreation room; Erholungsbereich*
battered *in a poor state, esp. by being used a lot*
armoury *a place where weapons and military equipment are stored*
infirmary *here: room for medical treatment*

is what Defenders called the room where everyone slept. It too was a bare concrete box. After standing in the entrance for about a minute, my eyes adapted enough to be able to make out the main details. There were thirty beds in the room, fifteen on each side, with plywood partitions separating them into cubicles. At the far end was the washroom. I was already familiar with the layout because it was the same as the barracks where I had done my training. One side had no external light source, the other had small square windows above head height. The beds along the right-hand wall were all empty, because that half of the company was on night duty. The beds along the left-hand wall were all occupied by sleeping bodies, except the ninth bed along, which had been empty and was now mine.

plywood *Sperrholz*
partition *Aufteilung*
cubicle *Schlafzelle*

I put my bag down in the back of the cubicle. I took off my shoes and my outer layers of clothing and got into the bed. The sheets were rough but the two blankets were thick and I quickly warmed up. I could hear snores and muttering from my new squad companions. Being hungry makes me speedy; I realised I hadn't eaten since setting out, and that my mind was whirring too fast to sleep. Tired, wakeful, apprehensive, I lay there and looked at the ceiling, and thought, I only have two years of this, 729 more nights, after I get through this one. That's if I'm lucky and nothing goes wrong. I must have slept, because I was woken up. Or maybe it was a new kind of sleep where you have none of the good part of being asleep but all of the bad part of being jolted awake. I heard an alarm and a few moments later felt the bed shake and opened my eyes to see a man's face leaning down over me, close enough to smell his hot, faintly rank breath. The face was all beard, eyes and wool cap. On the upside, he was smiling.

snore *Schnarchen*
to mutter *brummeln*
squad a small group of people trained to work together as a unit
to whirr *brummen*
apprehensive feeling worried that sth. unpleasant will happen

to jolt to move suddenly and violently

rank smelling unpleasant

"New meat," he said. "I'm the Corporal. Also known as Yos. Five minutes to wash, fifteen to breakfast, then we assemble." He shook the bed one more time, as if for luck, then stood up and headed towards the washroom. He was another tall man, well over six feet. Around him other squad members were getting up, grumbling and scratching. I saw that most of them slept more or less fully clothed. The Corporal stopped a few metres away and turned to me.

to assemble to come together

"Don't look so worried," he said. "You know that thing they say, don't worry, it might never happen? This is different. You're on the Wall. It already has." He laughed and left me.

Thirty in a company, divided into two squads or shifts of fifteen. In addition, five-odd permanent staff at each guard station, cooks and cleaners. Companies rotate, two weeks on the Wall, two weeks off.

-odd to show that the exact number is not known; roughly

One of those weeks is training and maintenance and whatever, the other is leave. Squads only change members when people have finished their time on the Wall. That's a rolling process, so there are always Defenders who are coming up to the end of their time, mixed in with others who've just started. Those are the two twitchiest groups, the ones who've only just begun and haven't got a clue what they're doing, and the ones at the end who feel they can reach out with their tongues and taste the freedom of life after the Wall, and who can think of only two subjects, how great it will be to get away and what a disaster it would be if anything went wrong in the last few days. The Defenders in the middle, some distance from both the beginning and the end, are more stoic.

In my squad I'd already met the Sergeant and the Corporal: they were always easy to tell apart, at whatever distance and however thickly swaddled in cold-weather clothing, because the Sergeant was heavy and the Corporal was tall. We called the Sergeant Sarge and we called the Corporal Yos. His hobby was whittling, and when we weren't on the Wall he was usually working on a piece of wood with a wicked-looking curved knife. As for the other members of the squad, that first morning and for several days to come, telling people apart was an issue. It was the layers. So many layers! At breakfast, their heads down over porridge, silent, my new companions were difficult to distinguish even by gender. Everybody goes to the Wall and the balance overall is fifty-fifty, so by probability half of my squad should be women, but there was basically no way of knowing who was who except by asking, and it didn't seem an ideal ice-breaker.

After breakfast we went to the wardroom for a briefing from the Captain. The battered, unloved desks and chairs made it look like a school. There were two maps behind him, one a detailed 3D projection of our section of Wall and the other at a smaller scale showing the nearest fifty kilometres of coast. I was to learn that the briefing almost always had no relevant news, other than the temperature and the weather forecast – though that was very important information. Sometimes we would be told about a flotilla of Others who had been spotted and attacked from the air, just in case some of them had survived and might still be coming in our direction. Occasionally there would be some big-picture news about crops failing or countries breaking down or coordination between rich countries, or some other emerging detail of the new world we were occupying since the Change. Sometimes there would be news of an attack in which Others had used new or unexpected tactics, or attacked in surprising strength. If Others ever got through, we were told about it. The room would go very quiet. We'd hear when, where, how many.

---

maintenance work needed to keep a building, machine, etc. in good condition
and whatever and so on

twitchy nervous and worried
to have not got a clue (*idm.*) to be completely unable to understand or deal with sth.

stoic not complaining or showing emotions

to swaddle to wrap a baby tightly in cloth

whittling *Schnitzen*

wicked *here*: dangerous

probability *Wahrscheinlichkeit*

ice-breaker sth. you say or do that makes a situation easier
wardroom *Offiziersbereich*

flotilla a large group of boats or small ships

to emerge to appear, to become known

to shuffle *schlurfen*
to fidget *herumzappeln, herumhampeln*
tight *disciplined*

There was no news like that on my first day. We sat shuffling and fidgeting and then the Captain came in. We stood up: not to attention, but we stood up. The Captain ran a tight company; there were lots of posts where nobody bothered to do that. He nodded and we sat down again and the room became still. 5

high of *maximum of*

"Nothing special today," he said. "No sightings of Others reported from the air or sea. No news of any relevance from the wider world. It's two degrees now, high of five later, which will feel like about zero with the wind chill. Good news: we have a new Defender with us so we're back up to strength. Kavanagh, stand up." 10
I did. I looked around the room and all fourteen members of my squad looked back at me.
"He's starting his two years with us. Two years if he and you are lucky and we all do our jobs. Remember, the first two weeks, he's still training. Also remember, this isn't a drill. We could be at- 15 tacked today and he and you need to be ready. OK, that's it. I'll see you during my rounds."

to make for somewhere *to go directly towards somewhere*

We stood up again and started to make for the door. The Sergeant came over to me and pointed in turn at a grumpy-looking red-headed woman chewing gum sitting in the front row who'd been 20 cleaning her fingers with a penknife during the briefing, the heavily bearded man who'd been sitting beside her, and a gender-indeterminate blob in a balaclava who'd been sitting behind me.

penknife *Klappmesser*

indeterminate *not clearly known*
blob *round mass or shape*
balaclava *Sturmhaube*
lot *here: group*

"Put him in the middle of you lot," he said. "Posts eight to fourteen. Hifa on the big gun. I'll come and see you there in thirty 25 minutes."

rampart *Festungswall*

We went out onto the rampart that led to the Wall. The Sergeant looked around us and then he gave the order, the one which was once famous as the most frightening command in the army, the scariest sentence you would ever hear, because it was the imme- 30 diate precursor of close combat; words which meant, there is a good chance that you will kill or die today. In the new world, it was a sentence Defenders heard at the start of every single shift. He said:

precursor *Vorbote*
close combat *Nahkampf*

"Fix bayonets." 35
And that's how it began.

2

I think they used to call it concrete poetry, that thing where the words on the page look like a physical object, the object that the poem is trying to describe. You know, a poem about a tree in the shape of a tree, like this:

⁵   a

                               poem

                           about a

                       tree in the

                   shape of a tree,

¹⁰   in this case a Christ-

                mas tree, not a very con-

            vincing tree and not a very good

        poem but it's not trying to be a death-

    less masterpiece it's just to show the idea

¹⁵   yes?

A concrete poem. It feels like an appropriate form for life on the Wall, because for a start life on the Wall is more like a poem than it is like a story. Days don't vary much; there isn't much a-to-b. There isn't much narrative. You do have the constant prospect of
²⁰ action, the constant risk of sudden and total disaster – but that's not the same as stuff actually happening. Most days, it doesn't. The thing a typical day most resembles is the day before and the day after. It's less like a form of time and more like a physical element. Time as a thing, an object. And then because the Wall is the
²⁵ dominant thing in your life and the life of everyone else around you, and your responsibilities and your day and your thoughts are all about the Wall, and your future life is determined by what happens on the Wall – you can, fairly easily, lose your life here, or lose the life you wanted to have – the two entities start to blur
³⁰ together, Time and the Wall, Time and the Wall, the Wall and your day and your life sliding past, minute by minute.
Add in the fact that so much of the time, what you're mainly looking at is concrete. You stand on it, you sleep in it, your home and office and the place you eat and the place you shit
³⁵ and the place that gets in your dreams – concrete. Concrete ... there it is again. You could talk about the Wall in prose, or you

appropriate *angemessen*

to determine to control or influence sth.
fairly *ziemlich*
entity *Gebilde, Einheit*
to blur together to grow into sth. whose shape is not clear

prose language in its ordinary form; *Prosa*

could talk about it in poetry, but either way concrete would be prominent.

sheer absolute
scale the size or level of sth.;
Ausmaß

In prose it's a question of sheer scale. The Wall is ten thousand kilometres long, more or less. (This country has a lot of coast.) It is three metres wide at the top, every centimetre of the way. On ₅ the sea side it is usually about five metres high; on the land side the height varies according to the terrain. There is a watch house every three kilometres: three thousand-plus of them. There

-plus in excess of, over
helipad a place where a helicopter
can take off and land

are ramparts, stairs, barracks, exit points for boats, helipads, storage facilities, water towers, access structures, you name it. All of ₁₀ them made of concrete. If you had the stats and the time and were

stats short for statistics
sufficient enough of sth.
suffice it to say it is enough to say

sufficiently bored you could calculate just how much, but suffice it to say, that's a lot of concrete. Millions of tons of it. That's prose.

Prose is misleading, though, when it comes to saying what it feels ₁₅ and seems like. The days are the same, with variations in the

visibility *Sichtweite*

weather, and the view is the same, with variations in the visibility, and the people either side of you are the same, so it's static; it's not a story, it's an image which is fixed-with-variations. It's a poem and as I already said, it's a concrete poem with a few re- ₂₀ peating elements. One would be concrete itself:

concrete concrete concrete concrete concrete

concrete concrete concrete concrete concrete

concrete concrete concrete concrete concrete

concrete concrete concrete concrete concrete　　　　₂₅

concrete concrete concrete concrete concrete

concrete concrete concrete concrete concrete

But then there's also water, sky, wind, cold, Always water, sky, wind, cold, and of course concrete, so it's sometimes concretewaterskywindcold, when they all hit you as one thing, as a single ₃₀ entity, combined, like a punch, concretewaterskywindcold. Except it isn't always like that and you sometimes are affected by them distinctly, as separate things, and in a different order, so it might be

cold:::concrete:::wind:::sky:::water　　　　₃₅

or sometimes it's slower than that, they take time to sink in, so it might be a freak clear calm day (they happen, not often, but they happen), in which case it's like an even shorter haiku

haiku a short three-line Japanese
poem with 17 syllables

sky!

cold

water

concrete

5 wind

and then sometimes your perceptions slow, especially when it's
cold, deep cold, and you're already tired, and it's towards the end
of a watch, and then it's more like

cold

10 concrete

cold

water

cold

sky

15 cold

wind

cold

Ah yes, the cold. The physical feeling of being on the Wall varies
all the time, but varies within a narrow framework. It's always
20 cold, but there is more than one type of cold, you soon learn,
type 1 and type 2. Type 1 cold is the kind that's always there. It
begins when you wake up in the barracks, as I did on that first
day, and it's already cold, and it stays cold while you wash and
use the toilet and put on your day clothes, layering up from ther-
25 mal underclothes, inner layers, outer layers, all your indoor gear,
you go and eat, always porridge and sometimes protein and a
warm drink, and you grab as many energy bars as you can face
the thought of eating during the day before you go to the wardroom for a briefing, which sometimes has information about new
30 threats but more usually tells you that today will be the same as
yesterday, you go to the armoury and get your weapons, then get
your outer layer of clothes on, windproofs and waterproofs and
hat and gloves, everyone using a different rig so by this point you
look like the most disorganised army in the world, which in a way
35 you are. Then you go out on the Wall and immediately you're hit
by type 1 cold, the cold which is always already there, which you

framework *Gerüst, Rahmen*

gear the equipment, clothes, etc.
you use for a particular activity

rig *Ausrüstung, Montur*

blindfold *mit verbundenen Augen*

fart *Furz*

sod *(offensive) a person*

off duty *when sb. is not working*

hypothermia [,haɪpə'θɜːmiə]
Unterkühlung

flask *Thermosflasche*

to slice *to cut into sth.*

to seep into *durchsickern*

to displace *to take the place of (as if) by pushing out*

know so well and hate so much it's like being in one of those bands where they've been playing together for years and spent so much time together that they know each other so intimately that they can't bear to be in each other's company for a second longer, they can identify each other blindfold by the smell of each other's 5 farts, and yet they have no choice because this, after all, is what they do and who they are. Then you walk to your post for the day (or the night if you're on night shift, which is exactly the same except twelve hours further on) and relieve the lucky sod who is now off duty while you've become the poor sod who is on duty in 10 their place. And by the time you've walked to your post, which can be a kilometre and a half away, you're generating some body heat and you've started to fight back against the cold and you realise that as long as you keep moving you're going to be just warm enough. That's type 1 cold. 15

Type 2 cold starts the same, except that as you move through it, it gets colder. After walking to your post for twenty minutes, you're colder than you were at the start. The cold gets through to you deeply and intimately. It feels dangerous because it is dangerous. People have died of hypothermia on the Wall. You have no choice 20 with type 2 cold except to keep moving as much as you can and, mainly, to try to find out in advance if it's going to be a type 2 day and plan accordingly. That means double layers of everything, double porridge, double warm drinks. Sometimes someone will run back to the barracks and bring more clothes, a big flask of 25 warm liquid, anything. I've even heard of units where they make fires and gather round them on the coldest nights, but the Captain would never let us get away with that. Type 1 cold can come to seem familiar, almost friendly, because you get to know it so well – the rest of your life, any time you feel cold, it will remind 30 you of the Wall, and of this kind of cold, and because you're now remembering being miserable at a time when you're less miserable (by definition, you're less miserable, since you're no longer on the Wall), it will be not exactly a happy memory, but a memory with a happy effect: hooray, I'm no longer on the Wall! Somebody 35 said there was no greater misery than recalling a time of happiness when you're in a time of despair, and that's true, but let's focus on the positive and remember that the opposite is also true. When you remember the bad place, and you're no longer in the bad place, it feels good, like waking from a nightmare. 40

There are no positive thoughts about type 2. It cuts and slices and seeps into you. The other cold feels like something outside you that you have to cope with and overcome; type 2 feels internal. It gets inside your body, inside your head. It displaces part of you; it makes you feel as if there's less of you. Type 1 you can fight by 45 moving, you can fight by thinking about something else. Type 2, there is nothing else. At times there's not even you. Type 1 people complain about. Type 2 makes them go silent, even afterwards. Type 2 is a premonition of death.

5 That first day was a type 1 day. We climbed out on the ramp and started down the Wall towards our posts. Cold, horribly cold, but not dangerously so. Cold and medium clear. You can always tell the visibility on the Wall by how many watchtowers you can see. That day I could see the next two but not the third: they're three

10 K apart so that meant six kilometres but not nine. Call it seven. Medium visibility. It's the first thing you check because it tells you how far off you'll be able to spot Others. Clear days are better, unless you are looking into the sun at sunrise or sunset, in which case they're neither better nor worse. Attacks often come at that

15 time and from that angle – which would give the Others better odds, except we know that that is a time they're likely to be coming and so tend to be prepared. At least that's what you'd think. Of the attacks which succeed, though, about half happen at dawn or dusk.

20 My fellow Defenders grumbled and muttered and bitched as we walked. The Wall has gravel on the top, along some sections anyway, to help with grip in the wet. This was one of those sections. We crunched as we trudged. Every two hundred metres, somebody stopped at their post, peeling off from the shrinking group

25 and taking up position beside whoever had been on guard from the other squad. There were sometimes a few words of abuse or relief, a mixture of Thank God and About Fucking Time; all of the Defenders leaving their posts looked grey with exhaustion. They walked heavily. One or two of the guards at the furthest posts

30 were already walking back towards us, notwithstanding the fact that we hadn't got to them yet and their stations were technically unmanned in the interval. They wouldn't have done that if the Captain had been there, and if he had seen them he would have automatically added a day to their time on the Wall.

35 It was already light. The sun was low but, thanks to the layer of cloud, not dazzling.

The posts were numbered in faded white paint at hundred-metre intervals. Each post had a concrete bench, big enough for two people, facing the sea. The bearded man stopped at 8, the woman

40 he'd been sitting next to – maybe they were in a relationship, there was something about their unspeaking ease with each other – took 10. At 12, Hifa, the blob in the balaclava, pointed at me and said, "Here," and kept walking towards the next station, 14, the last one attached to our watch house. The Defender who'd been

45 at my post, a bulky man of about my height, picked up his

---

premonition *Vorahnung*

K (*abbr.*) kilometre

odds the likelihood that a particular thing will/not happen; *Wahrscheinlichkeit*

dusk the time before night when it is not yet dark
to bitch (*infml.*) to complain and make unkind remarks
gravel *Kies, Schotter*

to crunch *knirschen*
to trudge *stapfen*
to peel off *here*: to leave

words of abuse rude and offensive words
about fucking time (*sl.*) strong expression used to say that sth. should happen very soon

notwithstanding despite; *nichtsdestotrotz*

to dazzle *blenden*

ease *Ruhe, Leichtigkeit*

bulky big and heavy-looking

rucksack and slung his rifle over his shoulder and walked away
without a word or gesture.

I took off my backpack and put it against the rampart. I stood and
looked out at the sea. Twelve hours here felt like it was going to
be a very very long time. Some companies divide their time into 5
two shifts of six, but our Captain was one of the old-school ones

binary [ˈbaɪnəri] consisting
of two parts, either/or

who were more binary about it: you're on or you're off. That
seemed like the worst idea in the world right now, but I knew that
in eleven hours and fifty-five minutes I'd be all in favour.

Although everybody always calls the Wall the Wall, that isn't its 10
official name. Officially it is the National Coastal Defence Structure. On official documents it's abbreviated to NCDS. Guard tow-

Ilfracombe small town in the
English county of Devon

ers have a name and a number. This tower was Ilfracombe 4. We
were on the outermost stretch of a long coastal curve. Straight in
front, and for the ninety degrees to each side, there was nothing 15
to see except the ocean. If straight in front was twelve o'clock, it
was nothing but water from nine o'clock to three o'clock. Turn a
further ten degrees to either side – turn to eight o'clock or four

to undulate to rise and fall,
like waves

o'clock – and you could see the Wall undulating into the distance.
The engineers who built it tried to keep it as straight as possible, 20
because straighter = shorter, but there were many places where
the natural shape of what used to be the coastline meant that it
was more economical, in time and effort and concrete, to use the
existing shape of the coast as the guideline for the Wall. This
must be one of them. My new home.   25

3

In every walk of life, every job and every vocation, there is an experience which distinguishes actually doing the thing from the training and preparation, however extensive. You don't know what boxing is until somebody punches you, you don't
5 know what doing a shift in a factory feels like until the bell has gone at the end of the day, you don't know what a day's march with a full backpack is until you've done one, and you don't know what the Wall means until you've stood a twelve-hour watch.
10 Time has never passed as slowly as it did that day. Time on the Wall is treacle. Eventually, after you have put in enough hours on the Wall, you learn to cope with time. You train yourself not to look at the time, because it is never, never, ever, as late as you think and hope and long for it to be. You learn to float. You be-
15 come completely passive; you let the day pass through you, you stop trying to pass through it. But it takes months before you can do that. In the first weeks, and especially on your first day, you look at the time every few minutes. It's like there is a special slow time on the Wall; you can't believe it; you check and check again
20 and that only makes it worse.
After two hours, at nine o'clock, a member of the kitchen staff brings around a hot drink. Sometimes it's tea, sometimes coffee, but really, who cares? It's a hot drink, it's a sign that you've done your first two hours. Somebody comes round on a bike, bringing
25 a big heated flask. That first day, it was a woman, one of the cooks, who came along the Wall. I watched her stop for a minute or two at each post as she came. She was chatting with the Defenders. I felt my eyes fill with tears: the thought that someone was going to stop and talk to me suddenly seemed like the great-
30 est act of compassion and empathy I had ever encountered. As she got to the post before mine, where the woman next to me was on guard, I could hear both of them laughing. The sound of laughter on the Wall – it felt like an intrusion from another world. And I'd only been there two hours.
35 "Hello darling, I'm Mary," said he cook, as she stopped her bicycle next to me, her curly hair peeking out from under her cap. "Got your mug?"
I hadn't. I put my rifle down on the bench and got the standard-issue tin mug out of my backpack. She poured hot brown liquid
40 out of the flask.
"First day, isn't it? Poor thing. It always hits people hard. You get used to it though. And at least it's not raining or blowing a gale or night-time so there's always that."

to distinguish sth. from sth. to make a difference between two things

treacle Melasse, Sirup

to float here: sich treiben lassen

empathy Mitgefühl

intrusion Eindringen

to peek out from to stick out slightly

gale a very strong wind

to stew to be left to brew for a long time

to wear sth. out etw. abnutzen
keep them peeled! (saying) keep your eyes open for sb./sth.; remain watchful
rocket launcher Raketenwerfer

to occur to sb. to come into your mind

to get the hang of sth. (infml.) to learn how to do or deal with sth.

power bar Kraftriegel
oblong rectangular
to take time sich Zeit nehmen

lucky dip Glücksgriff
dense closely packed
chewy schwer zu kauen
acidic säuerlich
dotted through durchsetzt

"I'm Kavanagh," I said. The liquid was dark brown tea, stewed and bitter, with so much sugar in, it was as sweet as ice cream. I had never drunk anything so delicious.

"I know you are, darling. Well, we'll be seeing each other at least three more times today, so we mustn't wear out all the chat now. 5 Keep 'em peeled!"

And with that Mary was back on her bike, heading off towards Hifa, who had already put down the rocket launcher and turned to her in expectation. I kept watching while I drank my tea. It occurred to me that if the Others were able to work out a way of 10 attacking during a tea break, their odds would be good. Mary got to Hifa and they gave each other a quick, very unmilitary hug. Mary got off her bike and leant it against the bench. Then she poured out Hifa's tea and awarded herself a mug too and they settled down to talking. I was jealous. Mary didn't seem to be 15 worried about wearing out the chat when she was talking to Hifa, did she? They talked for about five minutes and then Mary got back on her bike and pedalled back down the top of the Wall, with a little wave for each one of us as she went past. It was three hours until lunch. I decided to break the time up into two sections 20 of ninety minutes, with an energy bar in the middle.

"They put something in the tea to stop you thinking about sex," somebody said on the communicator.

"Yeah," said somebody else. "They put tea."

The next ninety minutes went past slowly, but not as slowly as 25 the first two hours had done. I said to myself: maybe I'm starting to get the hang of this Wall. Mistake. Having done some maths to make myself feel depressed the night before – two years on the Wall if I'm lucky – I now did some maths to cheer myself up. Two years = 730 days but it's two weeks on, two weeks off, so that's 30 really only 365, and a day is really only a shift, since if the Others attack during somebody else's shift it's not your problem, so that's 365 shifts of twelve hours each, which by another way of looking at it is 187.5 full days, which is only six months, so my two years on the Wall is really only six months on the Wall, which 35 isn't so bad.

After eighty-four minutes, I started counting down towards my power bar. 360 seconds, 359, 358 … all the way down to 1. I took the waxed paper oblong out of my upper left pocket and un-wrapped it slowly, trying to take my time. The bars they give you 40 on the Wall aren't labelled so you don't know what's inside them. Lucky dip. This one was nutty and dense, with what seemed to be particles of red fruits, chewy and sweet and acidic, dotted through it. I don't normally pay much attention to what I eat, but on the Wall, where for a lot of the time there isn't much to think about, 45

I became obsessed with food. This power bar, for instance, was unlike anything else I had ever eaten – more intense, more important. The nuts had a different texture from the fruit. The bar was chewy and dry but also soft. Objectively and soberly, you would have to say that it was fairly nasty. Maybe you could go so far as to say it was horrible. At the same time it was the best thing I'd ever eaten. I tried to eat slowly, chewing each bit for as long as I could, thirty chews, forty, fifty, the flavours changing as I chewed, the fruits taking over from the nuts. I was glad when there was still three quarters of the bar left, calm when there was only half left, starting to feel regretful when I'd got down to the last quarter, then the last eighth, then the last mouthful, no crumbs left in the wrapper because the bar was too densely constructed for that, even when I tipped it up into my mouth, chewing fifty times, fifty-one, fifty-two, see if I can get to sixty, nope, there's nothing left, nothing in my mouth except saliva and a faint tang of dried raspberries.

When I looked up from the bar, the Captain was about a hundred metres away, walking towards me. I say 'walking': that was significant. Most of us trudged or shuffled along the Wall, and almost everyone, almost all the time, moved with their heads down. We all of us spent enough time looking out at the sea. You put off as long as you could the moment when you had to turn your attention outwards. Head down, eyes down. Nothing good to see if you look up.

The Captain wasn't like that. He stood straight and looked around him when he walked – or at least most of time he did. On this occasion he was looking directly at me. He was wearing his uniform outers, which were bright green, because the Defenders' uniform is the opposite of camouflage: instead of trying to hide from an enemy, we're trying to be as visible as possible, to the Others and to ourselves. The idea is that it will scare them and reassure us. The Captain for his part certainly did look scary enough, or reassuring enough, depending on your point of view.

I took my eyes off him and pretended to scan the horizon. Nothing to see. I wouldn't have minded a boatload of Others, just to break the suspense.

"Kavanagh," he said when he arrived. His voice was deep and naturally severe – he was one of those men whose default mode sounds like an order or a rebuke.

"Sir." "We're here to look out at the sea," he said. I took that to mean that he had seen my long absorption in my midmorning snack. The Wall is not a place where people blush, but I felt myself flush red.

"Sorry sir."

---

obsessed with sth. *besessen von*

texture *Konsistenz*
soberly seriously, reasonably
nasty bad or very unpleasant

regretful showing that you feel sorry

nope (*sl.*) no
saliva *Speichel*
faint not strong; slight
tang a strong, sharp taste

to shuffle to walk slowly, dragging one's feet

camouflage *Tarnkleidung*

severe not kind or friendly
default mode *Standardeinstellung*
rebuke *Tadel*

contrails *Kondensstreifen*

He stopped staring at me and turned to look at the water. Concrete sky wind water. A few moments passed. Directly above us I could see the contrails of a plane. Energy is plentiful, thanks to nuclear power, but fuel isn't, especially not aviation fuel, so now only very few people get to go on planes. That would be members 5 of the elite, flying off to talk to other members of the elite about the Change and the Others and what to do about them. At least that's what they say they do. I felt the familiar longing to be up there, one of them, instead of down here, one of us. The Captain and I both watched the plane move into the distance. If he had 10 been a different kind of person, he would have spat.

"Everyone finds the first day hard. The second is easier. The third

to get the measure of sth. to get used or accustomed to sth.

easier still. Eventually you get the measure of it."

He turned to me again.

"This is my fourth tour on the Wall. No Other has ever got over 15 the Wall on my duty. I've never lost a company member, I don't intend those things to change." He looked at me again to make sure I got the point, then nodded and marched off towards Hifa at the end of our section of Wall.

I thought: he's an impressive man, our Captain. He's a leader. 20 Four turns on the Wall: that meant he had done three supplemen-

supplementary additional, extra

perk an advantage that you are given because of your job

tary tours of duty, each one of which earned perks and privileges for himself and his family. Better house, better food, better schools for his children. They say this is one of the ways people rise up and become members of the elite. So, a family man. A brave man, 25 a family man, a leader, an athlete. A person with a sense of duty and responsibility. A good man to follow into battle. If you had asked me right then and there what was the least likely thing I could think of about the Captain, it would be that he was also, above and beyond any other thing, the biggest fucking liar I've 30 ever met.

4

I took so long over my power bar and my chat with the Captain that the ninety minutes until lunch was actually only eighty minutes. I started to get the hang of the fact that looking at the time made it pass by more slowly. Another plane went past,
5 heading in the other direction this time – more members of the elite, coming and going, talking their talk. Oh how wonderful it would be to be up in the air … The wind rose, not to gale force but to something a little stronger than a breeze, and the sea swell was both rolling and choppy. The sky cleared and I could now
10 see four watchtowers: visibility twelve kilometres. I began to understand just how hard it could be to see what was in the water, even on a clear day, when the wind and waves and sun did not cooperate.

The drill at lunch varies from watchtower to watchtower. At Il-
15 fracombe 4 the routine is that people are allowed to gather together for ten minutes with the two Defenders in the nearest posts. The furthest anyone is from their post is two hundred metres; the biggest gap between a group having lunch is six hundred metres. Safe enough to have a gap of that size for ten minutes
20 twice a day. You'd have thought. At three minutes to twelve, I saw Hifa at post 14 put down the grenade launcher and take something out of his or her rucksack, then pick up the weapon again and begin walking towards me. I turned and looked the other way and the red-haired woman from post 10 was heading towards me
25 as well.

They arrived at the same time and both of them sat down on the bench without speaking. They put down their weapons and started opening their packed lunches. The woman pulled back the hood of her outer coat, and I could see some strands of red hair escap-
30 ing from underneath her beanie. She looked less irritable than she had earlier in the day. Not a morning person. Hifa was still entirely wrapped up, and all I could see was the eyes and the tip of the nose. If you had asked me beforehand, I would have said it was impossible to eat a meal without taking off your balaclava,
35 but that was clearly what was about to happen.

I got my food out too and sat down at the end of the bench.

"So, how's it going, new meat?" asked the woman.

"Kavanagh," I said, sticking out my hand. Both of us still had gloves on. She gave it a quick firm shake.
40 "Simpson," she said. "Or Shoona."

"Shoona. It's OK. The Captain caught me staring at my power bar."

"Yeah, he does that. Catches people. That right, Hifa?"

Hifa grunted, mouth full.

---

gale force *Sturmstärke*

swell rolling movement of the sea; *Dünung*
choppy with a lot of small, rough waves caused by the wind

grenade launcher *Granatwerfer*

strand *Strähne*
beanie small hat that fits closely to the head; *Mütze*
irritable easily annoyed; *reizbar*

new meat (*sl.*) person new to a situation

"Wouldn't you rather have lunch with …?" I said, and gestured towards the man she'd been sitting next to at breakfast. He was in the next group of three, four hundred metres away. Shoona shrugged.

"You know what they say. For better, for worse, but never for 5 lunch."

Hifa snorted a laugh.

breeder *Gebärende*

"You're Breeders?"

This time both of them laughed.

"No of course we're not fucking Breeders. Do I look like a Breeder? 10 Don't answer that. Cooper and I are just having sex."

equidistant equally far or close
tease *Scherz, Necken*

"You like him," said Hifa, at some point equidistant between a statement and a question and a tease. I was sorry to hear the question, because what I wanted to ask was something else: where did they have sex? There was no privacy on the Wall. Only 15 Breeders (i.e. people trying to be Breeders) and officers got separate accommodation. The showers?

sodding (*sl.*) *Scheiß-*

"Well enough," said Shoona. "More than I like this sodding sandwich, anyway."

It was hard to disagree with that. The sandwich bread was dry 20 and what was supposed to be a layer of cream cheese was thin-to-invisible. The food on the Wall is pretty good, on the whole; they take trouble over it because they know how important it is in a Defender's twelve-hour shift.

"Chewy," I said. For some reason that was very very funny. Both 25

to cackle to laugh in a loud, high voice
to thump to hit sth. and cause a noise

of them bent over, cackling, thumping themselves first on the legs, then on each other's backs.

"True," said Shoona, when she got her breath back. She took a long pull from her bottle of water. "Well, Chewy, time to get back

gonna (*infml.*) going to

to it. This Wall's not gonna guard itself." 30

We put our lunch stuff away and picked up our weapons and Shoona and Hifa started trudging back to their posts. Hifa got about five metres away and the turned around and said, "See ya, Chewy."

Once Shoona and Hifa had got back to their posts, I let a few min- 35 utes go past before I looked at my watch. I was starting to learn. It was now twelve thirty. The good news was I had got through five and a half hours. The bad news was that I had six and a half more to go. With the sun higher in the sky, it was easier to see now, meaning that this should be a time of less risk. The Others 40 knew that too, which meant that you couldn't rely on it. If everyone knows it's a time of low risk, maybe that's a good moment to try something. So low risk is high risk. Bu not vice versa.

Mornings on the Wall, dawn and dusk and night, were times for poetry. Skyconcretewaterwind. Afternoons were for prose. Ten 45

thousand kilometres of Wall. A Defender for every two hundred metres: fifty thousand Defenders on duty at any time. Another fifty thousand on the other shift, so a hundred thousand on duty, day in day out. Plus it's two weeks on, two weeks off. Half of the
5 Defenders aren't on the Wall, they're on leave or on training or waiting for their two weeks' turn of duty. So two hundred thousand active Defenders at any given moment. Add support and ancillary staff, officers and administrators, add the Coast Guard and the air force and the navy, people off sick, whatever, and it's
10 more than three hundred thousand people involved in defending the Wall. That's why everybody goes to the Wall, no exceptions. That's the rule.

Except for Breeders. It's a paradox. Because the Wall needs so many people, we need people to Breed, so that there are enough
15 people to man the Wall. It's on a fine edge as things currently stand, and there's talk of the tours having to be made longer, two and a half or three years, to make up a shortfall. But people don't want to Breed, because the world is such a horrible place. So as an incentive to get people to leave the Wall, if you reproduce, you
20 can leave. You Breed to leave the Wall. Some people say that this isn't fair to the children, who are born into a world where they have to do time on the Wall in their turn. Maybe they won't, though. Maybe all the Others will have died off by then and we won't need the Wall. Who knows? And besides, the children can
25 always Breed in their turn, and get off the Wall that way. Prolonging the life of our species too, as a side effect. Breed to Leave, that's the slogan.

I should say that people don't despise or look down on Breeders. They just think they're a bit weird. It's not so much, that's
30 wrong, it's more, why would you? Why don't people want to Breed? It's an idea that caught on after the Change: that we shouldn't want to bring children into the world. We broke the world and have no right to keep populating it. We can't feed and look after all the humans there already are, here and now; the
35 humans who are here and now, most of them, are starving and drowning, dying and desperate; so how dare we make more of them? They aren't starving and drowning here, in this country, but they are almost everywhere else; so how dare we make more humans to come into this world? There are lots of different an-
40 swers to that. Nobody can predict the future; that's one answer. God tells us to; that's an answer which works for some. Maybe the best answer, though, or maybe I'm just talking about the one that makes the most sense to me, is just, because. Because; the best/worst answer to most human questions. Why are we here?
45 Because.

ancillary providing support or help

to be on a fine edge *Spitz auf Knopf stehen*

shortfall amount below what is needed

incentive *Ansporn*

to prolong to make sth. last longer

to despise sb./sth. *jdn./etw. verachten*

to look after sb./sth. to take care of sb./sth.

to dare do sth. *wagen zu tun*

to starve to die of hunger
to drown *ertrinken*

Back to the prose. Most Defenders stand on the Wall because that's where the manpower is needed, but the Wall isn't the only form of border and coastal protection. The Flight scans the sea for the Others, locates them, sometimes 'takes them out' then and there. It's funny, only Defenders on the Wall talk about 'killing' Others: we're the ones who do it face to face, and we're the only ones who don't use euphemisms for it. The Flight consists of some people in planes and many more people operating drones. Sometimes the Flight marks their location for the Guards, full name Coast Guards but everyone calls them the Guards, who use ships of two main kinds, medium range and short-range. They patrol the coast and the seas and their job is to sink the Others' boats. The Defenders are there for the rest of the Others: the ones who get through, which is a significant number, because there is a lot of sky and sea to watch, and because ten thousand kilometres of coast is a lot of coast. They come in rowing boats and rubber dinghies, on inflatable tubes, in groups and in swarms and in couples, in threes, in singles; the smaller the number, often, the harder to detect. They are clever, they are desperate, they are ruthless, they are fighting for their lives, so all of those things had to be true for us as well. We had to be clever and desperate and ruthless and fight for our lives, only more so, or we would switch places. I didn't want to die fighting on the Wall, but if it came to it, I would rather that than be put to sea. One in, one out: for every Other who got over the Wall, one Defender would be put to sea. A tribunal of our fellow Defenders would convene and decide who was most responsible, and those people, in that order of responsibility, would be put in a boat that same day. If five Others got over the Wall, five of us would be put to sea. It was easy to imagine being those people. Your old comrades pointing guns at you while you pushed your boat out into the water, the only feeling colder and lonelier and more final than being on the Wall.

Members of the Flight and the Guard don't get put to sea, so people would rather do that than be on the Wall. As a result it's much harder to get in. To get into the Flight you have to pass lots of biomechanical tests. (I wear glasses so I didn't even bother applying. I learnt afterwards that was a mistake, because the Flight has lots of ground staff and support staff and I could have got a job there.) To get into the Guard it helps to have family connections with boats and the sea. I didn't bother applying for that either, because I've hardly ever been on a boat and I was worried I'd get seasick. No, it was the Wall for me. It was always going to be the Wall.

That first afternoon went by slowly. Planes passed overhead a few times; once, about two o'clock, I saw a boat on the horizon, got excited and called it in, but I was shouted down by my fellow

euphemism ['juːfəmɪzəm] *beschöningende Umschreibung*

ruthless cruel; *skrupellos*

tribunal [traɪ'bjuːnəl] *Tribunal, Strafgericht*
to convene (*fml.*) to bring together a group of people for a meeting

Defenders, who said it was a Guard ship. They said they could tell by the shape. After Yos finished calling me an idiot over the communicator, Sarge came on and told me I would soon be able to recognise Guard ships on sight and that it was better to call in
5 something I didn't know about than keep quiet and risk something worse. I felt better after that. At three, I had another power bar, this time made of savoury ingredients, chickpeas I think and maybe sesame and carrot. It wasn't especially nice but I was glad of it, and more glad of Mary's second visit on her bike with her
10 flask of hot liquid, coffee this time.

"Nearly there," she said, as she pedalled off. But that wasn't true, and the last few hours went by just as heavily as the rest of the day. It began to get dark at around five. The day had clouded over. It was one of those evenings which seem not so much a transition
15 from day to night as from light grey to thicker grey to darker grey to darker still, the light fading by increments, until dark wins. Lights came on automatically, a hundred metres apart on the Wall. The lamps threw a narrow patch of blazing illumination, which only made the dark around more intense. Some sections of
20 the Wall were said to disable their lights and use night-vision instead; I could see why. There was no moon. I suddenly realised just how hard it would be to see Others coming at night, if the weather and light conditions were at all difficult. I also realised why they always start you on the Wall on a day shift: so you've
25 had a chance to get used to the twelve-hour stint of duty before you have to do one when it really matters, at night, when the Others come.

For the first time that day, I grew anxious, not about fatigue or cold or whether I would get through it, but about the Others. It
30 was not difficult to imagine a black-clad figure hopping silently over the Wall, knife in its hand, murder in its eyes, nothing to lose. No warning; no mercy. I tried to look straight ahead and then move my head from side to side, using my peripheral vision, the way we had been trained to do. All I could think of was how
35 easy it would be for the Others if they attacked now.

"Different at night, isn't it?" said a voice into my ear. I looked across and could see Hifa looking towards me. I raised an arm in acknowledgement.

"You get used to it," Hifa said. "Sort of."
40 The wind dropped at dusk, and the swell settled down. I could hear a motorboat in the distance. One of ours, I assumed – no Others would mount an assault in something so noisy. It would be a Guard patrol going home after dark. I could hear a plane far overhead too; that would be the Flight, also on their way home. The
45 wind and the waves were quieter now, but I was more aware of

---

savoury salty or spicy
chickpea Kichererbse

by increments slowly; schrittweise

blazing (lit.) brightly lit
illumination (fml.) light

stint a fixed or limited period of time spent doing a particular job

black-clad dressed in black clothes
to hop over to climb over

peripheral vision periphere Sicht

to mount an assault to prepare and make an attack

pattern *Schema, Muster*

liminal (*fml.*) belonging to two
different places
consciousness *Bewusstsein*

choir [kwaɪər] a group of people
singing together
to chant to sing a regularly
repeated text
demon [ˈdiːmən] an evil spirit

dirge lament; *Klagelied*

woozy confused

to leap (leapt, leapt) to make a
large jump or sudden movement

to clump to walk noisily with slow,
heavy steps

to flip to change

ecstatic experiencing great joy

dismissal farewell

to ache to be sore
fatigue extreme tiredness

them, because they were less constant. I started to think I could
hear patterns in the sound, whispering or singing or voices muttering not-quite-words. An image began to run through my mind,
not quite a hallucination or a waking dream, but like a guided
fantasy, like the kind of story you tell yourself in the liminal in- 5
between consciousness just as you're falling asleep or just after
you've woken up. The noises, the near-voices, were being made by
a choir, hooded and robed in black, chanting a ritual, appeasing
spirits or gods or demons or the ancestors. There were two rows of
them and their faces were in shadow, and maybe they themselves 10
didn't know the meaning of what they were chanting. Maybe it
was a dirge, a funeral dirge. They were monks or nuns or a mixture of the two. They were chanting because they wanted something to happen, or not to. The chanting was a lament or a prayer.
"Here they come," said the Sergeant over the communicator. I was 15
so woozy, so out of it, that my first thought was that the black-
robed figures were coming, had leapt out of my imagination and
were here on the Wall with us. The adrenaline helped me snap
out of it: he meant, the night-shift was coming. The next shift of
our company had come out of the watchtower and were clump- 20
ing down the ramparts towards us. I don't think I've ever felt my
mood flip so abruptly and completely. Relief broke over me like a
great wave. Relief is maybe the purest form of happiness there is;
in that moment, anyway, I'd have said so. I'd never been happier;
I'd never been more purely and ecstatically in the present. Cold? 25
What cold? Here comes the next shift! Slowly, admittedly, very
slowly, heads down, trudging and grumbling, the same way we
had twelve hours ago. Take your time, guys, I thought, take it as
slow as you like, as long as you keep coming.

There was no ceremony and not much small talk at the moment 30
of handover. The Defender I'd seen twelve hours before arrived at
my post. He was chewing gum. He did not speak but instead
flicked his head up at me in a combination of greeting and
dismissal. I already had my pack on and my rifle slung over my
shoulder. I flicked my head back at him and started the walk back 35
to the watchtower and the barracks. I realised that I had stiffened
up with the cold and immobility. My legs hurt from standing. The
wind, which had got up again, was directly in my face. It felt like
it didn't matter. The shift was over. That was the only thing that
counted. 40

When you're on the Wall, the division of time is very simple.
Twelve hours on duty, twelve hours off. In practice that means
four hours for you, eight hours for sleep. I don't really remember
what I did that first evening, but I do still remember the physical
sensation of coming in out of the cold, aching with fatigue, and 45

taking my pack off and dropping my rifle at the armoury and then just sitting, sitting in the dry and the warmth, and thinking that I had never really appreciated sitting before, had never fully got the point of it, but that now I did, and I would never again
5 underestimate how good it is to have nothing to do, no demands on you, except to sit. Most of the patrol sat around too. We were in the mess hall. There was tea and biscuits – the best tea, the best biscuits. Nobody spoke much, or made a great deal of sense when they did. Then there was hot food – I don't remember what, but I
10 do remember going back for thirds. Some of the shift went to clean up, others to call home and check in with whoever it was they'd left behind. A few of us were gaming on our communicators, a few went through to watch television. I did all of those things in sequence and then woke with Yos shaking my shoulder.
15 "You fell asleep," he said. "Daft bugger, you might have been here all night," his tone kinder than his words. The TV was on but the room was empty; it was a chat show with the sound turned right down. He laughed. "The first one is a long one. Bedtime."

in sequence one after the other

daft bugger (offensive) silly person

I followed him through to the barracks bedroom. There were dif-
20 ferent generations of design at different points along the Wall; some watchtowers had individual bedrooms. This design, with everyone in one big room, was from a period when the theory was that Defenders should share things, so that they understand they're all in it together. My shift was in bed or getting ready for
25 it, the other shift's beds were empty. It was the same as when I'd arrived only the day before, though that fact – that it was only twenty-four hours since I had walked into this room – made no sense. It felt more like twenty-four years. I washed, stripped off my day clothes, then put on my night clothes, starting with a
30 thermal inner layer. The lights went out.
I took off my glasses and got into bed. But then I realised there was one last thing I wanted to do before going to sleep. I put my glasses back on and got back out of bed. I walked down to the far end of the barracks. Most of the squad was already asleep, one or
35 two of them snoring. Someone, I couldn't tell who, was reading under the blankets with the help of a pen-light. The moon had risen by now and some sharp light was coming in the narrow high windows. I stopped at the last cubicle beside the washroom. I looked down and saw what I was looking for: caramel-coloured
40 skin and short waved hair and a button nose peering over the thickly stacked blankets. I thought I had got away with it, but just as I turned, I saw Hifa's eyes were open, looking narrowly at me, glinting and amused. But I had got what I wanted.

button nose a small, flat and round nose; *Stupsnase*
to stack *(auf-)stapeln*

to glint *glitzern*

Hifa was a woman. I went back to bed, and that was my first day
45 on the Wall.

5

On the Wall, one day is every day. At least, it is in terms of the big-picture items such as the shape of the twenty-four hours, your duties, where you go and what you do and who you do it with. Lots of variation within that, but the architecture of the days is the same. That's the way you want it to be, too, because on ₅ the Wall, any news is bad news. They're never going to say, guess what, the Others have stopped coming and you can leave the Wall now. Guess what, we've decided we like your face and you don't have to do two years on the Wall, in fact you can leave tomorrow, in fact, wait, why not, you can leave right this minute! Off you go! ₁₀ Wait, you forgot your cookies!

That's not going to happen. The only things that can happen are bad things. So you want nothing to happen. Except it's more complicated than that. Somewhere in the dark cave-mind there's a gremlin, saying, But wouldn't it be interesting if something did ₁₅ happen, if they came, if you had to fight for your life, if you had to do that thing you dread and train for, have nightmares about but maybe just are a tiny bit curious about too, and you have to kill or be killed? Wouldn't it be better to do that, to feel something other than cold and hunger and boredom and fatigue? Wouldn't ₂₀ it be exciting to use that bayonet you clamp on your gun every morning? You'll get to find out something about yourself, what you are like when the worst happens. Whether you are still you. Only the louder and stupider Defenders will ever talk about this, but we all think about it. We half-fantasise about the worst that ₂₅ could happen.

Mostly, though, what happens is nothing, and mostly, that's the way we like it. My first two weeks on the Wall were like that. Every day was the same as the first day, with the main variable being the weather. Most days were about as cold as the first. Two ₃₀ were warmer – not warm enough to be warm but warm enough to go out with one layer less. One day was type 2 cold, dangerously cold, frighteningly cold, but the weather forecasters had told us it was coming and we were prepared. The really lethal cold is the kind that comes on when you aren't expecting it. ₃₅

I saw the same people every day, the members of my squad. I walked out to the Wall with Shoona and Hifa and we had lunch together. The nickname Chewy, I am sorry to say, stuck. Yos and the Sergeant took turns pointing out things I was doing wrong, things I could do differently, things to watch out for. I realised that ₄₀ this was ongoing training, and though I didn't really like being found fault with all the time, I could see why there were doing it. Shoona began to tease me and Hifa about being an item, singing

gremlin Kobold

to dread [dred] to be extremely afraid of

to clamp on aufstecken

lethal ['li:θəl] able to cause death; tödlich

to be an item (infml.) to be in a relationship

'Hifa and Chewy sitting in a tree, k-i-s-s-i-n-g.' There was nothing personal about the teasing, it was almost pro forma: if a male
Defender and a female Defender were in any way friendly to each
other, if they were anything other than fridge-temperature indif-
ferent, they could expect to be accused of being 'at it.' In this case,
though, Shoona was on to something, because I was starting to
have thoughts about Hifa. Even though I had never seen her in
anything other than multiple layers of baggy clothing. Actually,
maybe that was part of what was getting my attention – looking
at all those shapeless clothes, it was hard not to wonder about the
shape underneath them … formlessness which you know isn't
really formlessness, which you know for sure has a definite shape,
an unmistakable glow … and also, it is a conclusive human truth
that the only thing which makes the time pass better than daydreaming about food is daydreaming about sex. So, yes, Hifa and
Chewy, but not necessarily sitting in a tree, k-i-s-s-i-n-g.

One day the Sergeant properly yelled at me, when he made an
impromptu inspection and found that I didn't have my spare ammunition rigged correctly. He was right: there was a particular
manner in which we were supposed to do it, magazines folded
back over each other in a set sequence, which made it quicker to
load the ammo in combat, but it was laborious and boring to do,
and so I sometimes skipped it.

There was nothing particularly unusual about being shouted at,
so that wasn't the main point of interest. The thing which made
me focus was what Sarge said when he'd calmed down a little.

"You're lucky it was me," he said. "The Captain sees that, you get
extra days on the Wall. That thing you did right there, that's an
extra two weeks on the watch. You want that?"

It didn't seem to be a rhetorical question. I had to admit that no, I
did not want that.

"I didn't think so," said Sarge. "Most people, their bark is worse
than their bite. For pretty much everybody, that's true. Their bark
is their bite. Yelling or bollocking or calling you names is the
worst they'll ever do. Not him. His bite is worse than his bark. You
don't have to worry about him giving you a bollocking. You have
to worry about him doing you real damage. Bite, not bark. Do you
get it?"

I said that I thought I did. That didn't seen good enough, and
Sarge came closer, confidentially close, as if we were in a crowded
pub and he was whispering a secret, not as if we were on the
Wall, in the middle of nowhere, two hundred metres from the
nearest human ears.

"I'll tell you something about the Captain. It's not a secret, but it's
something he prefers to tell people for himself. When he does tell

eavesdropper *Lauscher*

you, do me a favour and act like it's a surprise." He looked around, as if he was worried about eavesdroppers, and he lowered his voice so that I could barely hear him over the wind. "The Captain was an Other. He got here ten years ago, before the laws changed. That's why he is so hardcore. That's why he's so strict. He knows ₅ what it's like out there. He knows he's not going back. He's done four turns on the Wall because he's obsessed with keeping them out and proving he is worth being allowed to stay." He let it sink in then hissed: "The Captain was an Other!"

to hiss to say sth. in a quiet angry way

It was one of those things you're told which make no sense and at ₁₀ the same time you immediately know, right down in your cells, are true. The Captain was an Other! Of course he was. Until about ten years ago, Others who showed they had valuable skills could stay, at the cost of exchanging places with the Defenders who had failed to keep them out. The law was changed because this fact ₁₅ became known to Others and started to act as a 'pull factor', a reason they came here. Now, today, Others who get over the Wall

to euthanise sb. [ˈjuːθənaɪz] to kill painlessly using medication
Help servant

have to choose between being euthanised, becoming Help or being put back to sea. There's no escape and no alternative, now that everybody in the country has a chip: without one, you'd last ₂₀ about ten minutes. So even if they get over the Wall and then get away, they're always caught and offered the standard choice. Almost all of them choose to be Help. The attraction is that if they have children, the children are raised as citizens. That's after being taken away from their parents, of course. Others tend to be ₂₅ Breeders. You see the kids all around the place, often with older parents, or parents who are a visibly different ethnicity from their

ethnicity belonging to a racial, national or tribal group

children. The Captain must have been one of the last to get through before the new laws. No wonder he was a fanatic. No

tribal scars *Stammesnarben*

wonder his bite was worse than his bark. His scars were tribal ₃₀ scars, and yet he had left behind his tribe and was now a Defender, one of us.

"I get it," I said to Sarge. "I get it." I refolded the magazines of ammunition, the way I had been taught to do it, while he watched. The Captain used to be an Other ... of course, of course, it made ₃₅ complete sense. There was something abnormal about his

implacability *Unerbittlichkeit*

implacability. It was easier to understand once you started to think about the things he must have seen, the things he must have done. That day was the last time I cheated or took a short cut or

to take a short cut *eine Abkürzung nehmen*
to cut a corner *etw. nicht so genau nehmen*
to do sth. by the book to do sth. exactly as the rules tell you
human margin *menschlicher Spielraum*

cut a corner or did anything not one hundred per cent by the ₄₀ book. I became Mr Rules. I realised that even though I was on the Wall, a part of me had been assuming there were still small human margins here and there, room for interpretation, space for forgiveness or acceptance or, less nobly, the chance to talk yourself out of any trouble you might have got yourself into. I now ₄₅ saw that that was wrong. No leeway, no space, nothing but black and white, the rulebook or anarchy, nothing but the Wall and the Others and the always waiting, always expectant, entirely unforgiving sea.

leeway freedom to act within particular limits
anarchy lawlessness, lack of control, chaos

6

After that first two-week shift on the Wall I went home. The trip was the reverse of the one I'd made to the Wall: lorry, train, second train, bus, walk. It might sound similar but it couldn't have been more different, and the main difference was that the whole company was travelling back with me. A company of thirty-plus, heading off together after two weeks of what amounted to hard labour and semi-incarceration. We were a little, I think the word would be, *rowdy*. No alcohol is allowed on the Wall, a strict rule strictly enforced: if you're caught you and anyone else involved, or thought to be involved, automatically get extra days to serve. Somehow, though, as soon as we were on the lorry, two-litre bottles of spirits magically appeared. We passed them around, swigging happily, and again I felt the pure joy you sometimes got on the Wall, the joy of relief, when something horrible is over. One of life's great pleasures, deeply loved by all Defenders: the moment when you get to say: I hated that, but now it's finished. This was the first chance I got to interact with the other shift. A strange thing: we were all in the same place at the same time, doing the same thing, but we hardly ever had anything to do with each other, apart from those few fumbling moments of handover at either end of a watch. That could make you hate each other, because your emotions, at that moment, couldn't possibly be more out of sync: starting a shift meant depressed, resentful, apprehensive, bitterly doing the worst thing in your life; finishing one meant euphoric, ecstatic, relieved, skipping off to the best bit of the day. Going off shift, you felt no ill-will to your doppelgänger, but that wasn't true in reverse, because he hated you. In twelve hours it would be the other way around. Nothing personal: when you came on shift, you always hated the person you were relieving. The fact that you knew the other set of emotions so completely, that you knew exactly what the other person was feeling, made it worse. Your shift twin was a person you met twice a day, about whom you had very strong views, whom you didn't really know.

After the lorry, we got on a train, a civilian train, which ran from the nearest town up to the capital. I felt sorry for the other passengers: we were loud, we were rude, we didn't care what anyone else thought or what they needed – that was our train. People were used to that kind of behaviour from Defenders, and tended to give us a lot of space. (Good idea.) When we piled into our carriage, a Breeder with a small child at the far end picked up her child and her bags and moved elsewhere. (Also a good idea.) It was warm, indeed verging on overheated, after the two weeks I'd

incarceration the act of putting or keeping sb. in prison
rowdy loud, rough

to swig (*infml.*) *gierig saufen*

fumbling *ungeschickt*

out of sync (*infml.*) unsynchronised
resentful *missgünstig*

to have strong views about sb./sth. *eine eindeutige Meinung zu jdm./etw. haben*

to pile into sth. (*infml.*) to go into sth. in large numbers and in a disorderly fashion
to verge on sth. (*phr. v.*) *an etw. grenzen*

spent on the Wall. I'd forgotten what it felt like to be hot; it was nice for the first couple of minutes, and then I could feel myself starting to sweat. We all took off multiple layers of clothing. There was yet more booze – someone had taken the chance to
5 pick up another couple of bottles at the station. We got stuck into the drinking. The train set off. Some of the company were singing. Shoona and Cooper, after two drinks, were sitting and holding hands and occasionally, when they thought nobody was looking, kissing. You could see that they liked each other more than
10 either let on. I had found myself, not by chance, a seat next to Hifa at the end of the carriage. Hifa minus ten layers of clothing was lithe, skinny, tough and frail at the same time. Her black hair stuck out in all directions. It was only about the third time I'd seen her without a beanie or cap. We were sitting there talking
15 about nothing much, when a man, a Defender, came and dumped himself in the seat across from us and held out a bottle of vodka. I took it, nodded thanks, took a swig, handed it to Hifa, who took a swig and handed it back to the man. All through this he kept looking at me. Then I got it.
20 "You're him!"
He laughed. A hot waft of alcohol came across the train table.
It was indeed him, my shift twin. It was no surprise I didn't recognise him, since he was another Defender I'd never seen out of his Wall clothes, swaddled in layers of cold-weather protection,
25 wearing a beanie with a hood pulled down over it. Take four sets of outwear off him, and he was a slim dark-haired man with brown eyes and a four-day beard. My age. That was to be expected, most Defenders were.
"Hughes," he said.
30 "Kavanagh," I said.
"Chewy," he said.
"I don't love it, but I suppose so."
"You're skinnier than I thought, Chewy."
"Same. It's the – "
35 "Yeah, I know."
"How long?"
"Fifty-eight weeks."
In the middle. Hughes didn't ask how long I'd been on the Wall. He didn't need to because he knew first-hand. He started to get
40 up.
"So, see you at training week. Just wanted to say hello."
"Thanks. Yes."
He stood by our seats for a moment and raised the bottle in a toast.
45 "Well, if you are going to Breed, you could both do worse."

booze (infml.) alcohol

lithe [laɪð] young, healthy, attractive
frail zerbrechlich

to take a swig (infml.) to take a large mouthful; einen großen Schluck nehmen

waft (Duft)Wolke

in unison *einstimmig*

to sway to swing

defiant *trotzig*

In unison, Hifa and I said: "Fuck off."

He laughed and headed off down the carriage towards the sing-along, him and the train both swinging and swaying from side to side. The company had run through the repertoire of old pop songs, switched to obscene favourites (which had emptied the 5 carriage of the few remaining civilians – we now had it entirely to ourselves), and then started singing the all-time Defender classic, melancholy and defiant and nihilistic all at once, not so much a song as a chant or dirge:

> We're on the Wall because 10
>
> We're on the Wall because
>
> We're on the Wall because

We're on the Wall because [stamp three times, pause for three beats]

> We're on the Wall because …

opaque *(fml.) undurchsichtig*

perception *Wahrnehmung*
to alternate *wechseln*

fitting *Ausstattung*

and so on. The effect was hypnotic, self-transcending; you never 15 felt less of an individual, more of a group, than when you were singing that song/chanting that chant/dirging that dirge. There was no sign that the song was going to stop, so Hifa and I, a few seats from the rest of the company, joined in. I can't sing, not even slightly, but with that particular song it doesn't matter. Hifa's 20 singing voice was unexpectedly high and delicate. We're on the Wall because We're on the Wall, because …

Night had settled, and the train windows were now half opaque, so you could choose whether to look out the window into the dark landscape outside, or keep your focus on the reflection back 25 into the train carriage. I've always liked that trick of perspective and perception. I alternated between the reflection and the view through the window. Moon, cows, trees, a river; my own face with Hifa behind me, the battered train fittings, the other Defenders, singing and swigging. The view beyond or the view within, 30 the landscape or the reflection, inside or outside. The cold out there, the warmth in here.

to josh to joke, often in order to tease sb.
to disperse to spread across a large area

to sneak (snuck, snuck) a look to look at sb./sth. secretly

At London, we split up, after a certain amount of hugging and joshing, and carrying each other off the train, and throwing up. The company dispersed to take a variety of different trains to our 35 various parts of the country. For me it was a shot hop across town on the underground and then a two-hour stopping train to the Midlands. This time I was the only Defender, and instead of running away to other compartments, people snuck looks at me, until I looked back at them, and then they acted as if they'd been 40 caught doing something they knew they shouldn't. Then it was a wait for the local bus, last one of the evening, then the bus, then a walk from the terminus, a mile or so but feeling longer with my rucksack and my emotions about home both bearing down on me. My parents had left the porch light on, so I could spot our house from a long way off, the only semi in our street which was still illuminated on the outside. They'd be waiting up. I squared my shoulders and knocked on the door.

Home: it didn't just seem as if home was a long way away, or a long time ago, it actually felt as if the whole concept of home was strange, a thing you used to believe in, an ideology you'd once been passionate about but had now abandoned. Home: the place where, when you have to go there, they have to take you in. Somebody had said that. But once you had spent time on the Wall, you stop believing in the idea that anybody, ever, has no choice but to take you in. Nobody has to take you in. They can choose to, or not.

terminus *Endstation*

semi (*BE*) a house that is semi-detached; *Doppelhaushälfte*

to abandon sb./sth. to leave a place/person, usually for ever

7

None of us can talk to our parents. By "us" I mean my generation, people born after the Change. You know that thing where you break up with someone and say, It's not you, it's me? This is the opposite. It's not us, it's them. Everyone knows what the problem is. The diagnosis isn't hard – the diagnosis isn't even controversial. It's guilt: mass guilt, generational guilt. The olds feel they irretrievably fucked up the world, then allowed us to be born into it. You know what? It's true. That's exactly what they did. They know it, we know it. Everybody knows it.

To make things worse, the olds didn't do time on the Wall, because there was no Wall, because there had been no Change so the Wall wasn't needed. This means that the single most important and formative experience in the lives of my generation – the big thing we all have in common – is something about which they have exactly no clue. The life advice, the knowing-better, the back-in-our-day wisdom which, according to books and films, was a big part of the whole deal between parents and children, just doesn't work. Want to put me straight about what I'm doing in my life, Grandad? No thanks. Why don't you travel back in time and unfuckup the world and then travel back here and maybe then we can talk.

There are admittedly some people my age who are curious about what things were like before, who like to hear about it, who love the stories and the amazing facts. Put it like this: there are some people my age who have a thing about beaches. They watch movies and TV programmes about beaches, they look at pictures of beaches, they ask the olds what it was like to go to a beach, what it felt like to lie on sand all day, and what was it like to build a sandcastle and watch the water come in and see the sandcastle fight off the water and then succumb to it, a castle which once had looked so big and invulnerable, just melting away, so that when the tide goes out you can't see that there was ever anything there, and what was it like to have a picnic on the beach, didn't sand get in the food, and what was surfing like, what was it like to be carried towards the beach a wave, with people standing on the beach watching you, and was it really true the water was sometimes warm, even here, even this far north? There are people who love all that shit. Not me. Show me an actual beach, and I'll express some interest in beaches. But you know what? The level of my interest exactly corresponds to the number of existing beaches. And there isn't a single beach left, anywhere in the world.

Not everyone agrees with me on this. Maybe most people don't. Lots of people like to watch old movies where everyone is on the beach all the time. My view? Stupid.

---

formative *nachhaltig prägend*

to succumb to to accept defeat

invulnerable impossible to damage in any way

tide the rise and fall of the sea

My mother is hard going. She just feels guilty all the time; her expression in repose, whenever I'm in the room, resembles a grieving sheep. Just below the surface she's furious too, obviously, because feeling guilty all the time makes people angry, but she channels it
5 into martyrdom and being saintlike and doing everything and never saying a harsh word no matter how badly I screw up and never being angry, just sometimes (and never explicitly) the teensiest bit, you know … disappointed. The time I took their car without permission, got drunk, overrode the autopilot, slid off the road
10 and hit a tree and trashed the battery, which wasn't covered by the insurance because of the whole drunk + underage thing? Not angry, not at all, I'll just go and clean the kitchen and put out your school uniform for tomorrow, I know you didn't mean to let us down darling and I'm sorry I can't help it if I feel a little bit … sad.
15 My father is worse than my mother. The thing about Dad is he still has the emotional reflexes of a parent. He wants to be in charge, to know better, to put me straight, to tell me about back in the day, to start sentences with the words "When I was …" He used to do this when I was little, at school, helping me with home-
20 work or showing me how to do small practical things. Shoelaces at five, wiring plugs at fourteen, that sort of thing. To be fair, he was pretty good at it. In a different world he'd have been a good father. But it stopped working once I became a teenager and it started to sink in that the world hadn't always been like this and
25 that the people responsible for it ending up like this were our parents – them and their generation. I don't want to know their advice or to know what they think about anything, ever.
So a week at home is as you'd expect. My mother manages to make the task of running the household and feeding three adults
30 seem like the world's most demanding job. We aren't rich enough to have Help – Help is free but you have to feed and clothe and house it so the costs still add up. It's fair enough that there is a lot of work, though we have a washbot and a cleanbot so it maybe isn't quite as much work as all that. Maybe not as much as my
35 mother makes it seem, when I'm at home. Basically, she acts like she's the bravest, keenest, most willing slave in the salt mine. We hardly ever speak, except for her to ask whether I liked it, if there's anything special I'd like for [next meal], do I want to see any of my friends [to which the answer is, why is that any con-
40 cern of hers?], can she get me anything? Would I like a cup of tea in the morning? It's like staying in a well-run but emotionally suffocating B&B.
I'd be lying if I said this brought out the best in me.
As for my father, he's at work in the day at his office, and then
45 home in the evening to eat whatever my mother has cooked and

---

in repose the state of resting or lying down
to grieve trauern

martyrdom Märtyrertum; Opferbereitschaft
to screw up (infml.) to fail at sth., to ruin sth.
teensy (infml.) very small, tiny
explicit clear and exact
to override (-rode, -ridden) to take no notice of sth., to disconnect
to trash to damage or destroy

to wire plugs Stecker verdrahten

demanding anstrengend, anspruchsvoll

-bot short for robot

keen wanting to sth. very much, eager

to suffocate ersticken
B&B (abbr.) Bed and Breakfast; a small hotel or house that rents rooms

then watch television/movies/whatever. We don't talk much and both prefer it that way.

All of this was completely as usual; in the words of the song, same as it ever was. I tend to go out to see old mates. But there are fewer of them around than usual, because people my age are all 5 off on the Wall and some of them are still on shift, or on training, or at home. The main topic of conversation: being on the Wall. People compare complaints. Our company sounds like one of the strictest there is – some of them only have ten people on watch at a time, so you get one day or night in three off! That's against the 10 rules and if the Others come you're finished, but the thinking is that if the Others come you're finished anyway.

Let's just say, that's not how the Captain sees it. I bitched about my company for a bit and everyone said I was unlucky to be somewhere so hardcore. I agreed and joined in the moaning, but 15 I was, secretly, proud to be going through such a strict version of Defending. I was a real Defender. If you had one day in three off, that made you less of a Defender. Two thirds of one. Not that other people could see this distinction between real Defenders (i.e. me) and the others – all they could see was a group of De- 20 fenders in the pub, getting drunk. They steered well clear. Even the ones, maybe especially the ones, young enough to have done stints as Defenders themselves were careful to keep a distance. They knew that we knew how little we had to lose. What would anybody do – send us to the Wall? Besides, the courts are 25 notoriously lenient on Defenders. We get in fights, we bust places up, and nothing much happens. Quite bloody right.

Talking to my old mates, I came to realise that life was going to be divided into two, before the Wall and after the Wall. It was as if this thing we had in common was coming between us; the Wall 30 was the same for everybody, but it was different for everybody too. Maybe we'd go back to having our lives in common in two years' time (or rather in ninety-eight weeks' time, I'd gone fully over to the Defenders' habit of counting time not by the calendar but by the number of weeks you've put in), but for now, we were 35 friends because of things in the past, not the present. The main lesson I took from my week at home: my Wall company was what I had in my life now, instead of family and friends.

When I left on the return journey, walk bus train another train lorry, I said goodbye to my mother and father at the front door. A 40 shy hug from my mother, and a handshake from my dad. I could see in his eyes that he wanted to say something, dispense some advice, and he could see in mine that I wasn't having it. I picked up my rucksack and started out but when the door closed, I stopped and waited at the window for a few minutes. It was dark 45

---

to bitch about sb./sth. (*infml.*) to complain about sth.

hardcore extremely strict

to steer clear (*infml.*) to keep away

notoriously berüchtigt
lenient nachsichtig
to bust up to break or damage

to not have it (*idm.*) to not accept or tolerate sth.

out and they couldn't see me. The light in the hallway went off, then the light in the sitting room went on, then the television went on, then they started watching the programme they'd clearly been waiting a whole week to watch. I don't know whether it was a documentary or a film, I didn't wait to see, but the opening shots showed sand and blue sky and deeper blue water, and small figures climbing up onto boards and riding waves and falling off into the water. My parents had waited for me to leave and then turned on a programme about surfing.

8

Then it was back to the Wall. The second cycle was harder because our squad switched over and were on the night shift. I had thought the twelve hours of day watch was difficult, but the nights were worse. The dark makes it harder, obviously. The type 2 cold, which is much more likely to come at night, makes it harder 5 too – the cold which is like glue, like mud, which makes it so hard to move it's as if the Wall's concrete is still wet. But the real difficulty is because it's easier to be apprehensive at night. That deep, black part of the brain which by day secretly wonders what it would be like if the Others came, and wonders if it would really 10 be so bad, by night is given over to fear.

At night, on the Wall, imagination is not your friend. The distracting thoughts which help you get through the day – about being somewhere else, about what you'll do when you get off the Wall, about food, about sex – don't work as well. You see things 15 and hear things that aren't there. You know this, and you train for this, but at the same time you know that sometimes, these things are there, and that many times the following has happened: a Defender who thought for a moment he saw something which looked like moonlight gleaming off metal, and dismissed it, or 20 thought he heard something like metal scratching on concrete, and dismissed it, died coughing up blood with an Other's knife in his guts. You don't get through a twelve-hour shift without having your adrenaline triggered at least once. You tell yourself to calm down, then you tell yourself that there's maybe something 25 after all. Up down up, like taking pills. You never get used to it, and the best you can hope for is that you get used to not getting used to it.

We saw much more of the Captain at night. I know it doesn't sound possible that the presence of one man can make a differ- 30 ence to a fear that's as elemental and basic as the kind you get standing guard in the dark against the Others. It did, though. You knew that at some point in your twelve hours, he would be there, appearing either on foot, marching down the ramparts through the pools of illumination, or on a bicycle, which he never did by 35 day, and which always looked slightly incongruous. He was a big man and the bike looked as if it was a size too small for him. Sometimes he would just appear, popping up beside a post without warning, because he had come along the track inside the Wall, the same trick he had used on the first day to catch me 40 daydreaming. (I learned later he did it to everyone on their first day.) He never said much, just stood beside you and looked out at the sea. Then he would make some simple observation, something

to distract to take sb.'s attention away from sth.; *ablenken*

to dismiss to refuse to consider, to ignore
guts *Bauch, Eingeweide*
adrenaline [əˈdrenəlan]
to trigger to cause sth. to start

incongruous strange, out of place; *fehl am Platz*

basic and elemental, about the kind of night it was, dark or less dark, cold or less cold, moonlit or starlit, windy or still, harder to see or less hard, nearly over or just begun. He never told you anything you didn't already know, but it was always just enough
5 to let you know that he had stood on the Wall many times, far more times than you ever would, and he knew it better than anyone, and he was here with you. Then he would nod a farewell, and go on to the next post. Often, in the middle stretches on the Wall, halfway between one post and another, he would just stop
10 and stare out at the sea. It was as if he was stretching out his senses, extending the reach of his hearing and vision, out into the dark.

to extend to make longer or greater

"What do you think the Captain is looking for, when he does that?" I asked Hifa one night. At night we did the same thing we
15 did by day, and met in groups of three for a mid-shift meal. I hadn't realised that you stayed in your pattern of posts for the whole of your two years on the Wall, meaning you ate with the same three people every day, hundreds of times. If you didn't get on with your crew, if they were bullies or idiots or silent or coldly
20 hostile, or just if the chemistry was wrong, a twelve-hour shift which was already difficult became even more so.

hostile *feindlich*

"Maybe he thinks his senses are sharper when there's no one around," she said. "You know, the small noises people make. Distractions. Body language. Away from it all. Are you going to fin-
25 ish that?" she asked Shoona, who was making slow progress with that night's energy bar. It had something very sticky in it, maybe dates. In reply Shoona broke it in half and gave the bottom of the bar to Hifa. She took it without saying anything and started eating it. In any other context it would have seemed outlandishly

outlandish strange and unusual

30 rude, but on the Wall it was a kind of intimacy.
"Four tours ..." said Hifa. "Imagine doing four tours. Eight years on the Wall."
"He was a sergeant by the end of his first tour," said Shoona. "He just has a knack for it."

to have a knack for sth. to have a talent for sth.

35 "Yeah, well, imagine having a knack for it," said Hifa. "I mean, of all the things you could have a knack for."
"Juggling," I said.
"Knitting," said Shoona.
"Sex," said Hifa.
40 "Sleep," I said.
We didn't say much after that.
I finished my food and my hot drink and got up to go back to my post. At night, even the young and the fit stiffened up quickly, and I could feel how the cold had taken up residence in various
45 parts of my body while I was sitting – my hips, my knees. Hifa

and Shoona got up too and we split up. I went to the edge of the illuminated ground around my post, about fifty metres away, and jogged back and forwards to the far edge for a few minutes, getting out of breath and warming up but being careful to stop short of sweating. At one end of my circuit, looking out to sea, I thought 5 I saw something. A glimmer of light, was my first thought, out to sea. It was unlikely to be one of ours: the Guard did go out at night, but when they did, they didn't often use lights. I thought I must have been imagining it, but a few minutes later there was another glint, and then and then another. 10

glint a small, bright flash of light

"I think I can see lights," I said over the communicator. I felt embarrassed and frightened at the same time – embarrassed in case I was imagining things, frightened in case it was Others. "Out to sea."

embarrassed ashamed

"How far out? asked the Captain. Having his voice loudly in my 15 ear without preamble made me jump; normally he didn't use the communicator.

preamble here: warning

"It's hard to tell, sir. I'm sorry. Not close but closer than the horizon. Maybe a kilometre or more."

"How many?" 20

"Two or three. Winking on and off."

to wink to keep flashing on and off quickly
good spot gut gesehen

"OK. Good spot. Keep watching. Don't worry, it happens sometimes."

"Why?" I asked. "Sir. What's happening?"

"We don't know," said the Captain, not in his usual tone of com- 25 mand or rebuke, but as if he was asking the same question. "It's just something they sometimes do."

I didn't need to ask who he meant by 'they'. The lights were Others. That was my first encounter with them. Not a face-to-face encounter, because that would involve either them or me dying. 30 But an encounter nonetheless. The first time I saw them. I think that was also the first time I could imagine what it would be like to be another, floating in the dark, on some makeshift boat or raft or inflatable, staring at the shoreline, looking at the Wall, at the sprinkling of lights above and the steep black dark below. You 35 would be bobbing up and down with the sea swell. You would hardly be able to remember the last time you were warm or dry or safe. We were cold but the Others were colder. We were bored and tired and uncomfortable and anxious, they were angry and frightened and exhausted and desperate. God, the Wall must look 40 like a terrible thing from the sea, a flat malevolent line like a scar. So blank, so remorseless, so implacable. We were used to feeling frightened of them, hostile to them: if they came here, we would kill them. It was that simple. But – how we must seem to them! We must seem more like devils than human beings. Spirits, 45

encounter a meeting, esp. one that happens by chance

to float to move smoothly
makeshift temporary and of low quality
raft Floß
inflatable aufblasbares Boot
to bob up and down to rise and fall

malevolent [mə'levələnt] causing harm or evil
scar Narbe
blank showing no emotion
remorseless erbarmungslos
implacable unerbittlich

embodied essences, of pure malignity. If we would kill them on sight, what would they do to us, if they could?

I remember thinking: we don't owe them anything. I'm glad I'm one of us and not one of them. Twenty-six hours later, my second shift ended.

malignity *Bösartigkeit*

to owe sb. sth. *jdm. etw. schulden*

9

Lake District a mountainous region and popular holiday destination in the North West of England

coating covering on or over a surface

to prowl herumschleichen
to scowl jdn. einschüchtern

standby ready to do sth.

to latch on to sth. (phr. v.) to develop an interest in sth.

It was late afternoon and we were standing near the top of a valley in the Lake District. Our rucksacks sat on the ground next to us. The early part of the day had been cloudy, but the sky cleared and the day was now close to perfect: not too warm when we were walking, not too cold when we were still. The light was al- 5 most yellow, not fading yet but beginning to think about it, in that ideal moment when it's like an invisible coating of butter, making everything richer, deeper, more intimate. The hills seemed friendly. I took a drink of water and looked around the mountains and felt glad to be there. 10

Our next few turns on the Wall had been uneventful. We guarded the Wall, the Captain prowled and scowled, Sarge and Yos kept us in order. The days were longer, the nights shorter. The weather warmed up a little. The type 2 cold had largely passed – though when it did come, it was more dangerous than ever, because you 15 could be taken by surprise. One member of our squad, a quiet tall woman who had done a year at college and was about to go back, came to the end of her tour and we gave a party for her. Because we were still on the Wall, it was a sober party, but it was a happy occasion for all that, and it did make me think that time was go- 20 ing past. I was getting through my shifts. Every day that went past, every hour was bringing me closer to getting away, getting off the Wall, starting the rest of my life. Between those two-week cycles we went 'home' to our families and then did a week on standby duty, which was physically much easier than either Wall 25 shifts or training, but was so uneventful it brought other challenges. The next holiday, a group of us decided, we would spend together. So that is what this was: a holiday week with my new friends. I wouldn't have done it if Hifa hadn't been going, but once she had mentioned it, I latched on to the idea. 30

None of us had any money, so we thought we'd go camping. We wanted to go somewhere with no view of the sea; with attractive landscape; with nice pubs; with good walking but not too strenuous, or only strenuous for those of us who felt like it. Three men and three women: me and Cooper and Hughes, Hifa and Shoona 35 and Mary. Two tents borrowed from the quartermaster. We agreed to leave our communicators behind – a radical move, actually, the first time we'd tried anything of the kind. I hadn't spent a week away from my phone since I first got one at the age of ten. Nature! That was the idea. I'm not saying it was a good idea, just 40 that it was the idea.

Cooper researched the ideal camping spot, just along the hillside from a locally famous pub, but this was our first day, and it wasn't where he had thought it would be. The result was that we were standing here as the day gave signs of ending, no tents pitched. This was a beautiful spot but not necessarily a great campsite.

"Let's go over the hill and see if there's somewhere better," said Cooper.

"Oh come on," said Mary. "I'm knackered. I want my dinner."

"That pub is out there somewhere," Cooper said. "If we had our communicators ..."

"We all agreed," said Hifa and I together.

"OK, fine, we agreed. And now we're lost."

"We aren't lost, we just aren't sure where we are. There's a difference," said Cooper.

"I think I remember this place from when we were talking about it. I think it's just up and over. I could be a kilometre, not much more," said Shoona. In that mysterious way of group dynamics, her opinion decided the matter. Maybe her words carried extra weight because she was more likely to argue with Cooper than to go along with him, so there was no sense of a couple ganging up or siding together. We finished our water, picked up our packs. The Help, who had been standing silently a few metres away, did the same thing.

That was the other big, daring, innovative thing we had done for this trip: we had decided to bring Help. We had borrowed them from the ancillary services support section of the Defenders. Help is unaffordable for most ordinary people, but if you're camping, there's no extra food or shelter that the Help isn't carrying for itself, so you basically get the Help for free. It was me who worked this out and me who suggested it and I won't pretend not to be impressed by myself. This meant that instead of carrying exceptionally heavy, unwieldy rucksacks with all our food and gear with them, we were carrying much smaller, lighter, fun-sized holiday rucksacks. We could do whatever we wanted in the day and our campsite would be shipshape when we got back, fire lit, dinner cooking, clothes washed. It would be a taste of what it's like to be rich. I had thought it might be awkward for us, from the human point of view, getting used to Help when we weren't the kind of people who had it in our private lives. But it was interesting how little adjustment it took. The Help were a man and a woman, a couple I think, from their familiarity with each other and the way they hardly spoke. I didn't ask them their story and they didn't offer to tell it, which was perfect too. He did the cooking and she did everything else.

On the first day, Cooper's navigation turned out to be correct. We carried on the track we'd been taking up the hill, the sunlight at our back so the whole landscape looked blessed, flooded with

---

to pitch a tent to put up a tent and make it ready to use

to be knackered (*BE, sl.*) extremely tired

to argue with sb. *sich mit jdm. streiten*
to gang up on sb. to unite as a group against sb.

unwieldy *unhandlich, sperrig*

shipshape neat, clean, in good order

blessed *traumhaft*

gold. When we got to the top, the view opened out again: a lake stretched out in front of us, with mountains surrounding it on all sides: right in the middle of the lake a paddle boat was puffing out steam. There was a moment like one of those nineteenth-century paintings of a Romantic dude having conquered a peak and sur- 5 veying the world laid out beneath him, except the painting would have some additional details: six scruffy Defenders, two Help, and also the Defenders were all doing a little celebratory dance because they'd found the pub they were looking for. It was about half a kilometre down the other side of the hill, with a small, 10 perfectly sited campground sharing the same view we'd had from the top.

"Result," said Cooper, pleased with himself. We left our bags and went into the pub while the Help set up our camp. Yes, I thought – this must be what it's like to be in the elite. To have things done 15 for you. To be on the inside. The pub was an old-time fantasy of an English inn, with saloon and lounge and snug, wood panels, cosy: you could imagine arriving here on a winter night and immediately feeling safe and warm. The landlord was, we could tell after about ten seconds, a former Defender who gave special 20 treatment to people doing their time on the Wall. The first set of pints was on the house. We had one more round, then went back out to our tents, where the Help had begun cooking over the campsite fire. It was now dark, but a deep blue moonlit dark, the kind Defenders like. Fire, woodsmoke, mutton: everything was 25 perfect. The Wall felt a very long way off.

The next morning I woke early, not long after first light. I got out of the tent to stretch the sleep out of me and look for coffee. I wasn't wearing my glasses so things were blurry, and I had a sudden hallucination: a figure in white, backlit by the rising sun, 30 slowly dancing, aflame with light. I thought: an archangel! I thought: I'm going mad! I thought: sweet baby Jesus, that's Hughes doing tai chi. He didn't stop or turn to look at me but kept at his practice. It was impressive and also ridiculous – impressive in part because he must have known it looked ridiculous, but that 35 wasn't stopping him or slowing him down. Was he good at it? I think maybe he was. It looked rhythmical enough and he didn't fall over.

The Help wasn't up yet but Hughes had brewed up a pot of coffee on a stove and I took some. I sat on one of the camp stools and 40 looked out at the view. I got on well with Hughes, and the odd thing, apart from the fact that we were physically a little alike, was that he had grown up near me, a town about fifteen miles away. It turned out we knew people who'd been to school with each other. At handover once, Sarge shouted at Hughes for being 45 in the wrong place, then when he saw who it was apologised, or sort-of apologised. His exact words were "Sorry, got the wrong tall thin streak of piss."

By the time I finished a mug of coffee Hughes had finished doing
5 his exercises.

"Sorry," he said. "I know it looks stupid.

"No ..." I started to say. Then I shrugged. "Just different. From, you know, fix bayonet, point automatic weapon, pull trigger."

"I can't do it on the Wall, people would take the mickey. I'd never
10 hear the end of it."

"Yeah, I can see that."

"Also you're supposed to do it outdoors and most of the time it's too fucking cold."

"Yeah, I can see that too."

15 "My teacher would say I should just ignore it. The cold and the teasing. I can't, though."

"What is he, some ninety-year-old Chinese dude with whiskers, who's been doing martial arts so long he can, like, fly?"

"No, he's called Graham, about thirty-five, from Wolverhampton.
20 But he does know his tai chi."

"You planning to go back there?"

"No. I'm going to go to college." He reached down into a bag and pulled out a book, a paperback copy of Wordsworth's selected poems. "I want to study literature. I might stay on at uni and teach
25 if I can make a go of it."

I looked at Hughes. The bulky, looming, whiskery figure I usually met trudging down the Wall in twilight, muttering curses under his breath and glaring at me and carrying an automatic weapon in his right hand rather than slung over his shoulder – that per-
30 son was a skinny, gentle intellectual who did meditative martial arts and read Romantic poetry and wanted to be an academic.

"You?" he asked.

"I don't know," I said, and found, to my surprise, that the thought was true. I used to have secret ideas about what I wanted to do:
35 secret in the strong sense that I had never told anyone. I wanted to get away from home (that part was no secret), to get as much education as I could, to get a job where I made lots of money, and to become a member of the elite. All this was too vague to count as a plan. I didn't know anyone who had done it; I didn't know
40 the detail of how to do it; but I knew that it could be done. Elites have to let in some outsiders, that is a basic rule of how they work. It's how they spread just enough of the benefits around to stop disorder rising from below. Also: elites need new blood be- cause it's the newly arrived members of the elite who know how
45 the rest of the population are thinking, right now. Not in general

---

got the wrong tall thin streak of piss based on the phrase 'to get the wrong end of stick', meaning to misunderstand sth.

to shrug *mit den Achseln zucken*

to take the mickey (*BE, infml.*) to tease sb.; *jdn. aufziehen*

whiskers *here*: untidy beard
martial arts *Kampfsport*

Wordsworth William Wordsworth (1770 – 1850), an English Romantic poet
to make a go of sth. to try to make sth. succeed, usually by working hard
looming *sich auftürmend*

terms, but right in this specific historical moment. To find that stuff out, you have to let some of them in. Somebody like me, a bright ambitious provincial boy.

This was secret, dark, private. I knew enough to know that this was not a good thing to want, and not a good way to be: that at 5 the same time I was in the middle of my friends and peers and colleagues, my fellow Defenders. I was privately scheming to get away from them, to become somebody else. I was in effect saying that I was better than them – not saying it out loud, but doing something much worse, saying it in my heart. My deepest thought 10 was: I'm not like you. You don't know me.

And yet, to my surprise, I found that this secret of mine, about who I really was, seemed to be wearing off. The more time I spent with them, the more I realised I was more like the other Defenders than I was unlike them. At first I looked at those planes flying 15 overhead and I longed, physically ached, to be up there looking down rather than down here looking up. To see the world spread out below, to be up there in the blue, to be so far up above you could no longer see people – that was it. To go up above people, to be away from ordinariness, to live in the pure inhuman ele- 20 ment of height and air. I still felt the appeal of that, the thrill of it. To be up there rather than down here … but the problem was, that was the same as wishing to be above normal people, not one of them. To say, I'm more like those people up in the plane than I'm like Sarge and Yos and Mary and Cooper and Shoona and Hughes 25 and Hifa and even my parents. To be one of them and not one of us. But I was realising that maybe I didn't want to be one of them; maybe I liked us more than I liked them. Though those planes still looked very beautiful, and it must be amazing to be that far up, to be moving that quickly, to be able to look down as you fly … 30

"Yeah, I don't know. College. Then, I don't know."

"No point pretending to know when you really don't."

"No."

Mary was the next one up. She came out of the girls' tent yawning and stretching, her curly hair seeming to stretch too, up and 35 out. She came over and helped herself to coffee – she was one of those temperamentally cheerful people who are hilariously moody in the morning until they've had some caffeine. After she finished her cup she was ready to talk.

"I wonder what they're planning to cook tonight," she said. Al- 40 though one of the reasons we had Help was so that we didn't have to cook, cooking was Mary's hobby and chief interest as well as her job: it was just her favourite thing to do. No need to ask her what her plans were for life after the Wall. It was her favourite topic of conversation, a running reverie about what she'd do once 45

to scheme *Ränke schmieden*

to wear off (*phr. v.*) to gradually disappear

to long *sich sehnen nach*

to help yourself to sth. to serve yourself
hilarious extremely funny and causing a lot of laughter
moody *launisch*

reverie (*lit.*) pleasant dream-like thoughts

she had the money to open her own place. (That part, the bit where she put together the money, was a little vague. But she had faith.) When she could cook whatever she wanted, as long as it was in season. She loved to talk about it.

5 "The produce you could get before the Change," she said. "Everything all the time. Tomatoes and fruits, hams from you name it, meat whenever you liked, all of it all year around. Oils, spices, herbs all year round, anything you wanted from anywhere at any time. I read those old books, I think, it must have been too easy,
10 you know? You could just cook anything. Whenever. It just makes you think, how did people know what to want? I mean, if it's anything you like, any time, it's like science fiction, where they have a machine that just makes stuff. It does your head in. Press a button, and it's roast beef, pheasant mole, chickpea fritters in yo-
15 ghurt dressing aioli, prawn curry, mango soufflé, duck blood stir fry, consommé, you know, where does it all end? I mean, the idea is amazing, everything all the time, I get it, it's weird and wrong too. Now here's less, but maybe, I don't know, I wouldn't say it's better, that would be mad, obviously it's not better, but you have
20 to work with what you've got, you know, and even if it is, you know, turnips, turnips, fucking turnips yet again, at least you know you're working with turnips because that's what came out of the ground and that's what you've got to cook and that's what you've got to make interesting, because there's no choice, you
25 know? And then it's cabbages or celeriac or swedes or beetroot or berries, it is whatever it is that comes out of the ground and that's what's amazing and beautiful about it, you know, that's what's interesting, not just going to the shops and being able to buy, you know, stuff that just got off a plane from who knows where."

30 She found it hard to leave the Help to get on with it, and spent the first few days hovering over the cook and making suggestions which, to judge from his body language, he didn't entirely appreciate. A proud man, you could see that. And yet by the end of the week they were cooking together, despite Shoona telling her she
35 was an idiot and the whole point of the holiday was not to be doing the very same thing she spent all her time doing when she was on the Wall. Mary's reply: "But I want to." There's never any answer to that.

Another question pressed on me while we were on holiday. It
40 was: when did Cooper and Shoona have sex? This was a mystery at barracks, and even more so here. We had asked them if they wanted a tent of their own – well, I say we, it was Hifa asking Shoona in private – and they had said no. Fine, but when and where did they do it? It must have involved sneaking off out-
45 doors, or round the back of buildings, or something. They never

produce agricultural and other natural products

to do one's head in to make sb. feel really mixed up, irritated
pheasant mole spicy sauce served with pheasant
chickpea fritters *Reibeplätzchen aus Kichererbsen*
prawn *Garnele*
consommé *Fleischbrühe*

turnip *Steckrübe*

celeriac *Knollensellerie*
swede *gelbe Kohlrübe*
beetroot *rote Beete*

to hover over to be always near

made any public gestures of affections and were in no obvious sense a couple, except they were.

My own plans in that direction came to nothing. I tried a couple of times to go off for walks with Hifa, but one of the problems with camping, it turned out, was that there was almost no privacy. ₅ Every time I made a sneaky suggestion – fancy a trip to the pub? fancy seeing what's over the hill? fancy a walk down to the nearest village? fancy borrowing a couple of rods from the landlord and going to try some fishing? – she would either immediately ask the others if they wanted to come too, or they would see us ₁₀ heading off and join us without asking, as if everyone had automatic permission to join in anything anyone else was doing. I felt pathetic, as if I'd gone back to school and wasn't all that far away from the stage of sexual development where boys' way of showing girls that they like them is to go up to them and pull their hair ₁₅ and then run to the other end of the room.

I still often think of that week. Maybe it's in part because of what happened afterwards. But at least some of it is because it was a magical seven days. I can't say it was the happiest time I spent on the Wall, because the whole point is that we weren't on the Wall, ₂₀ we were on holiday; but it was the best time I ever spent with my new Wall family. We walked, talked, ate, read. Drank a fair bit but never so that we were too hungover to enjoy the day after. The landlord let us use the bathrooms of the pub; he even let us wash and shower there. We got to know each other differently. Being a ₂₅ Defender was a personality people put on when they went to the Wall. Their non-Wall self was closer to their real self, maybe. Or maybe not, I now think, maybe there isn't a real self, just different versions of us we wear in different settings and with different people. The me who deals with my parents is not the me who ₃₀ talks to Hifa and that is not the me who takes orders from the Captain and that is not the me I am inside myself during my shift on the Wall, counting down the minutes to the end of the twelve hours.

On the last evening I finally managed to get Hifa to go off on her ₃₅ own with me, by sidling up to her, raising my eyebrows and asking, "Walk?" And just like that we set off down the hill from our camp. We walked down and around a col, then up to the top of a long valley and stood looking back down at the view. We were across the far side of the bowl of hills from where we were camp- ₄₀ ing and we could just see the pub. There was a final-night feeling, that back-to-school, back-to-reality vibe which you always get in the moments before you set off home at the end of a successful holiday. I thought: this is my moment to say something. Or maybe, don't say anything, just make my move? Hifa was ₄₅

---

sneaky doing things in a secret and unfair way
to fancy sth. to want to do sth.
rod *Angelrute*

pathetic hopeless, useless

a fair bit *eine ganze Menge*

to be hungover feeling unwell and having a sore head after drinking too much alcohol

to sidle up to sb. to move gradually closer to sb.

col mountain pass

bowl *here*: ring-like formation

vibe feeling, sensation

panting slightly from the exertion of walking the last stretch up-
hill, her hair pulled back by her knitted cap, her skin flushed, her
lips full and pink.

"When I grow up I'm going to be rich enough to have Help," Hifa
5 said, not forcefully but as if she was daydreaming. And just like
that I felt my moment go. She had said something which I'd been
thinking, but felt was too private to say. Wanting to have Help
was on my secret wish list, or had been, and this experience did
nothing to change that. If anything it made it seem more desir-
10 able. I had thought that Help was a status symbol, a technique for
signalling that you're rich. But the thing I learned that week was
how much nicer life could be if you had somebody else to do all
the boring and difficult bits for you. Having Help was like having
a life upgrade. I also realised this was one of the differences be-
15 tween me and Hifa. Because she didn't think she'd ever be rich
enough to have Help, she felt free to talk about it, disguised as a
joke. Because I thought I would one day be rich enough, because
my whole sense of myself was that I was going to be the kind of
person who was rich enough, I'd never make a joke about it. That
20 would be giving away real information about who I was and what
I wanted.

"Time to go back, the sun's about to go down," she said, turning
from the view. I could lunge? No, too late, too desperate. I had
missed my chance. I also thought, wow, it's funny how I don't re-
25 ally know anything about you.

The last morning came: back to reality. We packed, and headed
off to the train station to make the trip to the Wall. Our packs,
which had felt light on the way to the holiday, were heavy as we
set out on the return journey. We'd spent the whole week talking
30 and arguing and joshing, but we were quiet on the train. I was
still brooding on the issue of Help when we said goodbye at the
big terminus in London. There was something I'd been thinking
about that week. I'd never really thought about Help before, either having it or being it, and the linked question of what their
35 lives had been like before and after the Change, and the journeys
they had made to get here, and how they had got over the Wall,
and what it had been like to be among the Others and now to be
Help. I could just about imagine burning sand, a huge yellow sun
close overhead, salt water stinging in cuts, the weak being left
40 behind, the bitter tastes of exile and loss, the longing for safety,
the incandescent desperation and grief driving you onwards …
no, I couldn't really imagine. And yet here they were.

I don't know why the thing I wanted to know felt like an awkward question, but it did and I'd been storing up my nerve to ask.
45 At the station, the Help were leaving us to go to their next

to pant *schnaufen*
exertion the use of a lot of physical effort; *Anstrengung*

to lunge to move suddenly forward

to josh (*infml.*) to make jokes

to sting (stung, stung) *brennen*
cuts *Schnittwunden*

incandescent [ˌɪnkænˈdesənt] (*lit.*) extreme
desperation *Verzweiflung*
grief very great sadness; *Gram*
to store your nerve to remain calm in a difficult situation

assignment. As we Defenders had agreed, I took the cook aside for a moment to thank him and slip him an envelope with a tip for him and his partner – you aren't supposed to do that, but we thought it was the right thing. He took it with an inclination of his head. The only time I'd seen him smile, or even change expression, was on the last couple of days of the holiday, when he was cooking with Mary. This was my last chance. The station was busy and crowded, which created a sense of intimacy around our talk: we couldn't be overheard.

"I have something I wanted to ask," I said. The Help was a thin man, economical in movement, and whenever you spoke to him he stayed impassive, his hands by his sides. "What happened to the World, we here have a name for it, we call it the Change. But what I've been wondering is what other people call it, if there's a word for the same thing, or if it's just something that happened. I hope you don't mind me asking, but is there a word for the Change, what we call the Change, in your language?"

"Coo-ee-shee-a," I thought he said. I didn't know if I'd heard that correctly and had no idea what it meant, but there was something in his eyes that stopped me from asking more. He picked up his bag and he walked off with his partner, not saying goodbye and not looking back.

We went to the safe deposit office and picked up the precious cargo we'd left there before heading north: our communicators. Hifa kissed hers before turning it on and said, "I've missed you so much."

I wanted to look at my communicator in private. I put it in my pocket and waited until the others had started off for our train back to the Wall. The station was still frantic, mainly with commuters rushing home: it was one of those moments when you remember just how much life there is away from yours, away from being a Defender. All these people had homes, pay packets, families, hobbies, taxes to pay, things on their mind, TV series to catch up with, heating bills, gardens to plant. I had none of those things; maybe one day I would. At the moment I didn't particularly want them. It was odd: I wanted to get off the Wall, I wanted this time to be over, yet when I tried to think hard about what would be next, there was a blank.

I switched on my communicator. There were lots of messages but before I looked at them I went onto the net to look something up: coo-ee-shee-a. I didn't get it right first time because I spelt it wrong, but on the third attempt I found what I was looking for. *Kuishia* is a Swahili word. It means "the ending".

inclination *Neigung*

economical *sparsam*
impassive showing no feeling or emotion

commuter sb. who regularly travels between work and home

odd strange

Swahili a Bantu language spoken in eastern and south-eastern Africa

10

When we went back to the Wall, it wasn't strictly 'back' but to a new location on the east coast. Remember, two weeks on the Wall, two weeks off, of which the first week is holiday and the second week is (usually) training. This was a training section.
5 Defenders looked forward to these. Basic training was generally felt to be hell – that was the whole point of it, to toughen you up, get you used to all the new norms of the Wall, break you down and build you up again as a Defender. Once you were on the Wall, though, training weeks were, relatively speaking, fun. For a start,
10 every week you spent training was one less week on the Wall. You were in a new place, not your usual watchtower. Also, training meant you were doing new things – no point training the stuff you can already do.

We were sent to an early section of the Wall on a river estuary.
15 Most of the old riverscapes have gone since the Change – it's another thing we see only in pictures. Here, though, accidents of topography mean it still looks more or less the same as it does in old photos. There are sloping riverbanks, trees overhanging in the water, a gentle curve of slow-moving water and greenery. This
20 was one of the very first bits of the Wall to be built, and it was never used. The reason: as the Change progressed, engineers realised that the Wall need to start further out, so the river mouth was concreted over and the direction of the Wall had been reshaped. The result was a section of the Wall built to the usual
25 specs, but not in active use. A perfect spot for training. Also, because this wasn't the Wall proper, there was Help. Kit-cleaning and barracks maintenance was done by them. Chores and shitwork? Not on this watch! Now that right there was a little holiday in itself. Mary and the rest of her crew were especially jolly, be-
30 cause they had nothing to do: the Help did most of the cooking. They just sat around all day watching TV and playing games on their communicators. It would have been more annoying if they hadn't been so openly gleeful about it that they were hard to resent.

35 "This is a defend-attack exercise," said the Captain, the morning after we got to the watchtower. We were sitting in the barracks training room, which was the same as our own main room, except here you could see trees through the window – which made it feel very different. "We have a five-kilometre section of Wall to de-
40 fend for three days and three nights. Note that that's two K more than our usual distance. We'll be stretched. Each Defender will be guarding three hundred and thirty metres of Wall, not two hundred. Trust me: it's harder. Much harder. The other squad will be

estuary *Flussmündung*

riverscape *Flusslandschaft*

topography the physical appearance of the natural features of an area of land, especially the shape of its surface
to slope to go downward or upward in a angle

to concrete sth. over *etw. zubetonieren*

specs (*infml.*) short for specifications; *Vorgabe*
kit-cleaning the cleaning of clothes, tools, etc.
chore [tʃɔːr] an often boring job that needs to be done regularly
jolly cheerful
to annoy to make sb. angry

gleeful happy, excited, pleased
to be hard to resent *jdm. etw. kaum verübeln können*

attacking at some point over the next three days. Maybe more than once. I don't know anything about them, who they are or where they're from or what their numbers are. I'm guessing they're the same size unit as us, but I don't know that and we can't act on that assumption. We have to treat them exactly the same way we would treat Others. Except," he gave us one his rare, startling smiles, "with blanks instead of live ammo. You have a detector on your jacket. If it flashes, you're wounded but can keep fighting, if the light turns solid, you're dead. There are assessors to watch the fight. White armbands. If they tell you you're dead, you're dead. Don't mess with them, they have the power to give you extra time on the Wall. They film the fight with static and head cams too, and the ruling about who's dead and who's got through is made by combining what the assessors say with what they see on the footage. Any questions?"

We shuffled about a bit. Sarge eventually said, "Tell them about the fun part, sir."

The Captain actually laughed. It was clear he loved this kind of training – loved being active and doing things, as opposed to waiting for something to happen and being permanently on guard. He was still smiling.

"Yes – the fun part. After our three days we have a day to swap locations with the other squad, and then to make our own plans. Then, we're the attackers." I noticed he didn't say we're the Others. I was glad of it. The words would have seemed wrong; would have triggered a superstitious twinge. Nonetheless, it's what he meant, and was obviously what he was most looking forward to. The Captain, who had been an Other, loved the idea of playing at being an Other again, and play-acting at doing the thing he had once done for real.

"We're going to make their lives hell, for three days, and some of us are going to get over the Wall. I've done this exercise a number of times and I've never failed to get some of my squad over, and this time will be no exception. Think about it when you're on duty and we'll discuss and make plans on the turnover day. We're going to get over the Wall. You can all contribute ideas about how to do that. And I," he smiled again, "I've got some ideas too."

The session then became a general briefing about our section of the Wall, the peculiarities of its geography and topography. The headline news was that the riverbanks around here had been high and had descended to the river almost like cliffs, but cliffs which went up in stages, say five metres straight, then a small flat section, then another five metres. The steep banks were why the engineers had at one point thought the Wall could run here without much difficulty. They had turned out to be wrong, but only

---

assumption *Vermutung*

startling surprising
live ammo real, deadly ammunition
solid continuous, shining without a break

to mess with sb. to get involved/ to argue with sb.

cam camera

footage what has been filmed

to swap to change

superstitious *abergläubisch*
twinge a sudden short feeling of physical or mental pain

peculiarity the specific quality

to descend to go or come down

after they built the Wall. The result was that there was a ledge of riverbank left at the bottom of the Wall, not exactly like one of the old world's beaches, but wide enough to stand and walk on. This made the old cut-off section of the Wall a very useful place
5 for attackers, since there was somewhere they could perch. It was going to be an interesting week.

I don't think I ever saw our company in a better mood than during those seven days training. It really was like a holiday, or a holiday camp, because there was a structure, the unforgiving
10 structure of shifts, but also the change of location, the extra freedom of having Help, and, crucially, new faces. The Defenders who'd been there longer than I had knew their opposite numbers, their shift twins, but I only really knew Hughes. The rest of the other shift I'd met solely on those drunk, civilian-frightening
15 train journeys at the end of our deployment. It was entertaining to see how closely they paralleled us, with a new one (like me), a funny one, a grumpy one, one who needed to be told everything three times. They even had one whose hobby was whittling, just like Yos.
20 I was nervous when I started my first turn on the training section of Wall, or fake-Wall. To mix things up we would do three days of nights and three days of days with a complicated mixed swing-shift in the middle. Our section started on nights, which was both good and bad, since it meant we were getting the hardest part
25 over straight away, but on the other hand was more of a jolt, given that we'd just had a week off. The fact that we were on a not quite real version of the Wall felt strange: I was nervous, while also knowing that deep down there wasn't much reason to be nervous, not really since this wasn't like really being a Defender
30 and so if I failed to do my job I wasn't going to, you know, die. Also the scenery here was much more interesting, basically because there was one, as opposed to none at all except concretesky-waterwind. Here there was also a river, a section of Wall curling round a far bend of river, even trees! Just visible on a clear day
35 beyond the far section of Wall was a low range of green hills. By moonlight on that first night the landscape looked like an exotic world of composition, something a person had put together to show what you could do with blacks and whites and whatever those other moonlit colours are, not greys, but not normal colours
40 and not black/whites either. Dawn is when you can tell a white thread from a black thread, it says in the Quran. But there are still shadow-colour differences before dawn, when there's moonlight. Also, it wasn't as cold as our section of Wall. I don't know if we were lucky with the weather or if it was something to do with
45 there being less wind in this direction, or some other trick of

---

ledge *Felsvorsprung*

to perch to sit on or near the edge of sth.

crucially most importantly; *entscheidend*

deployment *Einsatz*

jolt a sudden violent change

bend a curved part of sth.

thread [θred] *Faden*
Quran [kəˈræn] the Koran

vigilant always being careful to notice things, especially possible danger

microclimate. For whatever reason, it was several degrees milder. Add it all together and it was much less hard. Which made it tempting not to be as vigilant as we were supposed to be.

"This is the life," someone said over the communicator, that first night. I laughed, then after I had, wondered why it was funny. ₅ Eventually I realised: because the idea that standing for twelve hours in the dark and bitter cold with an automatic weapon, waiting for someone to attack you, with certain death the price of failure, marks you in such a way that standing for twelve hours in the dark and slightly less cold waiting for someone to pretend to ₁₀ attack you, by comparison, feels like fun.

The first attack came that night, at four in the morning. It was good tactics on the part of the other squad – a bright moonlit night like this would normally be the last you'd choose for an assault. Also, we thought they'd take at least a day to look at the ₁₅ maps, work out the topography, make a plan. What they did, more simply and more effectively, was to cheat. They didn't approach the Wall over the estuary: they just were suddenly there, pouring over it at well-spaced intervals, silently, like ghosts. I had about five seconds of warning – in the form of weapons fire from ₂₀ a kilometre away, where the middle end of our section was overrun. I looked over, just had time to think, Oh shit, and a strange kind of electric shock, not a thought but a physical sensation, like the one you get when you're watching a horror film and something terrible starts to happen – you feel it in your back, your ₂₅

spine *Rückgrat*
sensation a vague feeling

to kick in (*phr. v.*) to begin to have an influence
A/R (*abbr.*) ArmaLite rifle
to scan to watch over

spine, your belly, but it's a sensation rather than an idea.

But it's true what Defenders say. The expression we use is that 'your training kicks in'. You find you have these new instincts baked into you. I clicked the safety off my A/R and looked back to my own section to scan. About a hundred metres away I saw two ₃₀ of them half over the Wall: one of them had made it but the other had got stuck and the first man was reaching down to pull his partner over. I lit them up, short bursts, the way I'd been trained. The first man looked over to me, then finished pulling his partner over the Wall, then turned to me with his hands in the air. I'd got ₃₅ them both. While I was congratulating myself on that, though, I heard a cracking sound from behind me and the red light on my chest started flashing. Again, training kicked in. I dived to the ground and rolled right towards the concrete bench at my post. Another two attackers had climbed the Wall in the other direc- ₄₀ tion and were coming towards me. With part of my brain I realised that if this was going on all along our section of Wall, it must mean we were in the middle of a full-company attack, and we were outnumbered two to one: their whole company was attacking our half-company squad. With the rest of my brain I was ₄₅

burst *Salve*

trying to steady myself enough to aim. I got a long burst off, longer than we were supposed to fire in one go. If you shoot too many rounds at once, the muzzle of your gun travels, and you veer off the target.

5 I was – partly by luck and partly by training – in a good position with decent cover, mostly hidden by the bench, while both the attackers were out in the open. They should have split up and rushed me. Maybe they froze, maybe they thought they'd got me when they came up on me from behind. Mistake. After I got off a

10 long clip one of them raised his hands to put his gun down. The other, whose red light was blinking, jumped up and began running towards me, jinking from side to side. He was about forty metres away and closing rapidly. I was out of ammo and had to change the magazine, and was grateful for the time Sarge had

15 caught me and bollocked me about taping them together the right way, because I had the new clip in before the attacker got to me and was raising the gun to shoot when the light on my chest went red just as I heard shots from behind me. I couldn't believe it – but no doubt that's what it's like, in a real fight. When you get shot

20 your first thought is that you can't believe it. Ooh I've been shot. Ooh so this is what it's like to be shot. Ooh this is what it's like to be dying, dying, dead ...

Some philosopher said that death is not an event in life. Maybe. It doesn't feel like that in a fight. It feels very much the opposite:

25 that death, yours or your opponent's, is not just an event in life, but the entire point of life. The culmination and meaning of the journey.

I turned. Two of the attackers had come up behind me. A white-armband assessor was with them. I was officially dead. An eerie

30 feeling, or mixture of feelings. I was annoyed, in the way you're annoyed when you're playing a game, and think you're winning, but suddenly lose; I was a little proud, because I'd 'killed' three of them and it had taken six of them to 'kill' me, though it was that irritating kind of pride that you can't express without sounding

35 as if you're boasting, and I knew without having to think about it that boasting about an event which had ended with me being 'killed' would quickly lead to teasing and to a new nickname like, I don't know, Dead Boy; I was a tiny bit relieved, because the fight was over, the tiring bit of the shift was over, the worst had hap-

40 pened, I was done for the night.

The two attackers who had snuck up behind me now put their heads together with the one I'd been shooting at, and began debating what to do next; declare that they had got over the Wall and stop, or run to the next section, several hundred metres away,

45 and join in the ongoing fight there. There was gunfire, but it was

---

to steady yourself to become calm and controlled
to get a burst off to fire a number of bullets in quick succession
muzzle *Mündung*
to veer off to suddenly change direction

clip magazine of bullets

to jink *ausweichen*

to bollock *anschnauzen*

chest *Oberkörper*

culmination *Höhepunkt, krönender Abschluss*

eerie strange in a frightening, mysterious way; *unheimlich*

to boast *prahlen*

sporadic; it was hard to tell what was going on. I went over to the three 'dead' attackers, who were standing together. It was a rule of these exercises that the 'dead' couldn't talk to the living, but there was no rule to say we couldn't talk to each other.

"Hi," said one. He broke a piece of chocolate off a bar and gave it ₅ to me. Chocolate was a real Defenders' luxury, very hard to get if you were off the Wall, so this was an insider's gesture, a peace offering.

"Thanks. Didn't see that one coming. You were hiding, yeah?"

to conceal to hide

I'd worked it out: the only way they could have done what they ₁₀ had done was if they'd been concealed on the ledge below the Wall and were waiting for us when we came on shift. Cheating, in other words, since they could never have made it to that spot any other way on a clear moonlit night. My section of the Wall had been swarmed: I found out later that thirty of them, arranged ₁₅ in five groups of six, had attacked five sections of the Wall, and mine was one of them.

"Yup."

legit (*infml.*) short form of legitimate; allowed

"Well, if the assessors let you do it, it's legit."

"Yeah, that's what our Captain said." ₂₀

"Done this before?"

"Attack-defend? No. You?"

I reckon I think

"No. More fun than being on the Wall, I reckon."

no shit (*sl.*) absolutely right

"No shit."

The two heroes who had shot me in the back had ended their ₂₅

colloquy (*fml.*) a formal conversation; *Unterredung*

colloquy and decided to go 'over the Wall', so the fight was officially over. The assessor told the wounded man he wasn't fit enough to go with them, so he started jogging down the ramparts towards the fight in the near distance. The assessor went with him. The attackers turned and went off in the other direction, ₃₀ back towards the watchtower and the barracks. One of the men stepped forward to shake my hand. I returned the gesture to the other, who turned out to be a woman. We all seemed somehow to

chum (*old use, infml.*) friend

be chums.

lot a large number of people

"Where are you lot staying?" I asked. ₃₅

"Two barracks along. Just round the river bend so you lot can't see us."

"How are you getting back?"

"Lorry. At the end of the exercise. Should be there any minute now." ₄₀

They gave me another piece of chocolate. About halfway back to

to breach sth. to make an opening in a wall or fence, especially in order to attack sb. or sth. behind it

the watchtower, I saw Hughes coming towards me. Of course: the Wall never goes unguarded. This exercise was meant to be realistic, so if the Wall had been breached, the new watch would have to come on. As he came closer it was clear that he was too tired to be angry about being woken in the middle of the night.

"Sorry mate," I said as we passed each other.

"Got any food?" We were sent straight out, no time."

5 I emptied my pockets. Hughes took what I had. The assessors would have said this was against the rules, but there were no assessors there, so what the hell.

"You kill all this lot?" he asked.

"Three of them. The other two got me."

10 "No hard feelings," said one of the men I'd 'killed', smiling, his voice claggy from the chocolate he was eating. We carried on back to the watchtower. Their lorry was waiting, and we all shook hands again. "See you later," I said, which got a laugh, because if I did, it would likely be with me having swarmed over the Wall, 15 and them lying in wait for me, another fight to the 'death'. No hard feelings, the living and the dead, more in common than you might think; a tiny bit of luck here and there dividing them; taking turns to live, taking turns to die; all in the same boat. All the same really. Others, Defenders – what's the difference? I 20 couldn't decide if this was the opposite of what it would be like to fight to the death, or a good preparation for it.

claggy (*BE, Northern English, infml.*) thick

to take turns *sich abwechseln*

11

debriefing official discussion after completion of a job

sneak unexpected, surprise

to ambush sb. to suddenly attack sb. after hiding and waiting for them

At the debriefing, I thought the Captain would give us a giant bollocking, but that didn't happen. It turned out he'd been in on it all along. That explained why he hadn't been there the night before, which I have to admit I had been wondering about. The two Captains had discussed this sneak attack and ours had agreed ₅ to allow the set-up. It was a way of testing our combat skills: not how well we'd catch Others sneaking up on the Wall, but how well we'd do in an all-out fight with a big group who'd got over and ambushed us.

"Not fair? You're probably thinking that? No, not fair. That's the ₁₀ point of the exercise. We train hard to fight easy. This may save your life one day. If you are overrun, you won't be wondering how or why it happened. You'll be fighting for your life. Lessons learned today may save you. Any questions?"

Hifa put her hand up. I was surprised: in groups she was usually ₁₅ quiet. "Yes. Do we get to do it to them?"

The Captain smiled slowly. "Oh yeah."

"Good."

Thirty of them had attacked. The whole squad, as I'd thought. Eighteen of them had been killed, and seven wounded sufficiently ₂₀ seriously that, according to the assessors, they wouldn't have been able to get away. Five of them had got over the Wall and 'escaped'. In real life, if they really were Others, they wouldn't get far, of course: they didn't have chips. They'd last a few days at best. After being rounded up they'd presumably decide to be ₂₅ Help.

Seven of us had been 'killed', all five of the Defenders on the sections which were swarmed, and two others who went to help them. Five wounded. Out of fifteen of our shift, only three of us were 'unharmed'. In real life, if a breach like that had happened, ₃₀ everyone responsible would be put to sea. A Defenders' court would determine how many people that was. If the other squad, the day shift, were found to have been slow in reacting, and that had contributed to the breach, some of them would be put to sea too. The Captain went into detail about the attack and our re- ₃₅ sponse to it, what had gone right, what had gone wrong. The take-away was clear: if Others get onto the Wall in numbers, and you aren't waiting for them, you're screwed.

take-away here: message

to be screwed (sl.) to be in huge trouble

chill totally calm and relaxed

to be riddled here: to be shot multiple times

Hifa had been one of those 'killed'. Her section of the Wall had been swarmed. Whereas I was, I found, pretty chill about being ₄₀ 'killed' – as the Captain said, it was a set-up, the whole point of exercises was that you went through experiences like this – Hifa didn't feel like that. Being riddled with blank automatic bullets

had got to her. She was silent and had gone into herself. After the
debrief we went and sat in the mess and Help brought us a cup of
tea.

"It's fake," I said to her afterwards. "It's children playing let's
5 pretend. Think of it as being like a video game."

"I don't play video games," she said, which was true. We sat there
for a bit. "Let's pretend ..." she said. "I used to like that. Let's pretend ... Grown-ups don't do enough let's pretend."

"You're a grown-up?"

10 She chucked a peppermint at me. That meant she was feeling better.

"Anyway, this was a nasty version of let's pretend. We're never
going to get thirty Others hiding at the bottom of the Wall waiting when we come on shift. It's as much let's pretend as building
15 a blanket fort and saying it's a castle."

"What kind of castle?"

"One with many turrets."

"Who lives in the castle?"

"A happy ogre."

20 "Oh! On his own?"

"Not necessarily."

"A lot of space. Even for an ogre."

"He needs space."

"He has commitment issues."

25 "And his breath is toxic. Literally – it poisons people. Even other
ogres."

"Sounds a bit like Yos."

"Now that's harsh," I said.

"I bet the ogre whittles."

30 "He can't, his hands are too big, he wants to whittle but he just
busts things."

"Poor ogre."

"Then he takes the broken pieces of wood and assembles them
into sculptures which he sells for enormous amounts of money to
35 collectors. That's how he can afford the castle. But he would trade
it all for being able to whittle."

"I feel sorry for the ogre now."

"I think you're right to."

"What does he eat?"

40 I thought for a moment.

"Children."

Hifa had a very appealing laugh, half an octave deeper than her
speaking voice.

Sarge appeared at the far end of the barracks. "Oi! You're back on
45 shift in thirty minutes." The attack had meant that all the shifts

---

to get to sb. (*phr. v.*) to make sb. suffer

to pretend *here*: to imagine

to chuck to throw sth. carelessly

turret *Gefechtsturm, Schützenstand*

ogre (*infml.*) a fierce and frightening person

commitment issues *Beziehungsprobleme*

to bust sth. to break sth. open or apart

muddled badly organized or mixed up

spell a period of time

to give sth. a go to try very hard to succeed

chop and roll rauer und ruhiger Wellengang

trauma shock

to snipe to shoot at sb. from a position where you cannot be seen
abreast in a line
narwhal Einhornwal
Wagner Richard Wagner (1813 – 1883), German composer; referring to a scene from the Vietnam War film Apocalypse Now
penultimate second from the last

pleasantry humorous remark
to give sb. the finger to put your middle finger up

recreational amenity Freizeiteinrichtung

schedule-wise according to the plans

were muddled, and we had swapped with the day watch. I sighed, Hifa sighed, we both began to get up and get ready. Sarge was in a good mood because he was one of the people who'd survived the attack (mainly by accident of place, if you ask me, though I wouldn't say that to his face). 5

We got through the rest of our defensive turn on the pretend-Wall, five more days, without being breached again. That's not the same as saying it was uneventful, because the longest spell between attacks was eighteen hours. Respect to that other company, they really gave it a go. But none of them got over the Wall. 10 To be honest, none of them even got particularly close. A sequence of moonlit nights helped. The estuary landscape meant you didn't have the distant blurred horizons of sky-sea which at dawn and dusk could make the light so difficult. Also, the waves were small to non-existent, river waves, and there was nothing 15 like the chop and roll which would make it so hard at our usual post. So there were factors which helped. Despite that, it was reassuring, after the trauma of that first night, that well-trained attackers coming at you under normal conditions were relatively easy to track and kill. We would see them a few hundred metres 20 off and light them up. The assessors claimed that a few of us were shot by people sniping from boats, but we all thought that was bullshit. Others with snipers using automatic weapons from boats? Sure, and they also ride in seven abreast on trained narwhals, blaring Wagner over loudspeakers. Their best attack was 25 on the penultimate night. I slept through it. They swam in a kilometre and tried to climb the Wall solo. The crew on duty let them get close, then picked them off one at a time.

Then it was our turn. We sorted out our stuff, got on a lorry and drove off to the other barracks, which, as the guys from their 30 company had said, was around the corner of the river, two watchtowers away. Halfway there we passed their lorry heading in the other direction, and some pleasantries were exchanged: our entire company stood up and gave them the finger, in formation.

The other barracks was the same as every other barracks, except 35 with a few more recreational amenities: table tennis, pool tables, and it even had a gym and a cinema. Of course! The defensive watch had to be on duty all the time, every day, but as attackers, we could pick and choose. We didn't have to work shifts, we could do whatever we liked, schedule-wise. Well, not quite: we'd do 40 exactly what the Captain told us to do, exactly when he told us to do it. Still, by comparison, where the other shift had been a bit like a holiday, this really was a holiday.

The Captain, it goes without saying, had other ideas. We were given orders an hour after we got to the new site. The meeting 45 was held in the briefing room. He was standing next to Sarge and Yos and I wouldn't say he was rubbing his hands with eager anticipation while cackling with glee, because he just wasn't that person, but he was pretty close.

⁵ "The fun part!" he said. "Now, first, a little exercise. Hands up everybody who enjoyed the experience of being overrun by Others, killed and wounded, or surviving only to be put to sea?"

The contrast between what he was saying – naming everyone in the room's worst fear – and his super-jaunty tone was like a slap.

¹⁰ Nobody's hand went up.

"Didn't think so," he said. "It includes me, by the way. The officer in charge of a company which allows a breach is automatically put to sea."

I looked around the room. It was clear that most people had for-¹⁵ gotten that.

"The reason this is the fun part is, we get to do to them what they did to us. They get to feel what it's like. You're probably wondering how, given that the landscape round here makes the Wall unrealistically easy to defend. They got to ambush us. That was ²⁰ an advantage agreed in advance. In return, we get an advantage, like them, once and once only. A five-minute power cut,"

A shifting and sitting-up took place in the room.

"That's right. Total loss of power for five minutes and five minutes only, on a night of our choosing. The idea is that Others or ²⁵ their sympathisers have co-ordinated a spot of sabotage. You might say it's unlikely, but so was that ambush attack on the first night unlikely. In case you're wondering, that is the standard training exercise here. These two respective advantages are always given to the two companies training on his site. This is our ³⁰ chance to even the score. Except, I don't want to even the score. They got five over the Wall. I want to go not one better, not two better, but twenty-five better. I want to get an entire squad over the Wall. That would be a record and it's a record I want."

He looked around as if trying to catch someone, anyone, in the ³⁵ act of not wanting the record so much as he did. No takers.

"So how do we do it?" I have my ideas. I want to hear yours."

Silence. Shuffling. More silence.

"This is going to be a very long meeting if nobody has anything to contribute."

⁴⁰ Cooper put his hand up.

"We make it hard for them."

"Yes, good. How?"

Fidgeting. I think it wasn't so much that people were clueless as that we didn't want to say stupid things in front of the Captain. ⁴⁵ He had that effect.

---

anticipation *Erwartung, Vorgefühl*
to cackle with glee to laugh in a high, loud voice excitedly

jaunty cheerful, jovial
slap *Ohrfeige*

power cut *Stromausfall*

to even a score to treat sb. in the same bad way they treat you

over. The others got eleven between them. Nineteen over the Wall was an all-time record. The next best was fourteen. From the moment the lights went out to the moment the assessors said the fight was over was seven minutes. Combat is like that, an undanceable rhythm: slow, slow, slower, sudden pandemonium. When we got back to barracks, the Captain, unlike the rest of us, wasn't elated. He just went calmly round and shook everyone's hand individually, the only time he ever did.

pandemonium *wildes Durcheinander*

elated extremely happy and excited

5

12

The other squad came over and we had a few drinks. No alcohol on the Wall, but this wasn't the real Wall. Somebody put some music on and there was dancing. There was karaoke, and people took turns, then one of their squad, a woman, had such an amaz-
5 ing voice that we stopped taking turns and listened to her sing soul classics for a while. Then a few more drinks. And a few more after that. Like I said, a holiday. Their squad was supposed to go home to their barracks but it emerged that their lorry drivers had got into conversation with our lorry drivers, and had opened
10 some cans, and then further cans, etc. and they had ended up as hammered as everyone else so there was nobody sober to drive the lorries. They ended up crashing in our barracks, using spare beds, sofas, chairs, even the pool tables. Only a drunk Defender can think a pool table makes an adequate bed.
15 The next morning we were due to go back to our real posts. That would involve about five hours in the lorry, ash-mouthed, suet-faced, smelling of recent disinterment. The other squad had it even worse: they were going back to north Wales. Hifa, who I'd last seen dancing with the woman with the amazing voice, was
20 wearing a beanie, the same she'd worn in her indeterminate-sex phase when I first met her, and her small features were peeking out from beneath it, scowling with hangover. If I'd been less hung-over myself it would have been funny. My day began with an increasingly panicky fifteen-minute search for my glasses, which
25 ended when I realised I'd never taken them off. Before our journey of horror, in the briefing room, a lecture. Or rather a 'little talk' from a member of the elite, some politician or government official, a short shiny young man with a mop of blond hair in an also shiny suit. He came into the overlit room and stood at the
30 podium. We stand up for officers, but he wasn't an officer, so we stayed put. He looked a little surprised at the state of us. Sixty dishevelled and severely hungover Defenders, unimpressed and unimpressive: not the world's easiest audience.
"Well done!" he said, brightly. They always start by praising you.
35 "The world's best home defence force, participating in the world's best training programme!"
Both parts of that were news to us, but whatever.
"I've been hearing from your commanding officers. Remarkable!"
I looked across Hifa, who was sitting next to me. At this close
40 range I could see she was very slightly swaying. Her eyes weren't closed, but on the other hand they weren't fully open either. I gave her a nudge, which was a mistake, because she turned towards me and exhaled. Not only could I smell the alcohol, I could

to emerge to become known

hammered (sl.) very drunk
to crash (sl.) to sleep

ash-mouthed mit pelziger Zunge
suet-faced having a sickly pale or yellow complexion; blass wie Talg
disinterment Exhumierung

indeterminate not clearly known

to scowl düster dreinschauen

dishevelled very untidy

nudge the act of pushing sb./sth. gently
to exhale ausatmen

actually tell that she'd been drinking spiced rum. Her eyes were bloodshot, which didn't stop her rolling them at the politician. "We can truly say, this country has never been better Defended. And it is thanks to women and men such as you. I think you deserve a round of applause!"   5

He began to clap. I think the idea was that we would join in and start applauding ourselves too – yeah! go us! – but he had severely misread the room. We sat there waiting for the point of this, assuming it had a point. It was hard to imagine he'd done this often before. He was a baby politician, an infant member of 10 the elite. He still had his training wheels. I may have been sleep-deprived, I might possibly still have been a bit drunk, but I fell for a moment in a reverie, a kind of guided dream, in which I imagined baby members of the elite being born from chrysalises, already wearing their shiny suits, their ties pre-knotted, their first 15 clichés already on their lips, being wiped down of cocoon matter and pushed towards a podium, ready to make their first speech, spout their first platitude, lose their virginity at lying. They'd be made to do that before they were given any food or drink or comfort, just to make sure it was the thing they knew first and best, 20 the thing which came most naturally. They tell us that everyone goes to the Wall, no exceptions. Somehow, though, when I saw the politician, I knew for the first time that that couldn't be true. This man had clearly never been on the Wall. He had never been a Defender. You could smell it on him. It was sometimes said that 25 rich people rigged ID chips so that Help went to the Wall instead of them. You heard rumours about medical exemptions, exemptions for extra education. No one ever admitted to not going on the Wall, but we all suspected that there were rich and powerful people who got out of it.   30

He stopped clapping. You could tell that he could tell that this was going badly, and also that he knew he mustn't show that he knew it. His manner changed and became more brisk. He let some of his sense of his own power show.

"Unfortunately, being a Defender isn't all a matter of praise and 35 compliments. However deserved they might be! And we have some new intelligence. Information with a direct bearing on your –

"and it was very interesting the way he said this next word, because you caught a glimpse of something cold and dark in him, just for that tiny moment, a small window into what he really 40 thought of us, and the distance between his life and ours –

"duties." Our duties. Yes, OK, our duties, our long nights in the cold and dark, twelve hours at a time spent bored shitless and in fear of our lives. That was what, in his eyes, we were for. That was our use, our purpose.   45

---

training wheels *Stützräder*
sleep-deprived not having had enough sleep

chrysalis *Larve eines Schmetterlings*

to wipe sth. down (*phr. v.*) to clean the surface of sth.
cocoon matter *here*: larvenähnlich
to spout *ausspucken*
platitude *Gemeinplatz, Platitüde*
virginity *Jungfräulichkeit*

to rig sth. *fälschen*
exemption *Freistellung*

brisk quick, energetic, active

"As you all know, the Change was not a single solitary event. We speak of it in that manner because here we experienced one particular shift, of sea level and weather, over a period of years it is true, but it felt then and when we look back on it today still feels like an incident that happened, a defined moment in time with a before and an after. There was our parents' world, and now there is our world."

That was sly of him. He was close to us in age, close enough to know how sensitive and how universal this feeling was, about the gulf between us and the generation before. The energy in the room changed. He might be every bad thing we knew him to be but he also knew some truths.

"The Change – before and after. Elsewhere, though, it was not like that. The Change was not an event but a process, a process that in some places, some unlucky places, has not stopped. In many of the hotter places of the world, in particular, the Change is still continuing, still reshaping landscapes, still impacting people's lives. Men and women fled from it, fled from its consequences, tried to make new lives for themselves, to scramble for new shelter, to climb to higher ground, to find a ledge, a cave, a well, an oasis, a place where they could find safety for them and their families. But," he said, his tone changed again, and he really did sound like a member of the elite, a man used to giving orders and breaking bad news, "the Change did not stop. The shelter blew away, the waters rose to the higher ground, the ground baked, the crops died, the ledge crumbled, the well dried up. The safety was an illusion. So the unfortunates must flee again, and they have begun, again, in numbers, like the numbers from many years ago when the Change first struck. Big numbers, dangerous numbers. So that is the first thing I am here to tell you. The Others are coming. We have had years of relative peace and calm, but that time is now over. You will be busy. The things for which you have been training: you are likely, more likely than for some years, to do them for real."

Now this really did count as news. I suddenly felt a lot less drunk. Hifa was sitting up straight staring at the man. The rest of the squads were too. Whatever we had thought we were going to hear, it wasn't this.

"The Flight and our friends abroad have confirmed this. Others are on their way. That is my first piece of information for you. But," he smiled, "the Wall has been here for years, and your training is, as I've already said, the best in the world. You are the best in the world. This country is the best of the world. We have prevailed, we do prevail, we will prevail. This we know to be true. However," his tone sad now, regretful, more-in-sorrow-than,

sly clever

to impact to have an influence on sth.

to scramble to compete with other people
well *Brunnen, Quelle*

to break news to inform about sth. that has just happened, is just beginning to happen
crops *Getreide*

to strike (struck, struck) *here*: to cause suffering

calm a quiet or peaceful period

to prevail to continue to exist and remain in control
regretful showing that you feel sorry about sth.
sorrow a feeling of great sadness

"there are those among us who do not see things the same way. There are those who see our desire for security, for safety, for peace" – he stretched out his arms in a gesture people often made when they were talking about the Wall, as if the Wall was like a giant pair of outspread arms – "as a selfish desire. A selfish, self- 5 interested turning away from the world. A refusal of our responsibilities. A – well, there's no point going on. You can't argue with people who want you to drown, to be overrun, to be washed away. You can't argue! There's nothing you can tell them to make them change their mind. And yet, they are there, and we have informa- 10 tion that some of them, some of these deluded people, are doing something almost impossible to believe. They're taking the side, not of the ordinary decent people of this country, the people you Defenders guard and protect, the people for whom you spend your long nights and days on the Wall, the people whose security 15 is the meaning and purpose of what you do – no, they don't take their side." He was getting into it now. He dropped his voice to a loud, histrionic whisper. "They take the side of the Others!"

After dropping that, he leant back from the podium and let it sink in. "Yes. They take the side of the Others. The Others! They would 20 rather be on the side of the Others than on the side of their own people. It is hard to imagine such wickedness. Hard to imagine being so wrong, so morally lost, so ethically destitute. I know that decent people will find it difficult to believe. But we must accept that these lost souls exist and that they are, there is no other way 25 of putting this, on the side of the Others. And what is more, and this is the new information that we now have, they are taking steps to help the Others. There is intelligence that some of these, I would call them criminals except that most criminals are just citizens who have lost their direction in life, made some mistakes, 30 gone awry – I will instead call them what they are, traitors. These traitors are working on ways of helping the Others. Of getting the Others away from us if they succeed in getting over the Wall. Of communicating with the Others, of suggesting places and times to attack, even, and this is the most concerning development of 35 all, of helping them get chips, of helping them to disappear into our society if they succeed in breaching the Wall. Of helping to defeat the Wall, defeat the Defenders – that's right, helping them to defeat you!"

You know what: looking around the room, I could tell that the 40 feeling had shifted again. We weren't that bothered. The news that more Others were coming, and coming imminently – that was an issue for us. That was real. We knew what that meant. The fact that Others were getting help from inside, that they might get away from the system once they were over the Wall, that wasn't 45

refusal *Zurückweisung, Ablehnung*

to drown *ertrinken, untergehen*

deluded believing things that are not real or true

decent socially acceptable or good

histrionic *theatralisch, pathetisch*

wickedness evil

ethically destitute without moral values

intelligence secret information about foreign governments and enemies

to go awry [əˈraɪ] to not do things in the intended way
traitor a person who is not loyal; *Verräter*

bothered worried, concerned
imminent coming very soon

really our problem. I could tell that it was a huge issue for the baby politician and I could see why, but from a Defender's point of view, if the Other gets over you're dead anyway, so the fact of the Other getting a shiny microchip and successfully hiding from the state isn't your worry. A big deal for the Others, obviously, and for the elite, but for Defenders, an Other who had got away was no longer our concern.

He talked for a bit more but there wasn't any further new information. The take-away was, the Others were coming and they have assistance. When he finished, we packed our stuff and got in the lorry for the drive to our next shift on the Wall. About halfway there, my head started hurting and I began feeling sick: I had stopped being drunk and my hangover had kicked in. It was a long trip. When we got to our barracks, the previous watch was still on duty: we had some time to go before our shift started. I went to bed and slept for eighteen hours.

II
THE OTHERS

13

Back at the Wall, everything was the same. It always was, physically: the same sky, the same sea, the same wind, the same horizon. Same concretewaterwindsky. But the politician had been right too. Rumours were going around that there was increased
5 activity by the Others. More boats on the horizon, more lights at night. There was also news of attacks, three in the last two weeks. (Detailed briefings on any attack were given to all Defenders. You never knew when you might learn something that would later save your life.) The attacks had been very poorly planned and
10 inexpert, basically Others just coming up to the Wall in rowing boats, asking to be killed. Remember, though, on the Wall, low risk is high risk. The Captain brought us all together and gave a lecture on exactly this topic.

"So why is this bad news? Being under attack from untrained,
15 unarmed Others who have exactly zero chance of getting through." I held up my hand.

"Because it means they're desperate. And if the clueless ones are desperate, the clever ones will be too."

"Point to Chewy," said the Captain. "Don't let the thick ones make
20 you lower your guard. They're coming."

Hughes held up his hand. "Sir, any evidence of that support from collaborators that we were warned about?" he asked.

"No," said the Captain. It was impressive how he could, just by standing still with no change of expression, call something
25 bullshit without using the word.

So, they were coming. And yet, at any given time, on any given shift, they weren't. Not yet anyway. Three attacks on ten thousand kilometres of Wall wasn't all that many attacks, when you averaged it out. The year was heading into early summer. The
30 longer, marginally warmer days and shorter, marginally warmer nights made being on duty easier for both shifts. I had also, I realised, got through the first phase of being a Defender, the one where every shift was an assault on my sense of what was physically possible, and was now at the second stage, where you get
35 used to it, where the rhythm of shift is familiar, where you know that the twelve hours are going to go past, and the best thing to do is just let them: don't fight the passing of time, ride on it, float on it. Better: let it go its own way. Don't look at your watch. Think about something else. If anything happens, let your
40 adrenaline and your training take care of it. Don't live on the edge. Don't be on edge. Time will pass, all you have to do is let it. I spent many hours, that shift, thinking about the conversation I'd had with Hughes while we were camping. What did I want to

inexpert amateurish

clueless having no knowledge of sth.

thick (*sl.*) stupid

collaborator a person who works with an enemy who has taken control of their country

to average sth. out (*phr. v.*) den Durschnitt berechnen
marginally slightly

adrenaline [əˈdrenələn]
to be on edge to be nervous and tense

be when I grew up? If I wasn't going to be a member of the elite, what was I going to do instead? I might be comrades and friends with my fellow Defenders, might feel I had things in common with them, but that didn't mean I liked or had things in common with my parents. I wasn't going to go back home. Home 5 no longer felt like home. I'd go to college and then what? Hughes wanted to spend his life among books. I didn't. I quite liked the idea of going and living with some of my new friends, Hifa and Cooper and Shoona and Mary and Hughes, going off together and finding a new way of living, more communal, not family- 10 based but where we would live together and look after each other and maybe other like-minded people would join us. We'd maybe live on a farm, we'd maybe have, you know, goats. The kind of thing farm people had.

I had to admit that I knew nothing about farming. I just liked the 15 idea of trying something else. I didn't want to spend the rest of my life in a suburban hutch doing work I didn't even have the emotional energy to hate. Like my parents. When you're on the Wall, you're desperate to get off the Wall. It's all you think about: getting through your turn of duty, getting off the Wall. But then 20 you start to think, why? What do I want to get off the Wall for? What's waiting for me?

I could just – this was the terrible, unsayable thing, the thing I would have sworn an oath was impossible, just weeks before – I could just start to see why people sometimes signed up for more 25 than one shift on the Wall. People like Sarge and the Corporal, who were on their second turn; people like the Captain, who had done three and was now on his fourth. I'm not saying that I was starting actively to think about it. I'm just saying that I could see why people did. See that they liked the combination of long dull 30 uneventful days with a strong sense of purpose looming overall; the mix of aimless time, structured days and meaningful work. A bit like human life in general, you could say, the terrible regularity with which nothing happens, the genuine terror when something happens. Hurry up and wait. That's the motto which gov- 35 erns most lives. It's the motto which governs the Wall, for sure. The only thing worse when nothing happens is when something does.

Or maybe I'd do a bit of both, or all three: I'd do another shift on the Wall, which would be horrible, as horrible as this one, except 40 perhaps it would be a bit less so because I would understand what I was doing and I would be doing it not because I had to, not because I had no choice, but precisely because I did have a choice, because it was up to me, because it was in my control, and I knew what I'd be gaining by doing it. I'd be gaining a route up and out, 45

communal involving different social groups

suburban an area on the edge of a large town or city where people who work in the town or city often live

hutch *Stall*

dull not interesting or exciting in any way

aimless without any clear intention, purpose or direction

to gain sth. *erreichen, erringen*
route a method of achieving sth.

a chance to become someone else, a chance to win privileges, like the Captain – maybe I'd be offered a chance to train as an officer, then go to college, then fight my way into the elite and zoom around on planes for a bit, go to ... do whatever it is members of
5 the elite do, conferences or talks or meetings, big discussions about the Change, then go and start a commune and live with Hifa and the others and find a new style of living, a new balance. New things to want, new ways to be. Yes, that was a good idea, that was now my new policy, my plan: I would do a little bit of
10 everything.

That was how my mind would wander during those nights, nights which seemed to be appreciably shorter with every shift that went past. After ten days, the 'night' shift was starting in full daylight and ending in full daylight. The first coffee/snack break,
15 Mary coming down the Wall on her bicycle cart, was just as night fell, the last visit from her, with her last coffee of the shift, was just before dawn. Right from my first day I had liked Mary's visits – there was nothing original about that, everyone loved Mary. It's hard not to like the person who comes bringing chat
20 and laughter and company and a warm drink in the middle of a long lonely watch, but even so, her personality was perfectly adapted to the job. She was the kind of person who leaves most people smiling, most of the time. Even the look of her could make you smile, her round pretty pink face and curly near-ginger hair,
25 which always seemed to be trying to escape from whatever she was wearing to control and contain it – a kerchief when she was in the kitchen, a hood or a beanie or a cap when she was out, depending on the warmth and the wetness. Those long stretches of time made people cranky, and it was easy to have sharp swings
30 in mood, passages of time when you felt sure you weren't going to get through it. Mary never had that: her job was a relatively privileged one, by comparison, and she knew it, and made it part of her job to make everyone else feel better.

The tenth night of that shift, Mary did her second set of rounds
35 with dawn minutes away. I watched her on her usual routine, her bike stopping in each Defender's pool of light as she came along the ramparts, cup of warm drink and a few words for everyone. That night a gale was blowing. The waves and the wind were so loud that it was hard to hear even the communicator earpiece. A
40 roar, the sea as loud as I had ever heard it. The Captain had already been round twice that night, not saying anything much, just checking in. It was clear that he had taken the warnings from the baby politician seriously. I don't remember exactly what I was thinking, probably counting down to the end of the shift: four
45 more nights, meaning it was nearly over, and then two weeks

to zoom around to travel frequently

appreciably beträchtlich

ginger a red or orange-brown colour

kerchief Kopftuch

cranky (infml.) easily annoyed or upset

away and then two weeks of days, concretewaterwindsky, and then I'd be almost halfway through my first year on the Wall. It wasn't quite time to begin celebrating that the end was in sight, but I could at least know that I knew how to get through the time, that it would go past and then it would be over and I'd be off the ₅ Wall.

Mary stopped for a longer than usual chat with Shoona. There was a **faint** line at the horizon, dawn imminent, though the wind hadn't yet **dipped** as it often does at daybreak. She got back on her bike – or rather put her feet back on the pedals, she had been ₁₀ **straddling** it during her rounds, as always – and came over to me. I took a scan of the Wall and the water and prepared to give her my full attention for the next couple of minutes.

"Oof," she said when she arrived, "hello darling. I swear I'm getting more unfit the longer I do this, that doesn't make sense, does ₁₅ it, should be the other way round. Coffee and a biscuit, not in that order. Here, hold this." She reached into her shoulder bag and was holding out a packet of biscuits. I remember thinking: chocolate and orange jam, my favourite. I took them and put my rifle down on the bench, still within arm's reach **as per** the rules, and un- ₂₀ hooked my metal cup from the outside of my rucksack while she fiddled with the thermos flask. I was glad it was coffee rather than tea, because although the tea tasted better the coffee was more effective at keeping me awake. As she reached forwards to pour it I saw she had **spilt** it over herself, though spilt in a strange place, ₂₅ along her throat and the front top of her waterproof, and I thought, that's **weird**, I know she can be **clumsy**, but how did Mary manage to pour coffee upwards, somehow to **chuck** it up over herself? She made a small noise, a bit like the 'oof' when she stopped her bike, but quieter, more involuntary; she sounded surprised. She dropped ₃₀ the thermos and looked down at herself and the at all once several things happened, simultaneously, but also slowly:

The liquid was a strange colour. A strange **texture** too. Mary was backlit, a lamp behind her, so I couldn't see properly, and I realised, yes, it was the texture that was wrong, not the colour: the ₃₅ way the wetness was thick but also moving too fast for a mere spill; it can't be coffee, can she have spilt food on herself? but no it's a liquid, but no it's wrong for water, and it's not spilling it's pumping, it's not been poured over her it's coming out of her. There's only one thing it can be, it's blood. ₄₀

But how can it be blood? It's not a nosebleed, she hasn't thrown blood up on herself, my that would be a very serious illness, one that had you throwing blood up on yourself, anyway it's not coming out of her mouth it's coming from further down, it's pumping out of her, its – ₄₅

faint not strong and clear

to dip to go down to a lower level

to straddle to stand or sit with your legs on either side of sth.

as per according to

to spill (spilt, spilt) sth. verschütten, kleckern

weird strange
clumsy ungeschickt, tollpatschig
to chuck sth. to throw sth. carelessly

texture Konsistenz, Beschaffenheit

I swear I can remember this whole train of thought, a line of
argument running through my mind as if I was, I don't know,
defending a PhD thesis or something. It can only have taken a
tiny fraction of a second, and then I understood: Mary had been
5 hit by a bullet or a knife or something similar, it was a very bad
wound that she probably wouldn't survive. We were under attack. The Others had come.

I went for my rifle and dived back behind the bench, looking at
the Wall. I don't remember saying or doing anything to raise the
10 alert, but afterwards during the debrief they played back the recording of all communications that night, and the evidence is
right there in the form of my voice, slightly raised but not, I'm
proud to say, panicky: I sound the way you sound when you're
giving an order at the window of a drive-through fast-food place,
15 and you speak louder than usual to make sure they get the order
right. "Section twelve under attack, Others, code red" – code red
meaning this is not a drill, this is not a warning, they're right
here, right now. On the recording you can hear, about five seconds later, the full alert alarm go off: at this point the other shift
20 would be waking up, running to the armoury, and then running
for the Wall. I remember hearing gunfire off to my left, not far
away, maybe only one post over (that would be Shoona) and I remember looking – and at this I was a little frantic, for sure – to see
where the Others were, the Others who were near enough to have
25 killed Mary but not yet in sight. I saw a glinting metal thing on
top of the Wall and in that slowed-down, point-by-point analytic
process, worked out what it must be. Metal object, not there before. Must belong to the Others. Don't recognise it. Steel painted
black. A claw shape, like a crab: a grapple. Others coming up Wall
30 using grapple. I wonder, what should I do about that? I know, I'll
run to the Wall and shoot whoever is on the other side, because if
I wait until they get to the top, they will shoot me instead. I heard
gunfire, frantic uncontrolled gunfire, from further down the ramparts. Somebody was shooting on full automatic, not firing short
35 bursts the way we'd been trained, but emptying the whole magazine in one go. I stepped towards the Wall and then just at the last
moment, the very last moment, remembered my training, that if I
suspected Others at a specific point I should go a few metres away
and look from there, because they'd be waiting to see my head
40 pop over the parapet exactly above the spot they were climbing,
and would blow my head off.

I ran five metres down the Wall, knelt, and popped my head over
just enough to see, for the shortest fraction of a second. The far
side of the Wall was in deep shadow and I couldn't see well but
45 there were shapes on the Wall, one of them near the top: three of

to defend a PhD thesis to have
an oral examination about your
(written) doctoral thesis
fraction a small part of sth.

to dive to go down very quickly

frantic extremely upset, esp.
because of anxiety or fear

to glint *glitzern, funkeln*

parapet *Brüstung*

them, I thought, though it could have been four if there were two together at the bottom. I had a few seconds before the first figure would get over the Wall. I ran ten metres back the other way, so I was five metres past my post, on the other side from where I'd taken the sighting: the idea being that if they'd seen me they'd ₅ expect me to pop up and start shooting from the same spot. I took a breath, stood, and emptied half the magazine into the first figure, then the other half into the Others who were below. I was sure I'd killed the first one because, although he made no sound that I could hear over the noise of my weapon, he let go his grip ₁₀ and fell back into the sea. I wasn't sure if I'd hit the other two or three. I ducked back down the Wall and ran back to the first point I'd used to look over. I loaded a second magazine. As I stood to shoot, I felt a blow like a heavy punch on the upper right of my back, just below the shoulder. I turned, this was in Shoona's di- ₁₅ rection, and saw three Others, one of them kneeling and aiming a weapon, the closer two running towards me.

I tried to raise my rifle to shoot them but nothing happened. I was aware of how time had slowed down, so the first thing I thought was that this was just an extreme version of the same phenome- ₂₀ non, that my brain had sent the command for my arm to lift, but the arm hadn't responded yet. This thought seemed perfectly normal, as if I was in one of those video games where the protagonist can slow down time and the player has plenty of opportunity to aim, think, calibrate, during a moment which in real life ₂₅ would be mere hundredths of a second. My arm will be moving soon, I told myself, I've given the instruction, I've ordered it to move, so it will be raising the rifle to aiming position any moment now … and yet nothing happened, and I realised that time had not slowed down to the extent I thought it had, because the Others ₃₀ were still running towards me, and the one who had been kneeling to aim a weapon had now got up and was starting to run towards me too. I'd been wounded in my right arm and couldn't raise it. I reached across to lift my rifle with my left hand, but even as I did so I was thinking, who am I kidding, these guns ₃₅ aren't designed to be used one-handed, I can't aim and shoot with one arm, it just isn't possible, and that means I can't defend myself and that means I'm going to die here, today, in this very minute that I'm living through right now, so this is the last night I'll ever see. These are the last sounds I'll ever hear, the last thing ₄₀ in front of my eyes in this lifetime is going to be this Other forty metres away who has stopped and steadied himself and is aiming a rifle at me, here we go, he's aiming, I'm going to die right –

The Other's head disappeared. No other word for it. He was standing in silhouette, aiming, then he was still standing, except ₄₅

to duck down *sich ducken*

to calibrate *justieren*

to kid oneself (*infml.*) to fail to admit the truth to oneself

his body ended at the shoulders and neck. Time slowed again and
he stood still for the longest time, a grotesque statue, but while he
was standing still, or the thing which used to be him was standing still, everything else was noise and movement. A huge explo-
5 sion came from just below my position on the Wall, and then as I
was staggering and reeling from it, another. Earlier in the fight I
had had some understanding of what was happening, but by now
I had lost it, and had no idea what was going on: if I'd been more
aware, less disoriented and (to be fair to myself) not bleeding
10 heavily from the wound in my shoulder and back, I might have
realised that was Hifa, ignoring the rules about grenade launcher
use and shooting the Others who were climbing the Wall by my
post. In front of me, where the first Other had lost his head, I saw
the Captain, running up the inside steps onto the ramparts,
15 swinging a huge knife, not a standard bayonet but a giant thing,
a machete, into the back of one of the two surviving Others. He
had emptied his magazine into the head of the man who had been
about to kill me and now his only weapon was this knife. The last
Other turned towards him and started to raise his rifle. If he had
20 been running with it in his hands, the Captain would have died;
but that fraction of a second it took to raise-and-aim killed the
Other. The Captain jumped towards him and swung his machete
into the Other's neck. It was not a clean cut, the huge knife stuck
in the man's throat and he staggered sideways, dropping his gun
25 and raising his arms to his neck, apparently trying to pull the
metal out of his body. I watched this with what felt like objectiv-
ity and detachment, thinking: if I were in his position, I too would
attempt to remove the machete from my neck, so I understood
this man's reasoning, but I am not confident he will be able to
30 achieve his goal. He staggered back across in the other direction,
away from the Captain, and then fell forwards. He did not lie still;
he writhed around on the ground. The Captain stepped over to
the Other's rifle, picked it up, moved to stand over him, and fired
a short burst into him to kill him.
35 It was quiet, or rather, the gunfire had stopped. I could hear voices, Defenders' voices, from down the Wall. At some point in the
fight my communicator earpiece had become detached and was
cut off from the general chatter, if there was any. At some other
point I had sat down and leant with my back against the Wall. I
40 saw that I had taken my glasses off and put them down beside me.
I put them back on. The attack seemed to be over. I could tell because if it had still been continuing the Captain would have run
in the direction of the fighting. Instead he came over to me and
bent down. He was breathing heavily but otherwise seemed calm.
45 He reached to touch my arm then stopped.

to stagger to walk with difficulty
as if you are going to fall; *taumeln*
to reel *taumeln*

machete [məˈʃeti]

reasoning *Gedankengang*

to writhe *sich krümmen*

corpsman [korman] medical specialist in the military
to toggle a switch einen Kippschalter umlegen
anthology here: variety

to compress verdichten
dull not sharp
stabbing stechend
throbbing beating

stretcher Trage

tube here: Schlauch
to subside to become less strong or extreme

barrel Lauf einer Waffe

blur sth. you cannot remember clearly
prodding Drücken, Stubsen

gravely seriously

suction device Ansaugvorrichtung

crossbow Armbrust

bolt Pfeil

subsequent following

"You're wounded," he said. He stepped back and spoke into his communicator and it seemed mere seconds later that a military ambulance came alongside the inner ring and two corpsmen jogged up the Wall. It wasn't until this point that, like a switch being toggled, I was abruptly in pain. It started in my right shoul- 5 der and spread all down my right side. It was an anthology of pain types compressed together, at the same time dull and sharp and stabbing and throbbing and gripping.

"Take good care of this one, he did well tonight," the Captain said to the medics. I didn't know at the time, but that was to be the 10 only compliment he ever paid me. They put me on the stretcher and carried me down to the ambulance and hooked me up to various tubes, and the pain began to subside.

Time now began running at a completely different speed. During the fight each split second gave you time to think, to see what was 15 coming, to consider alternatives and consequences in the moment between pulling a trigger and the bullet coming out of the barrel. Then there was a short passage of time when I was in the moment, during the moment, time passing at the right speed, which was roughly now, as I got into the ambulance. After that, 20 the next few days went past in a blur of tubes and pills and tests and proddings and doctors, interrupted by passages when senior members of the Border Defence Force (too important to be mere Defenders) came and gravely, respectfully asked repetitive questions about what had happened that night. 25

While they asked questions, they also answered mine, or some of them. That's how I found out what happened. We had been attacked by twelve Others, who went after posts 8, 10 and 12, Cooper and Shoona and me. They had used inflatables to get within a few hundred metres of the Wall and had then swum the last bit. They 30 used suction devices to attach to the Wall initially, then the same kit climbers use on rock faces. The fact that it was a noisy, windy night had been crucial: they had probably been waiting for that. They were trained and competent. They were from sub-Saharan Africa. It was quite likely that they had been professional soldiers 35 in their previous lives. They had used crossbows as their first weapon, for the silence. Then they switched to guns. The guns had been taped and sealed to keep out the water. The plan had been to get as many of us as possible before they started making noise. A good plan. It was a crossbow bolt that had killed Mary 40 and another one that had hit me. Shoona too had been wounded by a crossbow and then killed in the subsequent firefight. Cooper had been shot and was badly wounded and might not survive. Two other Defenders had died. All of the Others had been killed. So none of us would be put to sea. 45

On the third morning, when I was still out of it, the Captain came around to visit, accompanied by the baby politician who had given the talk at training camp, and by a senior non-baby politician whose name I did not catch. "Well done," they said, with varia-
5 tions. They gave me a piece of paper which apparently was a form of official commendation. Not that it meant anything: the only prize worth having would have been remission from more time on the Wall, and that wasn't on offer. It was a pretty short visit and I was feeling woozy all the way through.
10 I woke up on the fourth morning with a clear head. Another toggled switch: pain subsided, brain fog gone. Hifa was sitting at the end of my bed, fiddling with her communicator. She was wearing a dressing gown. On the table beside her I could see she had brought a box of chocolates, which she had opened and was now
15 eating.
"I'm guessing those were supposed to be for me," I said.
"Oh hi," she said, looking up and blushing slightly. "No, they were for me actually. I've been in here too. Small wound but they kept me in for observation. Concussion. They're letting me out today."
20 "You broke the rules on use of the grenade launcher."
"I did, didn't I?"
She took another chocolate.
"It's surprisingly nice in here," Hifa said. I hadn't noticed this, but looking around, I could see that it was true. The bed and chairs
25 were much better made than anything we got as standard on the Wall; there was a view of distant hills. Even having a single room was a luxury. The room had a bath and toilet. There was Help. You were brought three meals a day. You had your own television. It was certainly a pleasanter place to be than the barracks. "Al-
30 most worth it," Hifa added.
"For concussion maybe, but some of us got shot."
"Well, by a crossbow – not sure that counts as being shot."
"Tell Mary that," I said, and then realised as soon as the words were out of my mouth that it was the wrong thing to say, horribly
35 wrong, not fair to Hifa and not fair to Mary, and if I thought about it for long enough, not fair to myself. Hifa's face changed and I could see her feelings churning, the fear and loss and grief, and by seeing them in her I could suddenly locate them in myself too. Mary was dead, had died in her own blood standing three
40 feet away from me, and Shoona had died too, in terror and pain, and maybe Cooper was going too, to join all the others who died that night, and me so nearly among them, death so near in those moments I could stretch out and touch the hem of its coat. I hadn't been having any feelings about what had happened – I
45 suppose I just hadn't been ready to. Now I felt terrified, of the

commendation (*fml.*) an official statement that praises sb.
remission reduction

dressing gown *Morgenmantel*

concussion *Gehirnerschütterung*

to churn to move violently

in terror in extreme fear

hem *Saum*

apprehension worry about
the future

apology the act of saying you
are sorry

banter conversation that is funny
and not serious

to banter with sb. to talk to sb. in
a friendly, humorous way

alternating *sich abwechselnd*

eventually finally, in the end

night itself – frightened of what I had already been through, which makes no sense, but that is what I felt – and with it had a sick sense of apprehension of going back to the Wall and living through it all again.

"Sorry," I said, but although she had tears in her eyes, she just ⁵ shook her head, apology not needed, she understood. It can happen, when you spend all your time with a group of people, that interaction between you gets stuck; there's a particular register in which all your exchanges happen. With Defenders, there was stand-your-ground joshing, banter which could be aggressive and ¹⁰ could be defensive but was never not there: a wall of its own. There were hardly any times when you were just plainly and defencelessly yourself with other people. That could make certain sorts of conversation difficult to have. Hughes talking about what he wanted to do after the Wall – that was an unusual thing. Now, ¹⁵ in this moment with Hifa, I felt a physical barrier between me and whatever was supposed to happen next. I didn't know what to say other than that I had no idea what to say. I hadn't meant to hurt her feelings. I hadn't meant to hurt my own feelings, for that matter. I didn't want to make a joke about Mary, whose death had ²⁰ been the worst thing I had ever seen, the worst thing I ever hoped to see. Hifa had been trying to banter with me, I had been trying to do the same thing back, and we had both messed it up. I could see that she thought, felt, the same; see too that neither of us knew what to say next. We sat for a little while, alternating look- ²⁵ ing at each other and looking at the floor, both feeling pretty miserable.

"I'm sick of the Wall," Hifa eventually said.

"Me too."

"If we stay on the Wall, and the attacks keep happening, and the ³⁰ attacks are like that, we'll eventually die."

"Maybe."

And then she said something which I have to admit I didn't expect:

"Do you want to Breed with me?" ³⁵

14

You may know in general that the nation needs more babies, and you may know that it encourages people to Breed, but you don't know the half of it until you actually set up in business as a Breeder yourself. Breeders, or people trying to Breed, get special
5 quarters on the Wall. They get rooms to share. In addition to the room and the extra rations you also get some say in where you want to serve your time on the Wall, and the ability to change shifts. In other words you can move away from the place and the squad you were previously with – as far as I know, becoming a
10 Breeder is the only way you get to have any say in that. A pretty sweet deal. If you could get used to the thought of bringing another person into the broken world. I can honestly say that the idea had never crossed my mind, before Hifa suggested it, and then as soon as she had, I knew I had no choice. It was the close-
15 ness of death – that was what did it. We could save ourselves from dying by bringing somebody new into the world. It suddenly seemed like the only thing to do.

There were lots of good things about Breeding, or trying to. Some of them I won't spell out here. I'll just say Hifa and I turned out to
20 be a good fit. Being wanted by someone who wants you, and then getting what you want ... nothing in the world is quite like that. There was only one downside to the new turn in our relationship, which was that the other members of our squad thought it was hilarious, and wouldn't stop teasing us about it. People were in a
25 bad place, after the attack and the deaths, and me and Hifa hooking up was the only other thing to talk and think about apart from how distraught everyone was, so that's all that they did: tease us and make jokes at us and ask us if the baby was on the way yet and if we were having fun trying and if we had tried do-
30 ing it this way, that way, would we like someone else to try in my place, would we like the whole squad to watch to make helpful comments on technique and form, had we given any thought to what we would do if the baby was Chinese, etc., etc., et bloody cetera.

35 During the next few weeks, it was as if I had two lives. One of them, the best and realest, was with Hifa. The two of us were excused training – my injury, plus our new aspiring-Breeder privileges – and we spent a whole week entirely together. We knew each other very well, had spent more time in each other's
40 company than a lot of couples who are just starting out; we had shared the most intense experience of our lives together. But from another perspective, we hardly knew each other at all. We had never had an argument. We had never seen each other

to hook up to be in relationship and have sex
distraught extremely worried, nervous, upset

realest most real

naked. I didn't know anything about her family other than that she was no keener on seeing them than I was on seeing mine. So we started to find out those things, to do those things, to get to know each other differently/deeper/better. I liked that, in fact I loved it.

In parallel: the Wall. That life which had felt like he realest thing I would ever do now seemed like a backdrop for my other, realer, private life. Many things changed. For a start, we were moved off it for a four-week section of training and reserve duty. With four dead and three injured from one squad of fifteen, we needed to be restaffed and retrained: to settle in the new people and wait for me and Hifa to be ready for active duty. In the middle of that period I was, of all things, given a medal. It turned out that the certificate from the baby politician was a promissory note telling me that there was more to come.

The whole company went in a lorry to a town about half an hour's drive away from our temporary barracks. We stopped around the back of the town hall and were met by some Help who led us through a winding series of corridors to suddenly come out on stage in front of a few hundred seated civilians. There was bunting above the podium; there was a television camera pointed at us. The loudspeaker system played pop music from the recent past while we waited. Then there was a bustle, a movement among the functionaries running the event, and a person who was obviously important came through the door we had come through and went up to the podium. People cheered and clapped. I had no idea who he was, but the civilians obviously did. He must have been a member of the elite who was clever at being popular with ordinary people. He held up his hands and people went quiet and then he made a mesmerising speech about the Wall (he called it he National Coastal Defence Structure) and the Defenders and how important we are and what heroes we are and how Britain is a nation of heroes and how our heroism is in the finest tradition of British heroism and how heroic that is. I may be misremembering some of this: we all agreed it was a great speech though afterwards we found it hard to repeat anything he'd said. Basically, there was lots in it about heroism and how we were heroes. Our names were read out, and we went up in order and were given the medals. The politician pinned them onto our uniforms. I was third out of five up to the podium. The Captain got a more important medal, and Hifa and one other squad member who had killed Others got smaller medals. I'd never stood in front of a roomful of people applauding me before, and I don't ever expect to do it again. It's embarrassing to admit (though why is it embarrassing?) but I really liked it.

backdrop a view behind sth.

to restaff to provide with new staff (*Personal*)

promissory note (*fml.*) *Schuldschein*

town hall *Rathaus*

bunting rows of brightly coloured small flags, often in the colours of a country's flag, that are hung up as decoration for special occasions or political events
bustle busy activity
functionary *Funktionär*

mesmerising completely holding the attention and interest of sb.

Then the ceremony was over and we were invited to a reception
room upstairs and a selection of the audience came up too and
there was Help serving everyone with drinks and small snacks,
and being Defenders, we tried to get as many of the drinks down
5 as we could. There was one glass of wine each, only the second
time I've ever had wine because it became rare and expensive after the Change, but there was plenty of beer and gin and whisky
and most of us managed to get properly hammered in the thirty
minutes we were there, the kind of abrupt, vertical-take-off
10 drunkenness where you get so much alcohol on board so quickly
you grow steadily drunker for the next couple of hours. A great
night out. Hifa started feeling ill on the lorry and when we got to
the barracks she went into our loo and I held her hair back while
she was sick and I realised that I loved her and that I'd never felt
15 so happy. I think that was the best day of my life.

reception *Empfang*

vertical-take-off *Senkrechtstart-*

loo (*infml.*) toilet

15

"We're going to Scotland," said the Captain. There was a rumbling and shifting in the briefing room. The entire company was there, in its new form, a mix of old Defenders and replacements. He let the news marinate for a few moments,

to marinate to allow sth. to settle; *einwirken lassen*

"You may be wondering why," he went on. Speaking for myself, I ⁵ wasn't, not particularly; if you look for logic on the Wall you're not far away from expecting the process to be fair, and if you expect it to be fair, you start to go mad. That's my take on it any-

take on sth. way of looking at sth.

way. So, no wondering why for me. "The reason is, this squad is considered to have done its fair share of the hard work of defend- ¹⁰ ing our frontiers. Here in the south is the first line of attack and the first line of defence." He meant, the first line of defence from the Others, but he didn't say so. I had noticed before that he used the word 'Others' as little as possible. It was the only sign he gave of sensitivity about his former life, his former self. "In the ¹⁵ north, it is different. The reasons for this are simple. The people attempting to cross the Wall are coming from a southerly direc-tion. The journey to the north is therefore longer and more dangerous. The north is also colder. That means there are fewer attempts to penetrate our defences from that direction. That ²⁰ means that defending the Wall is, in practice, less difficult in the far north. Sergeant, what maxim am I about to quote?"

to penetrate to move into or through sth.

Sarge had been cut on his face on the night of the attack, and the wound had not fully healed. It was spectacular, a double line of stitches down his right cheekbone. On either side of a livid scar. ²⁵ Half a centimetre higher and he would have lost his eye. As it was the scar made his expression look permanently contorted with disbelief: he looked like a stocky, angry, sceptical pirate.

livid of an unpleasant purple and dark-blue colour

contorted *verzerrt*

stocky *gedrungen*

"Less risky is more risky," he said.

"Yes. So bear that in mind. The idea that the north is harder to ³⁰ attack, easier to defend, may in itself be a factor which draws at-tacks. Still," he said, easing off the intensity a little, "we are being sent there for some respite, and it's to be hoped that we'll find it. As summer arrives the days are very long and the nights very short. We have a chance to get to know each other as a new com- ³⁵ pany. We may well, after a period in the far north and further training, be transferred back to the south. My advice would be to make the most of it. We train, then we go north at the next de-ployment."

respite a pause or rest from sth. difficult or unpleasant

"He seemed almost cheerful," Hifa said later. We were putting ⁴⁰ away our kit to go on a week's leave. The company had been on standby duty near our barracks. I wasn't fit enough to fight but I was on administrative duties while I recovered: which meant,

doing chores for the Captain, Sergeant and Corporal. It was unin-
teresting but not difficult. "I wonder what the secret bad news is."
"Cold?" I said. "Remote?" Hifa shrugged. She held out her hand to
me and I took it. We were setting out to do something we had
5 discussed and Hifa had long dreaded.
"Are you sure you're ready for this?" she said.
"I think so."
"You can say if you aren't."
"I know."
10 "I won't hold it against you and bring it up later."
"I know."
"I have doubts of my own."
"I understand."
"It's not guaranteed to go well."
15 "Yes, I understand."
"Not through any fault of yours – please don't think that. It's just,
it could go wrong."
"I know."
"I don't want to have misled you."
20 "Thank you."
"To make it clear."
"OK, Hifa, I've got it, I really have, and if you think it's a bad idea
and don't want me to do it that's completely fine, we won't."
"No need to be arsey."   arsey (*BE, sl.*) bad-tempered
25 "I don't think I was."
"Well, that's a matter of opinion."
"Hifa, for fuck's sake, we're only talking about visiting your
mother for a few days. She isn't Hitler. At least if she was Hitler I
assume you'd have said."
30 She exhaled, slow and long.
"I just, I don't want it to get in the way," she said, more subdued,   **subdued** not loud
less fighty.
"It won't," I said. "I promise."
We took the usual journey at the end of that shift, lorry to train to
35 London. We were leaving Ilfracombe 4 for ever. The company was
the quietest and soberest I'd ever seen it on a trip like this. The
new people hadn't really bedded in yet and the Defenders who'd   **to bed in** to become settled and
been there for longer were all thinking about the people who   part of a group
weren't with us. Absent friends. There was still no news about
40 Cooper. It was odd, because if you had pumped me full of truth
serum and asked me if there was anything about that section of
the Wall I would miss – the section where I'd spent the winter
months in the cold and dark, where I'd been the most frightened
I'd ever been, and the most bored I'd ever been, and had the most
45 intense experiences of my life, and nearly died – I'd have said no.

But as we left it behind and it moved into the past, moved into the category of experiences which were over, I realised I felt a sense of loss. I'd probably never see it again: that particular stretch of concretewindwatersky. That exact patch of damp over my bed, those precise stretches of ramparts where puddles would 5 accumulate in the gravel. The place where I met Hifa.

At London we split up as usual, said muted goodbyes. Hifa and I crossed the city to catch a train to the eastern town where her mother lived. The transport dynamic was always the same: on the train from the coast, where we outnumbered the civilians, we 10 were the dominant force, the top dogs, and people were wary, kept away and moved away. In the city, in small numbers and as individuals, we were objects of curiosity instead of fear: people snuck glances at us, observed us, would sometimes catch our eye. Nothing made you feel the gap between us and civilians more 15 than being in the middle of them. They just weren't thinking about the same things, didn't have the same priorities, had no idea how lucky they were.

You could tell pretty much without exception when the people checking you out had been Defenders: they were a certain age, 20 within a decade or two of us, and they looked both more empathetic and more assessing. They were probably wondering how long we'd been on the Wall, how long we had to go. I still had my arm in a sling and I was wearing my medal and I could see them noticing both of those things. The look in their eyes had 25 some pride in it, pride for you and a little bit for themselves too; some sympathy (it was easy to see them thinking, thank God I don't have to do that again, I wonder how long the poor sods have to go). Sometimes I thought I caught them thinking: when I was on the Wall, I used to tell myself I'd never forget how horrible it is 30 to be cold and tired and frightened and have months more of the feeling to go, and I promise I'll remember this moment, and if I ever get off the Wall and remember this moment I promise I'll never again take for granted being comfortable and safe and somewhere other than there. I didn't blame them for it, I'd had 35 the same thought many times myself. I hoped more than any-thing to get to a point in my life when I was like them – when I had the luxury and privilege of having been away from the Wall for so long that I needed external prompts to be reminded of it. When the Wall would be in the past, not the present and the 40 future.

The train to the east was old and slow. I liked it, the creakiness and old-fashionedness of it; the kind of train where people were going home with shopping bags, but had brought their own packed snacks for the trip rather than buying anything expensive 45

---

damp *Feuchtigkeit*

puddle a small pool of liquid

to accumulate to gradually increase

muted less emotional or enthusiastic than normal

top dog a person who has achieved a position of authority

wary careful, looking out for trouble

to sneak (snuck, snuck) a glance to secretly look at sb./sth.

empathetic *mitfühlend, verständnisvoll*

to assess to calculate or judge

prompt reminder; *Anstoß*

creakiness *Quietschen, Knarren*

in the big city. Hifa and I didn't talk much. I watched London go
past out the window and then blur into suburb and exurb, those
random tower blocks which spread on the outskirts of the city,
and then fields and country. I'm a city boy and the country al-
5 ways seems so empty, so underpopulated; even now when we
grow all our own food and there's more said about farming and
food than ever before, you never actually see any people working
on the land. Drones and bots, yes, people, no.

We arrived at the end of the main line and went to the station café
10 to wait for the train to the coast. We drank heavily stewed tea and
ate dry biscuits which were borderline inedible until you dunked
them. I felt sad, suddenly and unexpectedly, and couldn't tell why,
then realised I was having a near-memory of Mary, bringing her
hot drinks to us twice a shift. I didn't want to say that to Hifa so I
15 just sat there with the feelings for a moment, then looked over at
her and could see she was doing something similar, sitting there
staring down into her tea.

The train to the coast was even racketier and smaller and older
than the last one, no more than two carriages long. The fields
20 were big and dominated by huge single crops, most of which I
didn't recognise, apart from the loud yellow of rapeseed. The light
began to change as we got nearer the coast, and before long I
could smell the sea. The train made frequent stops and was almost
empty when it began to slow down and Hifa said, "We're here."
25 She swung her rucksack down off the space above her seat. Hifa
was not looking at all like herself, as if she had shrunk slightly.
I recognised the symptoms of familial dread.

At the end of the platform, a woman with a turban wrapped com-
plicatedly around her head and two different brightly coloured
30 shawls was standing waiting for us, leaning on a stick. She had
the same caramelly skin tone as Hifa but was taller and more
operatic, both in how she dressed and how she acted: she projected
drama. To the side of her and one pace behind was standing a
woman instantly recognizable as Help.
35 "Darling!" she said as soon as she saw us. "Darling! Let me look at
you." Hifa stood and submitted to this. Her mother reached out
and touched her face and turned it slightly from side to side. She
held her fingers over the place on the top of her head where Hifa
had stitches. She took a step backwards and looked at Hifa up and
40 down. She tilted her own head.
"As beautiful as ever," she said. She came over and stood in front
of me. She held the cane out behind her and the Help took it.
Then she held out both of her hands in front of her. I felt I had no
choice except to do the same. She took my hands and held them.
45 We still hadn't spoken. She did the same up-and-down thing she

exurb a region beyond the suburbs that is not highly developed and where wealthier people often live
random without any pattern
outskirts *Stadtrand, Vorstädte*

inedible not suitable as food
to dunk sth. (*infml.*) to put sth. into liquid for a short time to make softer

rackety noisy

rapeseed *Raps*

dread a strong feeling of fear or worry

operatic *opernhaft*
to project sth. to have a noticeable quality

to submit to sth. to allow another person or group to have power or authority over you

to tilt *neigen*

cane *Gehstock*

had done with her daughter, then let go of my hands, and without touching me held her fingers over the place where I'd been wounded. Then she stepped back and turned to Hifa.

"Yes," she said. "I understand." And to both of us: "Welcome!"

Hifa's mother lived in a cottage ten minutes' walk from the train 5 station. The little house stood in a row of similar properties just outside the coastal village. It was small and pretty on the outside, painted white, with a wooden gate, a **trellis** of flowers on the front wall and a small garden. The house would once have had a view of the sea, but that was now blocked by the Wall. The inside was 10 decorated with African art and bright paintings by Hifa's mother: she had been an art teacher but retired early and was now an artist. Her speciality was painting the spirit animals of her family and friends, and said that she was looking forward to painting mine, once she had worked out what it was. 15

Hifa's mother's big news was about her domestic arrangements. "I know it's terrible to have Help," she said, once we had got to the cottage and she had sent the Help to the shops in search of missing dinner ingredients. "If you had said when I was younger that I would have Help, not that it existed in those days, but had ex- 20 plained to me what it is and that I would one day be making use of it, I would not have believed you. Another human being at one's beck and call, just by lifting a finger, simply provided to one, in effect one's personal property … though of course they are technically the property of the state, there are all sorts monitorings 25 and safeguards, it isn't at all like such arrangements in the benighted past, it is a form of providing welfare and shelter and refuge to the wretched of the world – but no, still, I would not have believed you. It is a falling away, a lessening of one's own humanity. A decline in one's own standards. But what could I do? 30 I had you coming, I am not getting any younger, please don't say anything polite" – this was addressed to me, though the truth is I hadn't been going to say anything in the first place – "we both know it's true. The spirit is willing but the flesh is weak, and if we're being completely honest the spirit isn't always willing ei- 35 ther. Age is a terrible thing, a terrible opponent. People of your time in life don't understand this but you come to find it to be true, perhaps the only thing which is true for all humans everywhere, the terribleness of age. Our deepest piece of common humanity." 40

I suddenly got it. Hifa's mother was one of those people who like life to be all about them. With the Change, that is a harder belief to sustain; it takes much more effort to think that life is about you when the whole of human life has turned upside down, when everything has been irrevocably changed for everyone. You can 45

trellis *Rankgerüst, Spalier*

at sb.'s beck and call always willing and able to do whatever sb. asks

monitoring control

safeguard protection

benighted lacking morals; dark

wretched unhappy, poor

to sustain to keep alive

irrevocably impossible to change

do it, of course you can, because people can do anything with their minds and their sense of themselves, but it takes work and only certain kinds of unusually self-centred people can do it. They want to be the focus of all the drama and pity and all the stories. I could tell that she didn't like it that younger people are universally agreed to have had a worse deal than her generation. I understood Hifa's dread and found myself reaching for her hand. Hifa took mine, limply, reluctantly. I was about to find out why.

limply in a soft way
reluctantly zögernd

"Ah – love. The love of a partner. The sweetest thing in life, to have it, to be possessed of it. The greatest of sadnesses to look back on, in later life, in adversity, the cruel twist that your greatest happinesses became your greatest pain." Then she leant forwards – the cottage rooms were small, so our sofa and her chair were close to each other, catty-corner – and took my and Hifa's clasped hands in hers. "Enjoy it!" she said. She got up and left the room to get her communicator to ask the Help where she was and why she was being so slow.

adversity difficult or unlucky situation
twist complicated situation

catty-corner schräg gegenüber
clasped verschränkt

"Holy fuck," I whispered to Hifa.

"You get it now."

"Absolutely. Want me to do something? I can call Hughes, get him to call back, fake an emergency. Sudden summons back to the Wall. We can, I don't know, go and stay in a B & B."

summon order

"Or we could just kill ourselves, that would work too," said Hifa. Then she squeezed my hand and let go. "This too shall pass. She'll ease off from now, it's worse when she's nervous."

That proved true. The Help came back from the shops and served an absolutely delicious cream tea, an old-school treat I'd heard of but never had, with fresh scones (Hifa's mother: "made under my direction") and fresh clotted cream, and jam made by Hifa's mother the previous autumn. I made the mistake of asking for the recipe, out of nothing but politeness, which gave her the opportunity to say: "The balance of sugar and sharpness has to be just right, as sweet as love, as bitter as loss." There would be these moments when Hifa's mother suddenly went off on one. The rest of the time she was OK, and she could be very funny, especially about her neighbours. Also, as always, it was good to be away from the Wall and especially so to be with Hifa. We went for a walk down to what had been the seafront and was now a strange marooned parade of shops in the lee of the Wall, their façades oriented towards a promenade and a view which were no longer there. We did a lot of walking that weekend, as a device for getting out of the house.

cream tea a light meal of scones (= small cakes) with jam and thick cream
treat special and enjoyable experience
clotted cream a thick cream
jam Marmelade

to go off on one (BE, infml.) to suddenly start speaking in an exaggerated way about a favourite topic

marooned stranded
lee Windschatten
façade [fə'sɑːd]

"How come she can afford Help?"

"I haven't asked her but I can guess. Dad sends her money. He felt guilty about going off and leaving her – leaving us. He had to pay child support, but even when he didn't have to any more, he still sent cheques."

"She told you that?"

Hifa gave me a look.

"Of course not. He did." 5

"I thought you never saw him?"

"I don't. Hardly. Anyway, she's canny with money, always has been. When she was working she saved."

"I feel a bit sorry for the Help. More sorry than usual, I mean."

"Yeah – I wouldn't be at all surprised if she decided to swim for 10 it."

I laughed. Being with Hifa's mother made me think about my parents; about the difference between me and them, so different from Hifa and her mother, and yet maybe not, at the same time. Who broke the world? They wouldn't say that they did. And yet 15 it broke on their watch.

Hifa was right, though: it did get easier. Her mother dialled it down a bit. That gave Hifa the chance to relax a little and as she did she told me about her childhood, the dad who was great when he was there but was prone to go away without warning, until 20 one day he never came back; the charismatic, flaky, loving, difficult mother. The small-life country childhood which makes you need to get away so badly you can feel it in the roots of your hair. We wandered all over the town and the countryside around it. The paradox was that you couldn't see the sea when you were 25 close to it, because of the Wall, but if you went for a walk inland, and climbed up a bit, you could. So you went inland to see the sea.

I was at that point of recovery when you feel annoyed by your own weakness; when you are bored, as a prelude to getting better. Bored with my physical condition, I mean. In other respects I was 30 feeling better than ever. I was imagining a future off the Wall, once we were pregnant. We'd find work, take turns looking after the baby, maybe take turns going to college, and it would be onwards and upwards. There would be a new life, and we would be living a new life. It felt like too much to hope for, but not in a bad 35 way, more the kind of thing you stop yourself thinking about for superstitious reasons, because if you let yourself imagine all the details, it's less likely to happen. Breeders got good accommodation, so I wouldn't have to go back to live with my parents and Hifa wouldn't have to go back to live with hers. 40

By the fourth day of that week, my arm was out of its sling, and my shoulder, though it still hurt, hurt in a specific numb way which was unlike the access-all-areas pain I'd had when I was wounded. Unexpectedly catching a glimpse of myself in the mirror – there were lots of mirrors in the cottage – I thought, 45

---

cheque Bankscheck

canny clever and careful

on sb.'s watch during a period when sb. is in charge
to dial sth. down (phr. v.) to make sth. less extreme

prone likely to do sth.
charismatic having special traits that attract, inspire, or fascinate other people
flaky behaving in an erratic and strange way

annoyed slightly angry or upset
prelude Vorspiel

superstitious abergläubisch
accommodation a place to live, work, stay, etc. in

numb taub

who's that good-looking dude, then realised it was me, looking rested and well.

At the end of the week, Hifa's mother walked us to the train station. By now we were on nodding terms with the neighbours,
5 who waved or nodded back as we walked past. She stood on the single platform and waited until the two-carriage train came in. She held our hands together and looked at us for a long time.

"Courage," she said, tears in her eyes. "Courage, my brave, brave darlings. I feel for you. Courage!"
10 She squeezed hard and then let go.

"I cannot watch you go away. I will leave you now," she said. And she marched out of the station with her cane, a handkerchief in her right hand, dabbing it to her face as she disappeared back into the town. Hifa and I got into the train.

to dab to touch sth. with quick, light touches

15 "Well, she found a way of making it about her," I said, and then saw that Hifa was affected too, looking sad; I'd misread the moment. We found seats, sat heavily down, and off we were yet again on that train-train-lorry journey. We pulled away from the sea and set off towards the other sea, where we'd be standing
20 watch.

affected emotionally involved

She didn't get around to painting me, but she did manage to work out my spirit animal. Apparently I'm a goat. "A very resourceful animal – they can live on scraps." She said she'd paint it next time. There never was a next time, but of course I didn't know that
25 then.

scraps *Essensabfälle, Reste*

16

Defenders have a saying, "The Wall has no accent." It means when you're standing looking at the water, standing watching for Others, it doesn't matter where you are, it's all concretewater-windsky:

concrete   5

water

wind

sky:

it's basically always the same.

Like most sayings about most things, this is partly true, partly 10 not. Yes, the Wall is the Wall and the Others are the Others and a twelve-hour shift is a twelve-hour shift. You don't have any inter-action with the locals, wherever you are. The days tick down at **subtly** ['sʌtəli] not easily noticed   the same rate. But the light and wind and water are subtly differ-ent, and you get to know them so well that while you could say 15 that the Wall has no accent you could equally say the opposite: along the ten thousand kilometres of Wall, no two posts are iden-tical.

That was especially true in the far north. It just felt different. **slanting** *sich neigend*   Longer days, slanting light, different scents on the wind. It was 20 **scent** a pleasant natural smell   the best time of the year to be up north, no question, and I didn't love the thought of what it would be like in winter, but then if we'd been briefed correctly, we might not be there in winter, we'd be posted back down to the busy areas, once we were fully trained and ready. My view was: whatever. Hifa would be pregnant soon, 25 and we'd be out of there. We'd be living the Breeder life in our special state-donated Breeder accommodation.

I was glad of the change for all sorts of reasons. Hughes had been switched to our shift, to give us another experienced Defender in place of the people we'd lost; that was good. He was the person I 30 liked talking to best, after Hifa, and the quality of chat on the **exponentially** at an ever   communicator increased exponentially. But I missed Shoona. I **faster rate**   missed Cooper, who was still very sick and might recover, might not. I especially missed Mary. The new cook, Alan, was good at his job, in the sense that his food tasted good and there was plenty 35 **taciturn** tending not to speak   of it, but he was taciturn and made no secret of the fact that he **much**   liked cycling along the ramparts in the middle of the night to bring us hot drinks no more than we liked standing on the Wall. Our squad had several new members, so the group dynamics

were very different and I was, I found, now one of the elders,
wounded and decorated, a veteran of action, a potential Breeder,
a senior figure. That was weird. I was the one dispensing advice
to the new arrivals about how to get through a shift, I was the one
5 giving warnings about type 2 cold, I was the one telling people to
watch out for the Captain's small-hours inspections, and take
special care how you tape your ammo cartridges together. One
morning I caught Hifa in the mirror smiling at me as I was brush-
ing my teeth before shift.
10 "What?" I said.
"You're taller," she said.
"Piss off," I said, but what she said was true: I felt taller. I could tell
that I held myself differently. I wasn't the same person I'd been
when I arrived at the Wall.
15 A few days into that first tour up north, who should come for a
visit but our old friend the blond baby politician, dispenser of
intelligence briefings, platitudes and medals. He arrived on an
afternoon of clammy, close-clinging mist, a very unpleasant day
to be on the Wall. It was lucky that the north was quieter, because
20 this was good weather for the Others. Our shift gathered in the
briefing room, which was the same as every other briefing room,
except the maps were different. I found, sitting in front of him as
he stood at the podium, that my instinctive dislike had subsided a
little. That might be because he had been involved in giving me a
25 medal, which was pretty pathetic, really; but there we were. Also,
maybe, I was getting a glimpse of how a person made it into the
elite, and starting to see that it was possible – not easy, but
possible. A very good record on the Wall, followed by a record of
proven success at college, a Breeder, a young person on an upward
30 trajectory; that was the kind of man for whom elites would budge
up and make room. The kind of outsider/insider they needed. I
was taking more of an interest in him and seeing him more as an
object of study than of simple loathing.
"Hello and welcome," he started, as if he were our gracious host,
35 the man in charge of the far north. "We know each other of old,
some of us, and some of us are new colleagues. Welcome. Well
done! You are all members of the best defence force in the world,
the best trained and the best staffed and the best prepared!"
I realised it was his standard speech and tuned out. He would
40 have to give it twice, since this was a normal tour on the Wall, not
a training camp; once for us, once for the other shift. What must
it be like, to go around the country talking to Defenders and the
public, to not be part of their lives but talking to them about their
lives, to be up there in the plane? A metaphorical plane in the case
45 of this man, but still. To give orders while you were pretending

to dispense *here:* to provide/give

clammy sticky and slightly wet
close-clinging *dicht-anliegend*
mist *Nebel*

to subside to weaken

glimpse a brief look at sb./sth.

trajectory *Entwicklungsverlauf*
to budge up (*phr. v., BE, coll.*)
aufrücken

loathing a feeling of strong dislike
gracious behaving in a pleasant,
polite, calm way
host *Gastgeber*

to tune out to stop listening

just to be chatting, to boss people about b asking them if they could kindly do something for you ... Help, of course, there would be lots and lots of Help, cooking Help and cleaning Help and Help to look after the children if you had them, and driving Help and gardening Help for your big house with its self-sufficient food 5 supply (just in case), repair and maintenance Help and odd-job Help, electrical Help and painting and decorating Help ...

Now the speech had turned and he was repeating the warnings he had given at training – which, to be fair, had turned out to be true – about how there were more Others coming and they were 10 more desperate. He also repeated the warnings about how the Others were suspected to have secret networks of support, secret sympathisers, hidden in the general population. They were thought to have new ways of getting away from the coast, maybe even new ways of getting chipped. He went on for a bit more and 15 then stopped his general briefing and invited me and the Captain and Hifa up on stage and talked for a bit about how we had been decorated in action and how lucky this squad was to have three such resolute, able Defenders, and how we were the best defence force in the world, the best trained and the best staffed and the 20 best prepared.

We got down off the stage, and the baby politician stopped me for a word.

"Joseph," he said to me in greeting – which was odd in itself, nobody on the Wall called me by my given name, it was either 25 Kavanagh or Chewy. Even Hifa called me Chewy (as well as some other things). "Please – call me James."

"Er, hi James."

"How are you?" he said with the intensity dialled up. "How *are* you?" He had put on a concerned face.   30

"I'm fine, thanks."

"Wound better?"

"Yes, thanks."

"Change of landscape welcome?"

"So, there's a thing Defenders say, the Wall has no accent. Mean- 35 ing, it's sort of the same everywhere."

"Do they? Do they say that? That's good. That's really good. No accent – yes." He nodded two or three times. "Well, it's good to catch up with old friends. Good to stay in touch. Let me just give you this, just in case."   40

He took out a card of his top jacket pocket and handed it to me: a name and an email address. He reached out to give my arm a parting squeeze, then I saw him remembering that I had been wounded, and he wasn't clear for a fraction of a second what to do, then he either remembered it had been my right shoulder and was aiming 45

self-sufficient *selbstversorgend*
odd-job man *Handlanger*

resolute *entschlossen*

dialled up (*infml.*) to increase the intensity
concerned *besorgt*

fraction *Bruchteil*

for my left arm, or he remembered that he had just asked me if I had recovered, so if my arm was too sore to squeeze it was in a sense my responsibility not his, and went on with the gesture. I took the card, put it in my pocket, said goodbye. It was a small
5 thing but I took it as a sign, meaning that he saw in me some of the same stuff I saw, or wanted to see, in myself. He could smell the ambition, the get-me-out-of-here scent, all over me.

I was pleased. I also felt that I needed to have a shower. Sarge took a moment to talk to me as we were going through to lunch. The
10 rest of the squad had already gone ahead and sat down and were getting stuck in.

"You know what that plonker said. We're lucky to have you?"

I got my modest face ready and said that I did.

"Reckon if we really were lucky, we'd not have been attacked."

15 Fair enough.

Two tours went past without anything much happening. It was just past the top of high summer; short nights, with amazing northern sky colours I'd never seen before, shades of blue and purple shading into deep-blue-grey-purple and purple-off-black
20 and deep back. Once or twice, during nights when we weren't on shift, Hifa and I even went for a walk inland to get away from the light pollution of the Wall, so we could see the stars. There were so many lights in the sky that night seemed not so much a thing of darkness as an experiment in a different form of illumination,
25 an invitation to navigate by star.

"It's beautiful up here," Hifa said.

"In the summer."

"It smells different."

That was true – it did smell different. The sea smelt different. It
30 must be that the sea flora were different, the kelp and seaweed species were more pungent, vegetal and cabbagey, but not un-pleasantly so. Greener, basically, it smelt greener. Of living things. It was hard not to imagine what life would be like after the Wall, when you could go on a walk whenever you felt like it and goof
35 off whenever you felt like it and also work hard at clawing your way up in life and becoming a member of the elite and taking over the world. Also, a baby or babies plural. I liked those walks and that sky.

On our third far-northern tour, I didn't see the sky much, because
40 I was on nights and the lights spoiled the view. It was the least difficult night guarding I've ever done, because the dark was so short and the nightfall and sunrise so long and so spectacular, a protracted set-piece natural show. The danger and difficulty of

sore painful and uncomfortable

to get stuck in (*infml.*) to start doing with enthusiasm, like eating
plonker (*BE, sl.*) silly or stupid person

illumination (*fml.*) light

kelp *Seetang*

pungent smelling very strong and sharp
vegetal *pflanzlich*
cabbagey *kohlartig*
to goof off (*phr. v., AE, infml.*) to avoid doing any work
to claw your way up to reach the highest level of sth. by sheer willpower

protracted lasting for a long time
set-piece *Standard-*

edgy (*infml.*) nervous, not calm
to **bother** to make sb. feel worried

sodding (*BE, sl.*) *Scheiß-*

to **bicker** to argue about things that are not important
to **be off** to be not one's usual self

damp slightly wet
moisture *Feuchtigkeit*

clank *Klirren, Scheppern*

squally with sudden strong winds
gust a sudden strong burst

premonition a feeling that sth. unpleasant is going to happen

casual careless, not watchful

to **prowl** to keep moving about, restlessly

filthy very bad

the tour down south seemed a long distance off. The only person who didn't appear to like being where we were was the Captain, who was the closest he ever got to being edgy; as if the sense of quietness and peace and distance bothered him. He made his rounds more regularly than ever and had less than ever to say. ₅
"Maybe it's a post-traumatic thing," Hughes speculated one morning in the mess, after a night when the Captain had come round no fewer than five times. "He killed two people with a sodding machete. Practically cut them in half. People who maybe were not so unlike he once was. It's going to take a bit of processing." ₁₀
"He's not the type," I said.
"Everyone's the type sooner or later," said Hifa. We gently bickered for a while, without reaching a conclusion. The Captain was off, though, everyone agreed.
Eight days into that tour came the first really difficult weather we ₁₅ had seen up north. There had been days which were damp and still, and the air was so full of moisture it was like living inside a cloud that had sunk to earth, but from the Defenders' point of view, the great virtue of that weather was that in the super-humid silence, you could hear a cough or a metal clank from hundreds of ₂₀ metres away. You could talk to the Defender at the next post without raising your voice. There were other days with abrupt squally showers, gusts of wind and horizontal rain that you could see coming across the water towards you, which hit hard and overwhelmingly, and were gone in minutes. After the first one of ₂₅ these, you never forgot your waterproofs again. But that night was different, a hard rain and wind combined with a hard close fog; a sudden premonition of what it would be like up here when winter came.
"It's beautiful up here," I said over the communicator. ₃₀
"Oh shut up," Hifa said.
"Get a room," said Hughes.
"Keep it hygienic, said Sarge, meaning, keep off the communicator unless it's to do with business. It was a sensible thing to say on a night when it was so hard to hear, but we had got a little casual ₃₅ up north. I don't think any of us really believed in the possibility of an attack. Sarge added: "He hasn't been around yet, which means he'll be here any minute." In other words, the Captain, uncharacteristically absent from his prowling that night, was coming soon. ₄₀
I had long since given up checking the time when I was on guard, but it was some way in between 'lunch' (the midnight version of the main meal, that is) and the second cup of tea. Dawn was about an hour or more away. The weather was filthier than ever. It was hard to see. Specifically, it was hard to see straight in front of you, ₄₅

in the direction from which the wind and waves were coming, straight at the Wall. When you looked sideways towards the guard posts next to you, all you could see was flooding, streaming, torrential rain sheeting through the Wall lights.

5 I remember that I was thinking, it's hard to know what's going on out there, it's like a white-out, except it's pitch black, when the lights failed. It was a sensation so strange, and the disorientation was so total, that it took a few seconds to understand. There was lots of swearing and lamentation over the communicator.

10 "This is silver command," said Sarge, meaning, everyone else shut up. "Hold your posts. The lights have failed all along our sector. Stand still and shut up. The backup will kick in any second."

In drills and training, the backup generator usually started within fifteen to thirty seconds. That didn't happen. It was eerie, but I 15 wasn't worried, it was just one of those Wall cockups. The thirty seconds went past, no generator, no lights, no communication. Another thirty seconds. This was the longest period of dark I'd known on the Wall since the night in training when we had been playing at attack and had used a five-minute blackout to overrun 20 the Defenders.

The Wall lit up with gunfire. It was at the far end from my post, close to the watchtower. Several different sets of automatic weapons were firing and none of them sounded like the kind used by Defenders. Then there were three explosions, a big one, then a 25 bigger one, then the biggest explosion I had ever seen or heard, so loud it had a shockwave that hit a second or so after the light and flame. It came from the barracks. The brief glimpse of illumination showed me nothing that I could understand, but it was clear that there was fighting on the Wall. A voice came on the com-30 municator, saying, "Others, code red," which told me nothing that I didn't already know. Our training was to check if our own post was clear and then obey orders or, if there weren't any, to assess whether to run towards the fight or stand at post. I stood up to the Wall but in the rain and wind and dark I couldn't see what was on 35 the other side. There could have been an Other five feet below me, there could have been none in the next thousand metres. "Sergeant, orders please," I said, joining the three or four Defenders who'd made the same request, but there was no answer, so I said, "Kavanagh post thirteen engaging," and left my post to run to-40 wards the fight. There were two kinds of shooting now, our rifles and the flatter sound of the Others' weapons. Hifa said over the communicator that she was engaging too. I stopped to wait for her and thirty seconds later she was beside me, the grenade launcher at her shoulder, her eyes wild, the biggest I'd ever seen 45 them. We just looked at each other. Then we moved off, more

torrential very heavy
sheeting fast and heavy rain

white-out a weather phenomenon when snow and clouds, sky and earth merge into a single whiteness, dense blizzard
pitch black completely black
sensation *Sinnesempfindung*
swearing *Fluchen*

cockup (*sl.*) sth. that is done very badly

to make a request to officially ask for sth.

slowly, jogging rather than running, towards the gunfire, keeping as far away from each other as we could on opposite sides of the ramparts, to make a more difficult target.

People's eyes adapt to the dark at different speeds. Mine are pretty good. I think it took five minutes to get close to the fight and by ₅ then I could make out a group of Defenders with their backs to me, using the concrete benches as cover, and a group of Others beyond them, doing the same thing but also making darts across the Wall to cross the ramparts and get down on the inner side. When people say their blood ran cold, what they're describing is ₁₀ the feeling of being flooded with adrenaline; it's a sensation which hits all over the body, chest to guts to limbs to heart to head. In that moment I was soaked with cold. Others had got over the Wall and were getting away. The worst thing imaginable was happening on our watch. Some of us were going to be put to sea. ₁₅ When bullets come close, the noise they make as they go past changes from a zing to a crack. The bullets were starting to crack when Hifa and I got to the point where our people were fighting. Some of them were on the right of the Wall, behind a bench, and some were on the other side behind a concrete bulwark. Sarge ₂₀ and Yos were behind the bench. We took cover with them. Three of the new people in our squad were dead on the ramparts in front of us. Four other members of the shift were in cover behind the bulwark, taking turns to fire shots. The Others were about a hundred metres from us, in the direction of the barracks. There ₂₅ were two vehicles on the inner side of the Wall, people carriers. I assumed they were Defenders from nearby posts come to help us, but as Hifa and I arrived one of the cars drove away, fast. I realised that the Others had assistance; the rumours of support were true. Hence the blackout. Hence maybe the explosion in our barracks. ₃₀

"Where's the rest of the company?" I said to Sarge. He reached around the bench, fired off a few rounds, then turned to me.

"The barracks were sabotaged. They're dead or wounded. No help from there."

"How many have got away?" ₃₅

"Too many."

"What's the plan?"

"Kill as many as we can. Hifa, when the next car starts, hit it with a grenade. We'll give cover. That way we'll get as many of them as have got over. Two cars have gone already." ₄₀

Maybe eight per car. Sixteen Others. The worst breach anywhere in a long time.

For the moment it was a standoff. We couldn't get closer to them without coming out of cover and being easy to shoot. They couldn't get across the ramparts without being shot at. ₄₅

---

to make darts to make sudden rapid movements

guts *Eingeweide*
limb *Körperglied*
soaked *klatschnass*

bulwark *Bollwerk*

hence therefore, because of that

to sabotage [ˈsæbətɑːʒ] *sabotieren*

standoff stalemate; *Stillstand*

"Where's the Captain?"

"Dead. He must be or he'd be here."

But Sarge was wrong about that. A few seconds after he spoke, I
heard a scrabbling and scratching noise behind me and to the left,
5 the side furthest from the barracks and the Others. The Captain
came running up the nearest set of steps on the inside of the Wall
and dived into cover beside us. He was bleeding from a cut on his
head.

"Sir, we thought we'd lost you."

10 "I was caught at the far end when they attacked," he said, meaning he was past Hifa at the end of our section. I thought that I
would have seen him go past but I took it on trust, since in a fight
nothing much makes sense.

"We're going to wait here until the last of them has got over, then
15 Hifa's going to light up their vehicle," said Sarge. The Captain,
panting, nodded.

"Good plan," he said. He looked down for a moment. Then he
stepped back and shot Sarge in the head, twice. He turned the gun
towards the two Defenders who were standing nearest to the
20 bench and shot them both with a burst, side to side. Yos dived to
cover beside me. A hundred metres ahead of us I could see the
Others all sprinting across the ramparts. Hifa and I were on the
far side of the bench, largely protected from the Captain, and that
was what saved our lives, because he now turned to his left and
25 started shooting at the Defenders who were under cover from the
Others on the far side of the Wall, against the bulwark. I saw three
of them go down and without thinking, without processing what
I was doing – that training, when it kicks in, it really kicks in – I
ran forwards and shoved my bayonet into his back. He staggered
30 and fell and as he did I smashed him on the back of the head with
the rifle. He went down and stayed down. Hifa stepped past the
bench and took aim at the Others' vehicle, which was accelerating
hard on the inner peripheral road. Her first grenade missed, short,
but the second one didn't. The car exploded and swerved off the
35 road in flames. It was burning hard. No one would survive that.

I knelt down beside the Captain. Yos came over and joined me. We
looked at each other but didn't speak. The Captain was unconscious and bleeding heavily. Maybe he'd survive, maybe not. I got
up and went over to Sarge. He had two bullet holes in the front of
40 his face and the back of his head had gone. The two new people
against the bench were both multiply wounded and were bleeding out. I went over to the Defenders next to the ramparts but as
I was heading over I could hear engines and see lorries coming
from both directions, from the next watchtowers to the east and
45 to the west, and I knew that it was over. This part of it was over.

scrabbling *Scharren*

peripheral road
Umgehungsstraße
to swerve off to turn aside
abruptly

multiply (*adverb*) in various
places

17

We were arrested. Nothing personal: when Others get over the Wall, that's what happens next. The Defenders from the neighbouring unit were the ones who had to execute the order, and they didn't seem happy about it, but the rules are what they are.

handcuffs *Handschellen*

We weren't handcuffed or anything, but the surviving members ₅ of our unit, all seven of us, were put in a lorry and driven south for about four hours, and then locked up in a barracks room which was like a normal barracks room except instead of high small windows there were no windows at all, the doors couldn't be opened from the inside, and we had to ask permission to go to ₁₀ the toilet. Yos wasn't able to whittle, because he wasn't allowed a knife, so he fidgeted non-stop.

We spent a month in that room. I got to know it so well I could recognise every crack in the ceiling. When it rained heavily there were damp patches and I got to recognise them too, to watch the ₁₅ changing shapes they made as the water seeped in: map of small island, map of big island, map of continent; then back the other

parlour-game *Gesellschaftsspiel*

way when the rain stopped, shrinking, drying, gone. A parlour-game version of the Change. The barracks room was standard, built to house thirty people, and there were only seven of us. It ₂₀ was me and Hifa and Hughes and Yos and three new Defenders who I barely knew. We spent most of our time talking about what had happened in the attack and trying to work it out. I imagine we were being listened to, but we didn't really care. It's not like

reprieve *Begnadigung*

we were expecting a reprieve. We just wanted to try and make ₂₅ sense of it.

What was obvious was that the Captain had been working with the Others. They must have had other help too – lots of it. The talk of a network of supporters was true. Someone had cut the power, someone had helped dynamite the barracks, someone had ₃₀ arranged the vehicles. Maybe somewhere else, somebody was getting them chipped, hacking into databases, faking IDs. It was hard to imagine how anybody could do that to us; but the truth was

plain obvious

plain. While we Defenders were standing on the Wall, some of the people we were protecting were working to let Others over the ₃₅ Wall. It was like standing in front of a white-on-white painting and hearing the person next to you say that it was black-on-black.

betrayal *Verrat*

That's the main thing we talked about, the sense of betrayal we all felt. Hifa kept telling me to let it go, that people just did what they did and there was no explaining it, but I couldn't. I wanted to ₄₀ think about it, to try to understand it, but, at the same time, couldn't bear to. Betrayal by the Captain, betrayal by whoever it was that the Captain had been working with to help the Others. I

had never really thought about betrayal before; I knew the word
but not the meaning. Now I knew. Betrayal was like tasting a liquid, the bitterest thing you've ever put in your mouth, and holding the taste just long enough to fully understand how repulsive
5 it is, and then forcing yourself to drain the cup to the dregs.
Out of thirty Defenders in our company, only we seven in this
barracks room had survived. We spent quite a lot of time trying to
work out how many Others had got over the Wall and got away.
Two people carriers' worth, was the general view. The third vehi-
10 cle was fried by Hifa. Say eight to ten Others per vehicle. In the
chaos and fighting, though, maybe the escape vehicles weren't
full. Maybe one of the drivers had panicked, driven away with the
car empty. It was tempting to imagine ... say, one car empty, only
three people in the second car ... that would mean only three of
15 us had to be put to sea. Or if the Others had been lucky and we
had been unlucky, both cars had been full and twenty of them
might have got over the Wall, so we'd all be going to sea. No way
of knowing. But my hunch was that those cars had been pretty
full. A lot of Others had been seen running across the Wall.
20 The extent of the conspiracy, the level of organisation, the planning and resources involved – it was hard to get my head around
it. If the breach had happened to a different company I would
have been fascinated by the details. But you know what they say:
when it's someone else, it's theory; when it's you, it's practice –
25 and practice is very different from theory. And at the same time,
the unique circumstances of our breach, the scale of the planning
and the scale of the treachery, gave me moments when I did
something stupid: I entertained a tiny hope. We talked it over and
nobody could remember a breach that had involved people work-
30 ing with Others. Nothing like this – the breach, the assistance
from within, the Captain's betrayal – had ever happened before.
An extraordinary event would demand an extraordinary re-
sponse. Mercy might be shown. Maybe. My head knew that this
was very very unlikely, and that entertaining any hope would
35 cost me dear when hope was taken away. But my heart couldn't
stop itself. I wanted to be with Hifa, decades in the future, old
couple, much older than our parents were now, looking back at
this terrible crisis from a safe happy afterlife, the moment when
we nearly lost everything but were forgiven and brought back
40 under the big safe all-embracing blanket of life behind the Wall. I
couldn't resist the temptation of hope.
Every day or two I would be taken for interrogation. It happened
to all of us in turn. The routine varied: armed Defenders would
come and ask for us by name, or we'd be called to the door over
45 the loudspeaker, or people would just come in, set up at one end

repulsive extremely unpleasant or unacceptable
to drain to the dregs *bis zum Bodensatz leeren*

hunch an idea based on a feeling and for which there is no proof

conspiracy *Verschwörung*

treachery disloyalty, falseness

to cost dear to cause sb. terrible consequences

temptation *Verlockung*
interrogation questioning; *Befragung*

of the room and start asking questions. The same questions, over and over, about what had happened that night, about what we had seen and what we had done. There were also questions about what had happened before, and questions about the Captain – lots and lots of questions about the Captain. What did he do that night, where was he that night, where was he on the previous nights, what had we noticed about him, what did he say, what did he usually do, what did he do that tour that was different, what did we think about him, on and on and on. Did he ever talk about his life away from the Wall, did he have friends on the Wall, what else did we know about him?

After four weeks we were put in a lorry again and driven to a town and put in cells – separate cells. There was a small high barred window and a toilet in the corner of the room with a wash-basin next to it. I spent a day and a night there. Then two Defenders came and led me into a room with a long table at one end. Five senior Defenders sat behind it. I was marched to the front of the room opposite them and asked if there was anything I wanted to say before I heard the sentence. I already knew there would be no trial, that wasn't the way it worked. That **flicker** of wishful thinking which I'd stupidly allowed myself did not survive standing in this room and looking at these pale **solemn** closed faces. Hope is a mistake.

"Is there anything I can say that would make any difference?" I asked. They didn't seem to be expecting to be asked that and the officer in the middle, the senior one, looked from side to side and **muttered** something to his colleagues before turning his head back to me.

"No," he said. I shrugged.

"Then, no," I said, though I was tempted for a moment to say that I knew all the details of how the Others had done it, their secret network of supporters, just to see what would happen. I thought of something. "One thing, though: how many of them got over the Wall?"

It was obviously irregular to ask questions, but the man in the middle thought it over for a few moments and decided to answer. "We aren't sure but we think it was sixteen. Fifteen or sixteen."

That made it the worst breach in many years. It would be untrue to say this made me feel better, because it was still a death sentence, but it did make me take it less personally. It was a huge thing that had happened and we had been caught up in. I nodded to show that I was ready for what was coming.

"Joseph Kavanagh, you failed in your duty as a Defender, and you will be put to sea. May God have mercy on you," said the senior Defender. "Take him back to the cells."

flicker *Flackern*

solemn *feierlich*

to mutter *murmeln*

III
THE SEA

18

The third night at sea, I saw some lights in the far distance as we
bobbed up to the top of a swell. I wasn't sure I could believe my
own eyes, the first time I caught a glimpse of them; your mind
sometimes plays tricks on you when you're on the Wall, but on
5 the open sea, it's worse. You have no physical equilibrium in a
small boat, and it can feel as if your mental equilibrium goes too.
You can't trust your senses, and you can trust your imagination
even less. You try to pin your mind down to the specifics of the
moment. But it's hard. You hear things, you see things. The wind
10 carried voices, fragments of song – not music in general, but specifically song, voices in chorus. I often thought I was hearing
someone call my name. Clouds in the distance coalesced as land,
as hills, before fading back into cloud. So my first thought when I
saw the lights was, I'm probably imagining it. I'm not used to a
15 black this complete; on the Wall we had the lights along the guard
posts. Here, until the moon comes up, it's blind-black. So maybe
my synapses were firing weirdly, unused to a dark so final. Then,
seconds later, on the crest of another rise, I saw them again. And
then, a minute or so later, a third time, more clearly and more
20 definitely than before. Lights on the open sea.
We had talked about this: what to do, what calculations to make,
if we saw evidence of other boats. The plan had been to row towards them and look for signs of whether they were benign or
not. By daylight that felt as if it made sense. At night, less so. We
25 had no weapons and our only defence if we came under attack
would be to try to get away as fast as possible. Given that we only
had one set of oars, that wasn't very fast. A boat with lights was
either a Coast Guard boat or a boat of Others so confident that
they weren't worried about being seen. That meant that they
30 were either stupid or well armed. Either was dangerous.
The swell was two metres or so, not enough to be frightening, but
more than enough to be uncomfortable. It was the swell which
made it hard to be certain about the lights; they winked into view
at the top of each wave and then disappeared again as we went
35 down into the trough. Everyone else in the boat was asleep. It was
a lifeboat, or it had been. A waterproof awning covered the back
half of the boat, and that's where the others were sleeping. It was
also where our food supplies were stored. The water tanks and
water catchment traps were in the front of the boat, with me.
40 I wanted to wake someone up to talk about what we should do.
Hifa would under normal circumstances have been the obvious
choice, but she had been seasick for two days – not feeling-queasy
seasick, but repeatedly vomiting in a way which would be

equilibrium calm mental state

to coalesce *sich verbinden*
to fade to disappear gradually

synapse ['saɪnæps] the point at which electrical signals move from one nerve cell to another
crest top

benign [bɪ'naɪn] *here:* friendly, not dangerous

oar *Paddel*

to wink to flash on and off

trough [trɒf] *Wellental*
awning *Plane*

water catchment trap
Wasserauffangvorrichtung

feeling-queasy wanting to vomit

genuinely dangerous if it kept on – and had only just gone to sleep. It would not be the right call to wake her up. I chose Hughes. He was the only other person I trusted and he had done a little sailing with an uncle in his childhood, so he wasn't as ignorant about boats as I was. By which I mean: he knew almost nothing, 5 but I knew nothing-nothing, so he won. It felt like a desperate thing to be doing, to rely on the tiny amount he knew about the sea, but there was no choice. I bent over double to get under the awning and into the back of the boat. You learnt the hard way to be careful when you did that, because if you brushed against the 10 roof you were likely to get several litres of water decanted onto you. I shoved Hughes with my foot, then again, and he woke up. I held my fingers to my lips. He sat up and crawled out of the sleeping space. There was just enough starlight to see that he looked terrible, his lips cracking with salt and his face abraded red 15 with the sea winds. I realised I must look like that too.

"This had better be good," he said. I handed him a water bottle and pointed into the middle distance as we swayed up and down. He saw the lights as we got to the top of the second set of swells. He said nothing and looked at them for a while as they came in and 20 out of view. I noticed he too was taking some time before he felt sure he could trust his senses.

"Wat I'm wondering is, if you think about who that might be, how many of the options are good for us?" I said.

He nodded. We stood at the prow and looked into the distance 25 while the boat bucked up and down on the swell and the lights winked on, winked off. Once I had had a few chances to study the lights I thought I could see they were arranged in a triangu- lar pattern of five, one at the top and two lower down on each side. 30

"Same. Guards probably aren't out here at this time, but if they are and they see us, they'll sink us straight away, no question. So we can't go anywhere near them if they're Guards. If they're Oth- ers, how come they're making such a spectacle?"

A boat full of Others who felt confident enough to be fully illumi- 35 nated on the sea in the middle of the night – to be that unfright- ened, they would have to be very frightening.

"So we leave them be?"

He thought for a moment. It felt impossible that we would encounter the first sign of life out here, the first sign of company 40 and possible salvation, and turn away from it. But when we thought about it, saw the risks, there was nothing else we could do.

"Plus, I think they're further away than they look. The horizon at sea level is about five K. The swell is coming from that direction. That's a lot of rowing into a lot of waves." 45

to decant to pour

abraded rubbed

prow [praʊ] the front part of a boat or ship
to buck up and down to move sharply up and down
triangular [traɪˈæŋgjələr] dreieckig

to encounter sb./sth. to meet

salvation being saved from danger, loss or harm

"And only three of us to do the rowing."

We looked at each other. We had been physically inactive for six weeks while we were waiting for sentence, and the rowing was hard. My hands were blistered and split and I was getting out of breath within minutes. Even if we wanted to row to the boat we might not be able to do it.

"OK. Thanks. Go back to sleep," I said.

Hughes started to go back towards the covered part of the life-boat. He stopped.

"In a few days we may be so desperate we have no choice," he said.

"I know," I said.

So this was life at sea. After the sentences were passed, we were taken in another lorry to another barracks. This time we travelled in handcuffs. I imagine the authorities' thinking was that we now had nothing to lose so were more likely to make a run for it. The lorry journey was the worst moment of my life so far, worse than the moment of sentencing, worse even than when I knew the breach had happened and the Others had got away. I knew what the rules of the Wall were – like everyone else, I had known them my whole life. I don't remember having them explained to me because there was no time before the rules, before the facts of life: the sun comes up in the morning and it goes down at night; if you throw something in the air, gravity makes it come back down; if the Others get over, you get put to sea. And yet, for all that, I felt sick with the injustice of it. Physically sick. I knew for certain that I, that we, had done nothing wrong. More: I had done everything I could to guard the Wall to the best of my capabilities. I had fought hard and watched my friends die. We all had. And this was our reward.

I had heard the word 'despair' and thought I knew what it meant; thought also that it was one of those states of mind that resembles a weather system, something which sets in and then you live with it or under it. Now I found that despair can also be something that happens to you, that it can hit you in a single moment. And then it settles down with you for the duration. This is the thought I had in those days: that at some times in our lives we should, all of us, take some time to think about the worst possible thing that we can imagine happening to us. Your worst fear: track it down inside yourself. Take a good look at it. And face the fact that it will happen. The thing that you dread most will happen. When it does, the name of the thing you're feeling is despair.

Our guards offered us the opportunity to write letters to our 'loved ones'. This wasn't a special dispensation: it was clear that

blistered *mit Blasen bedeckt*
split *aufgerissen*

gravity *Schwerkraft*

to resemble sb./sth. to look or be like sb./sth.

duration the length of time that sth. lasts

dispensation (*fml.*) *here*: exception

there was a protocol, agreed procedures, for occasions such as this. Agreed procedures for the worst thing that could ever happen to a person. In my case 'loved ones' meant my parents, and I decided I didn't want to write to them, because I had nothing to say. Hifa talked me out of that. I put down some platitudes about being sorry, even though I wasn't. I said I loved them, even though I didn't, at least not in that moment. But I felt better for having written the letter.

We stayed in that new barracks for several days and one by one were brought to the medical centre and put under general anaesthetic while we had our chips removed. No biometric ID, no life. Not in this country. No turning back ... After the operation we were held in recovery for a day, then returned to barracks. I could feel an itch deep in my arm where the chip had been and when I asked the others said they had the same feeling. A phantom chip. On the sixth afternoon, Hughes and Hifa and I were called and taken to another lorry; we'd have said goodbye to Yos and the other Defenders, if we'd known that was the last time we'd see them. From the angle of the light through the side of the vehicle I got the impression that we were heading south. We were driven until it was dark. Another barracks, but this time we were there hardly any time at all, an hour at most, before some Guards came into the room. From the look on their faces I could see this was what the Help had called *kuishia*: the ending. They seemed sad rather than angry; also implacable. We were taken down a series of concrete tunnels and then suddenly were out in the open air, and a Guard ship was waiting, with a lifeboat tied to the side. As soon as I saw it I realised it was going to be ours. We were led across a gangway to the ship. The Guard captain was waiting for us and he, weirdly or generously, I'm still not sure which, maybe both, saluted us and shook our hands. The ship cast off and we headed out to sea and we were led downstairs to a small unfurnished cabin and the door was locked behind us.

Up to that point my despair had left me numb to other feelings. Despair, grief, numbness, blankness. But not much else. I felt there was nothing I could do, and as a corollary (maybe) that there was therefore nothing else that it was necessary to feel. Everything that happened had been inevitable. Now and for the first time, I felt afraid, very very afraid. The boat would be lowered into the water and we would be lost, with the same complete lack of agency we had had ever since the night of the attack. The feeling that I had been relying on to keep me numb – that there was nothing I could do – suddenly became a source of overmastering fear. There's nothing you can do. That thought can be a

anaesthetic [ˌænəsˈθetɪk] *Betäubung, Narkose*

itch *Juckreiz*

implacable *unerbittlich*

to cast off (*phr. v.*) to leave the shore

numbness lack of physical or emotional feeling
blankness emptiness
corollary *Begleiterscheinung*
inevitable *unausweichlich*

agency power, influence

comfort, or it can be a terror. Panic, the need to flee, the impossibility of fleeing, the desperate need to escape combined with the certainty that you can't escape, the sense that you are going to die of dread right there in that moment. My heart was beating
5 fast and erratically. There was no air in the cabin. The lights had been turned up and were flickering. I was frying in my clothes, where I'd felt cold only seconds before. Hifa saw me freaking out and put a hand on my arm. I flinched, as if I'd had an electric shock, then thought, why am I flinching, and that new idea was
10 just enough, turned my attention just enough, to allow me to start slowing down.

"It's OK," said Hifa, which was so not true it was a help. She wasn't looking at her best, pale and shaky, which turned out to be the start of her seasickness.

15 "Yeah, it's all great," said Hughes.

"So great," said Hifa. Her face was drawn. I could see that the attempt at banter between them was reflexive, a flashback to when we had been Defenders, when we had been on the Wall, and this is how we had talked to each other.

20 "I wonder how far they tow us?" said Hughes, who got his answer straight away, because the engines slowed to an idle.

When people are put to sea, they are taken out of sight of land, so that they won't immediately try to turn and go back where they came from and also so that they won't run straight into Guard
25 ships who would immediately sink them. We had been on the ship for about half an hour, so we couldn't be far from land. Say, fifteen K at most.

The door opened from the outside. Three Guards were standing there, with two behind them: the latter two were carrying guns.
30 Again, they didn't look grim so much as sad. We came out and followed the unarmed ones down the corridor with the armed guards behind. They led us clanking up the ship's metal stairs out onto the main deck. It was relatively calm and still and the night was clear. They walked us over to the lifeboat, which was a couple
35 of feet below the level of the deck, and we stepped across and down to get in. The whole crew came to the side of the ship and, on their captain's command, saluted as the lifeboat began to be lowered into the water. I swear that was almost the worst moment, the solemnity and finality of that salute.
40 The lifeboat swung a few feet further out as it was lowered and then, when we were just above sea level, was abruptly dropped into the water. We went crashing to the floor of the boat. When we'd got up and straightened ourselves out, the ship was moving away from us on a curving trajectory back towards land, alight
45 like a floating cathedral in the pitch black of the ocean. It was

comfort *Trost*

erratically irregularly, unexpectedly, chaotically
to fry to feel boiling hot

to flinch to make a sudden movement out of fear

drawn stretched
reflexive *reflexartig*

to tow sth. [təʊ] to pull a boat along
idle ['aɪdəl] not in use or operation

to clank *scheppern*

solemnity *Feierlichkeit*

alight lit up

immediately clear how different it was when you were centime-
tres above its surface on a pitching small plastic boat, as opposed
to a metal ship's deck ten metres high.

Having stood up, Hifa sat back down again. "I'm not sure about
this," she said. It was my turn to be reassuring so I told her to sit ₅
where she was while Hughes and I sorted ourselves out. There
were many boxes and crates in the front of the boat, and we
started to open them and look into them. The Guard had been
generous, very generous, with supplies and assistance. We
looked to have enough food for weeks. They had put in water- ₁₀
torch *Taschenlampe*   proof warm clothing, torches and batteries and metal tools.
cask barrel   There were several casks of water too. I couldn't do the maths on
that straight away, and I knew that people always needed more
water than they thought they did; but it looked as if we would be
able to survive for a while. As long as we weren't drowned or ₁₅
shot.

That, though, wasn't all the Guards had left us. We didn't go into
the back part of the boat, under the awning, because the front
was so full of food and equipment it needed to be reorganised
before we could fight our way through. That made it confusing ₂₀
and weird when noises started coming from the back of the boat.
Looking at each other wildly, Hifa and Hughes and I simultaneously realised that we were not alone. Then a figure wrapped
to swathe *einwickeln*   in a blanket came out of the back and straightened up. He was
swathed in multiple layers of cold-weather clothing and had a ₂₅
hood over his head and I thought I was hallucinating, or having
aneurysm [ˈænjərɪzəm] a swollen   an aneurysm, or something. Because although I could recognise
area on the wall of an artery   who it was I also couldn't get my brain to admit that I recognised
him. The hair under the hood was blond. I know you but I don't
know you, my brain was telling itself. Then he spoke and I saw ₃₀
that although I couldn't believe it, I had no choice.

"Hello," said James the baby politician. "I imagine you weren't
expecting to see me."

Hifa and Hughes and I just stared at him. Their mouths were
open and no doubt mine was too. James nodded and looked as ₃₅
pleased with himself as it is possible to look if you are huddled in
a blanket on a lifeboat on the open sea. It wasn't comforting to
see him, not at all, but I did feel momentarily less alone – as if it
was a relief to find it wasn't just us Defenders who were put to
sea.   ₄₀

"Yes, and there are other surprises in store. Come and look."

Hifa got up and we moved towards the back of the boat, staggering and balancing on the boxes and gear as we went. The awning
was folded down over both sides of the opening so we couldn't
see in. James pulled it back and bent down and pointed. We ₄₅

crouched down to look. A person was lying on a foam mattress
on the floor of the boat, wrapped in several layers of clothing and
blankets. He was either unconscious or asleep. Despite the wrapping, we all recognized him at first glance. It was the Captain.
5 James gave us a moment to take that in.

"So," he said. "Shall we kill him?"

foam *Schaumstoff*

19

I learnt that I had nearly killed him once already. The night of the attack, the Captain came close to bleeding out from the bayonet wound I'd given him. I'd hit an artery. If it had been up to us, his company, we would probably have let him die. But the medic got to him in time and he was stabilised and now, six weeks later, he 5 was recovering, too weak to row but otherwise getting stronger. He did indeed look like a man who had nearly died; the skin on his face was stretched and the scars on his cheeks were now in

strain *Strapaze*   parallel with newly drawn lines of illness and strain. His eyes were open and he stared at us and we stared back, but nobody 10 spoke. It wasn't until the next morning that we talked to him.

That was a strange night, all crammed together in the back of the lifeboat. Three banished Defenders and their two companions. Companion number one was the member of the elite who had failed in his chance to stop what had happened. Companion num- 15 ber two was the man who had betrayed us. Sixteen Others had got over the Wall and escaped, and so sixteen people were put to sea. That was the seven members of the company who had survived and nine others in the chain of command, including several people in the next watchtowers along, who were judged to have re- 20 acted too slowly when the action kicked off that night. James said that the judgement had been passed on him because, according to the court, he should have realised that the Captain was part of the network of Others and their supporters. He thought that was

outrageous shocking and morally   outrageous. He was bitter and did not pretend otherwise.   25
unacceptable
"My question is, how? How was I supposed to know?"

My answer to that was that I didn't know and didn't care. I was glad that he felt the injustice of what had been done to him as much as felt the injustice of what had been done to us.

"A network of hidden support and I was meant to find one end of 30 it and unravel the network with what, the power of telepathy? I'm supposed to look into his soul and work out this plan they'd

to hatch sth. to make a secret   been hatching for years?"
plan, *etw. ausbrüten*
"How about you shut up?" Hughes said. James took the hint.

to retch *würgen*   Hifa spent that first night retching, at first over the side, then into 35 a bucket, then dry-retching where she lay. We lay there and I didn't feel as if I'd slept but I must have because I opened my eyes and the sun was some way above the horizon. Hughes and Hifa were standing at the front of the boat. The Captain was awake but silent under the awning. I woke James and went to the others and 40 that's when we decided to have it all out and get the story. Hughes went under the awning and said something to the Captain and he got up and came to the bow.

The Captain sat with his back against the front of the lifeboat. We stood in front of him.

"It was ten years. Seven of us set out to get over the Wall. Then there were further expeditions with messages backwards and for-wards. We had a set of signals with lights. I was the only one who made it. We all knew we would have to wait and in the end it was five years before I was able to get a message back. Then we moved to the next phase. I waited for three more years. Then I was a Captain and we could start to execute a specific plan. By now we had got in touch with a wider network. Some of your country-men don't agree with the Wall. They think you need the Wall to keep out the water but not to keep out human beings. Some of them don't agree with turning people into Help. They think it's slavery. It's a big network, much bigger than you realise. I don't know much about who is in it and I don't know who they're help-ing but I do know that my people are not the only ones who are coming."

He stopped. We wanted something more and I could tell that he knew it. The silence went on – the human silence, because the wind and waves and creaking of the boat never stopped. It is never silent in a small boat in northern waters. Eventually it was Hifa who spoke. Her voice was hoarse from the hours of retching. **hoarse** *heiser, rauh*
"Aren't you going to say you're sorry?"

The Captain was stiff and still, leaning back rigidly, and I felt there was a strong reaction he wanted to give but wouldn't. He thought for a long time.

"The thing we most despise about you, you people, is your hypocrisy. You push children off a life raft and wish to feel good **hypocrisy** [hɪˈpɒkrɪsi] *Scheinheiligkeit* about yourselves for doing it. OK, fine, if that's what you want to **life raft** *Rettungsboot* do, but you can't expect the people you push off the side of the raft to think the same. To admire your virtue and principle while **virtue** *Tugend* we drown. So, no, I'm not going to be like you. I'm not going to **principle** moral standard of good behaviour lie, I'm not going to be a hypocrite, and I'm not going to say I'm **hypocrite** *Scheinheiliger* sorry."

"Not even for Sarge?" said Hifa.

He blinked but said nothing. In that moment I did want to kill him. I looked over at Hifa, who mainly seemed as if she was going to be sick again, and at James, who was standing with his lips pursed shaking his head, looking like someone on a television **to purse** *die Lippen spitzen* debate panel trying to make it clear to the audience that he disa-greed with an argument being made by a fellow panellist. Then I looked over at Hughes, and what I saw on his face was the look of a man who was in the middle of suffering a huge, all-encompassing disappointment. My anger subsided and began to turn into a sense of loss. I felt sad. Loss, loss, there was just so much loss, in what had happened to us, in what the Captain had done, in what we had done to the world, in what we had done to each other and in what was happening to us.

"Let's kill him," said James. If he had said that same thing five 5 minutes before, and if I had had a gun or knife in my hand, I would probably have done it then and there. But a couple of minutes can have a big effect on how you see things, and the moment for revenge had, for me, passed. We were probably all going to die anyway, and in this boat. Sending the Captain on ahead of us 10 didn't seem like it was worth doing.

revenge *Rache*

"Yes, you could do that," the Captain said. "Or you could let me lead you to somewhere safe."

Safe. I wouldn't have thought it possible for a single word to have such an impact. Safe. To think of being safe meant to have hope, 15 and I knew, had learnt recently, how dangerous hope is. And yet, out here on the sea, we couldn't live without it. The Captain's plan was to head south. He said there were islands and stretches of coast where we could find somewhere to stay. He said we would never be able to get back over the Wall but there were other places 20 to live. He said he was the only one among us to have made a long journey in a boat and he knew how to do it and he could do it again. He said because we came from an island we thought the whole world had a wall around it, but that wasn't true and there were places, not many but some, where we could get to safety. 25 More safety than we would have at sea, anyway. He said again that the important thing was to head south. He said that apart from anything else, the cold here in the north was dangerous and once we got thoroughly wet, as we would when there was bad weather or when the season changed, it would become more dan- 30 gerous still.

"If we get drenched, we may never dry out. If the boat floods we die. If we capsize, we die. This is not the Wall. We can't go back to barracks and dry out. We have to go south."

to capsize *kentern*

Then he went and sat in the back of the boat while we sat at the 35 front and discussed it. When he moved, especially when he got up or changed position, you could see the effect of his wound was still strongly present. The wind and waves were now getting stronger. Every deeper plunge brought a slap of salt spray into the boat.

plunge *violent downward movement*
slap *Schlag*

40

"South," said Hughes.

"We have no reason to trust him," said James. "We have less reason to trust him than any human being alive."

"We have so little reason to trust him that we have no reason not to trust him," said Hughes. I thought that I knew what he meant: 45

the Captain would know he had so little credibility with us that
there was no incentive to lie. Also, the unspeakable truth was I
still felt an instinct to trust him and be led by him. He just so obviously was a leader. At the same time I felt that instinct was craven
and doglike. Follow master, follow, off the edge of the cliff, not
once but twice.

"South," said Hifa. It sounded like a tentative conclusion, a provisional verdict. What else, after all, was there to do? Rely on
Hughes's experience sailing with his uncle, mainly on a big pond
near his house but twice in a river estuary on family holidays?

"South," I said. So we had taken the Captain's advice. There was a
compass among the survival kit that we had been left by the
Guards. And now here we were, bobbing up and down on a two-
metre swell, hiding from lights in the dark. Hughes and I stood
looking at them for a few minutes longer and then he patted me
on the arm and went back towards the awning at the back of the
boat.

I let Hughes duck under the cover and began pulling at the oars
to move us in the opposite direction, away from the ship and its
lights. We took rowing easy, because it was hard work, especially
for the unfit, and because doing it too energetically made you
perilously hungry. It was a trade-off, calories for movement. I was
rowing backwards so, when the waves permitted, I could see the
lights in the distance. The ship didn't seem to be growing any
further distant; then, slowly, it seemed that it was. I must have
rowed for an hour, with frequent breaks at the start, and then
with longer periods of rest than bursts of rowing. I was using the
same technique we used to employ on the Wall, spacing out
glances at my watch to try and make it a pleasant surprise when
I gave in and looked at the time. When my four-hour shift was
over I went to wake James for his turn. In the back of the boat,
Hifa and the Captain and Hughes were all deeply asleep, and so
was James until I shook him. I stood back to let him wake in his
own time.

He got up slowly, rubbing not just his eyes but his whole face,
making chewing movements with his mouth. Then he came out
from under the awning.

"I saw lights," I told him. "A few kilometres away. A ship. Hughes
saw them too. We talked it over and decided to leave it. Too late to
do anything about it now. I wanted you to know."

He nodded, thinking about it. I didn't trust him but he wasn't
stupid. I could see him running through the same calculations we
had made.

"OK," he said. "I'd have done the same." He nodded some more. It
was beginning to be light, and I could see how tired he was, but

---

credibility the fact that sb. can be
believed or trusted

craven extremely cowardly; *feige*

tentative uncertain
provisional for the time being
verdict *Urteilsspruch*

perilously dangerously
trade-off *Abwägung*

to space sth. out to spread out

determined wanting to do sth.
very much
fatigue being extremely tired
stubble Bartstoppeln

to rummage kramen

to defecate (fml.) den Darm
entleeren
to wriggle sich winden
circumference Durchmesser

how determined too. Fatigue and his blond stubble made him look ten years older than he had before we were banished. I went to climb into the back and take my turn sleeping, but he stopped me with a hand on my arm. I looked a question at him and he held up a finger. Then he rummaged under his layers of clothing, 5 the layers he never took off except when he had to lower his trousers to defecate over the side of the boat. He wriggled for a moment and then brought something out, as if it were a birthday present. It was an object about six inches high with a circumference about the same size. It took me a few seconds to believe my 10 own eyes, though I knew very well what is was: a high-explosive grenade.

"Jesus, James," I said. He was smiling.

"The commander of the Guard ship gave it to me," he said. "In case we run into trouble or in case we, you know, decide we can't 15 go on any more. In case we want to choose fire over water."

I looked at him hard and saw something I had never seen before, never even suspected, which was the glint of madness. I said:

"You can't possibly be– " but he cut me off.

"I'm not, I'm not," he said. "I just wanted you to know." He began 20 putting the grenade back under his clothes. I wasn't worried about it going off by accident, that was impossible with the design of those grenades; in fact it was hard enough getting them to detonate when you wanted them to. What I was worried about, though, was his state of mind. I decided I would tell Hifa and 25 Hughes about the grenade – the next time I could be with them privately.

I went and lay down and replayed what had happened, not with James, but earlier, with the lights in the distance. Through the next days, through all that happened, I found myself often think- 30 ing of those lights; wondering who they were, what boat they had been on, Guards or Others, or Defenders put to sea, even, perhaps, sea ships going about their business, carrying precious

cargo Ladung
who knew where somewhere
or other
to bloom to develop
brigand pirate

merciless gnadenlos

cargo or passengers who knew where. I couldn't get it out of my mind. All kinds of alternative futures bloomed into being when 35 I thought about that boat, who had been on it, where they might have taken us. Friendly brigands, who would have made us part of their crew. Pitying Guards, with the convenient ability to issue us with new chips and fake IDs. Or, more likely, merciless pirates who would have robbed and killed us on sight. I'd never 40 know. In my old life, if I had wanted to find something out sufficiently badly, I could. I would put my mind to it, devote resources to it, find an answer. That was no longer true. There were now many things that I would never know and never be able to find out. 45

On the fourth day, we had our first piece of luck. (Always bearing in mind Sarge's maxim that if we had truly been lucky we would have never been there in the first place.) Hifa's seasickness had ended, thank God, as abruptly as it had begun, on the third day. She was washed out and her cheekbones were sharper and her nose pointy under her cap. She looked, if I had to put it in one word, purposeful.

It was mid-morning and she was on watch. I was sitting in the front of the boat because the air in the back would sometimes get stuffy. When the weather was dry and the pitching of the boat not too severe, it could actually be quite pleasant to sit in front, in the intervals when you weren't consumed with anxiety and apprehension and plain terror. Hifa was standing at the tiller looking forwards and Hughes was rowing, slowly, taking long pauses between strokes. Hifa was looking very fixedly at the horizon.

"Can you come and hold this for a minute?" she said to me. I took the tiller. Hifa came right to the front of the boat and stood staring into the distance.

"Right," she said. "I'm sure. There is land in front of us and about fifteen degrees to the left. At first I thought I was imagining it but I'm definitely not. It's an island."

Hughes stopped rowing, I let go of the tiller and we both joined Hifa at the front of the boat. My first thought was: she's wrong. There was a short smudgy line on the horizon but the thing it most looked like was a bank of cloud. One of those mirages, those imagined solid shapes which were so tormenting at sea. I stood and looked a bit more. I took off my glasses, thought about wiping them, thought better of it and put them back on. Actually, maybe ...

"It's land," said Hughes, and hugged Hifa. They did a clumsy little jig. I still wasn't sure. My desperate wish to believe them made me reluctant to believe them. I kept looking. The line did not move or wave or blur as clouds tended to. I kept looking. Almost with reluctance, I gave in to hope and admitted to myself: yes, it was land. Land!

Hughes and I went back to the oars and took one each. We started to row in the direction of the land. There was no immediate way of guessing its distance, since high ground would be visible from much further away than low; it could be thirty kilometres, it could be as little as three to five. My guess was that it was low land and not too far. My reasoning was that high ground might accumulate its own weather, wisps of cloud above the highest point.

The wind was from the side and the boat rocked and bumped as we headed towards the miracle of land. Sometimes the oars would

---

pointy *spitz*

purposeful showing that you know what you want to do

stuffy *stickig*
pitching *Stampfen*

to be consumed with to have so much of a feeling that it affects everything you do
anxiety [æŋˈzaɪəti] *Angst, Beklemmung*
tiller *Ruder*

degree *Grad*

smudgy having no particular shape
mirage [mɪˈrɑːʒ] *Luftspiegelung, Fata Morgana*
tormenting cruelly annoying

clumsy *unbeholfen*
jig an energetic dance
reluctant *zögerlich*

wisp thin line

catch too deep, sometimes they would miss altogether. It made rowing even harder work than usual. Since we were put to sea blisters had formed on my hands, then burst, and the raw skin underneath was acutely painful. We took the oars for half an hour at a time, Hifa and James joining in. The Captain came out of the back of the boat to watch.

All I could think of was how easy it would have been to miss the island altogether. It was pure luck. In the night we would have gone straight by without the merest inkling of its presence. So much of our new life was about luck.

We rowed for a couple of hours and the island was close now, a few hundred metres away. The next problem became clear to all of us at the same time. I looked at Hifa and Hughes and James and they looked back at me. The Captain was standing right at the front of the lifeboat.

"No no no," said Hughes.

It was easy to see what he meant. There was nowhere to land. The island – beachless, like every coastland in the world after the Change – rose vertically out of the sea. All that was left of the low island it had formerly been was the upper part of its main hill. Or rather, hills, three of them, a triple-peaked mass. The three slopes were bare rock. The wind and waves smashed into them and if we went in too close, we would be smashed against them too. Even on a sunny, calm day, with a powerful ship able to hold its own against the winds and currents, it didn't look as if it would be pos-sible to get a foothold, not on this side of the island. In our boat and with our resources we would have no chance.

The Captain turned around.

"This isn't the only possible angle of approach," he said. That made sense. We would pull back, give it some space, take a tour around the island and see if there was anywhere we could land. Hifa turned the boat to the side and I stepped away from the oars to let James go solo. There was no rush now; we'd take as long as we needed. This might be our best chance of medium-term survival and we didn't want to skip past it in any hurry. At the same time, I felt a deep, almost nauseous sense of dread. My gut was telling me that there would be nothing to look at. The island was too steep, too rocky, a cliff in the middle of the ocean; I desperately wanted there to be a landing point, but I couldn't imagine what it would look like. The rowing was hard, even harder than it had been before, and as we turned to manoeuvre around the island the waves came from all points of the compass so that the boat bucked and rocked more wildly than ever. This is impossible, I thought, we will never be able to land here.

---

acute extreme

merest slightest
inkling Ahnung

triple-peaked having three peaks
slope Abhang

current Strömung

nauseous feeling as if you might
want to be sick
gut Bauchgefühl

to manoeuvre [məˈnuːvər]

I was half right. As we went around it became clear that the island was variations on a theme: vertical stone. It wasn't just unsafe to land, it was unsafe to get too close. A shipwreckers' dream of an island. And yet I was half wrong too, because as we came round into the lee of the island, hidden from the wind, in the sudden still and quiet, I saw the first good thing I had seen since we were put to sea: a flotilla of boats, floating together in the unexpected calm.

shipwrecker pirate who lures ships onto rocky grounds using lights
lee *Windschatten*

flotilla a large group of boats or small ships

20

The strangest thing about the next few days was how quickly we got used to our new life. I tried to keep a low profile and set myself the task of finding out what this all was, what it meant – who these people were and how they had got here. The floating community had ten members, before we arrived. They had eight sea-going vessels tied together and a couple of floating structures which were not seaworthy, not in any kind of weather, but were float-worthy. The community had not been a plan, more a series of accidents and coincidences. The first three boats had arrived in the lee of the island before the last winter began and had taken shelter, and then had found that the supply of protein (fish) and water (rain) could sustain them, and had stayed. The other boats – the other Others – had arrived piecemeal and over time. Their crews were from nowhere and anywhere. I'd been brought up not to think about the Others in terms of where they came from or who they were, to ignore all that – they were just Others. But maybe, now that I was one of them, they weren't Others any more? If I was an Other and they were Others perhaps none of us were Others but instead we were a new Us. It was confusing.

Members of the floating community couldn't go ashore, but they, we, were safe in the calm. It was nobody's idea of an ideal life but it was a life that could be lived. Traps, catchments and lines were all over the floating craft, in their hundreds: for food, I saw to my amazement, they were quite well supplied. The big lack was in fuel: there were only tiny quantities of wood, which was too precious to burn, and an equally tiny quantity of diesel fuel brought by one of the boats. It wasn't clear what to do with that so it was being kept for emergencies.

The second day after our arrival, I was walking around the rafts trying to understand how it all worked and I came to side of the community furthest from the sunken island. This was the biggest of all the rafts. A woman with wild black and grey hair was squatting as she wrestled with something I couldn't see clearly but which was still alive and fighting.

"I'm not going to pretend that looks good," I said. The woman laughed. The sea life made it difficult to tell how old people were but she was maybe in her mid-forties, strong-looking and intent on her work. I now had a better view of what she was doing. She had trapped a seagull in a net; she broke its neck with a single expert wring. You could see that she had done this many times before. The bird went limp and the woman's shoulders dropped with relief. She gestured at me to sit so I did.

vessel (*fml.*) a large boat or ship
seaworthy *seetauglich*

coincidence *Zufall*

supply food and other things necessary for living
to sustain to keep alive
piecemeal at different times in different ways

catchment *Behälter*

to squat *hocken*
to wrestle with sth. *sich mit etw. abmühen*

wring violent twist/turn

"What's the worst thing you ever ate in your life?" she said, half smiling, as she started to pull feathers off the bird. She spoke good English with a lilt, an accent from somewhere far away and a rhythm which had something not-English underneath it.

5 "You mean, before I got here?"

She laughed at that too.

"I don't really remember," I said. On the Wall, thinking about food had been a means of escape, a technique for casting your imagination into the future, into a time when you weren't on the Wall 10 any more. At sea, thinking of food had become a form of nostalgia, of time travel back to a safer place. On the Wall, thinking about food made you feel better. Out here, it made you feel worse. "To be honest, looking back, it all seems pretty good now. I had some stews and things I thought were impossible to eat but I'd give 15 anything to have them today."

"Whatever it was, gull is nastier. Believe it. A rank taste and a bitter taste. As bad as you can imagine. Game bird and fish. At the same time. Tough too. Juice runs when you sink your teeth in. Blood, salt, duck, fish oil. Hard to swallow. And that's if you cook 20 it. We can't use fire so we have to eat it raw. That's so much worse. Trick is to leave it to dry. It's still hard to chew but the flavour changes. You can get it down without gagging. Like jerky or pemmican. Fish-duck jerky. We store it for when we're low on protein. No choice."

25 No choice. That made sense. It was true for most things on the sea. Her boat – it seemed to be hers, though the sense of ownership might be a function of her strength of personality rather than anything more formal – was a large improvised raft made of wood. There were nets strung in the air all around the boat to 30 catch birds, and lines hanging off it all around in the water to catch fish. Rainwater catchment vessels were dotted all over the vessel. Including me, there were six or seven people on this raft, two of them solemn children who had been given, or had given themselves, the job of finishing off any birds or fish brought into 35 the boat: they carried clublike sticks with a thickened metal piece at the end. The children took sidelong glances at me when they thought I wouldn't notice. It was as if I too was a form of non-human life which might at any moment need to be whacked on the head. Killed and eaten too, maybe. Did children have thoughts 40 like that? Or was imaginative darkness of that sort an adult thing? I didn't know enough about them to know. The next time I caught the boy peeking at me I smiled and winked back. He quickly looked away.

Beyond the children were three girls, older than the children but 45 not old enough to count as adults. I never saw them more than

---

lilt a gentle and pleasant rising and falling sound in a person's voice

to cast (cast, cast) to throw

nostalgia a feeling of pleasure and also slight sadness when you think about things that happened in the past

stew *Eintopf*

gull *Möwe*
rank *ranzig*
game *Wild*
tough hard to chew; *zäh*

to get down (*infml.*) to swallow
gagging *Würgen*
jerky strips of dried salty meat
pemmican food prepared by Native Americans from lean dried strips of meat pounded into paste, mixed with fat and berries, and pressed into small cakes

to string (strung, strung) *spannen*

to dot to be spread across an area

solemn serious-looking

to whack to hit sb./sth. noisily

to peek at sb./sh. to look, especially for a short time or while trying to avoid being seen
to wink *mit den Augen zwinkern*

a stride a long step
to conspire *sich verschwören*

interlocutor *Gesprächspartnerin*
desultorily without much
enthusiasm; *halbherzig*

to pluck to pull the feathers off

wiry *drahtig*

to skip *here: tänzeln*
brisk quick, energetic and active
delicate *leichtfüssig*

keen very active

adequate enough or satisfactory

a stride or two away from each other. They spent most of their time whispering to each other, conspiring or sharing secrets. It was hard to know what those secrets would be, in a place like this; but maybe that made having them all the more important. They were not sisters – their ethnicities were visibly different – but 5 they spoke a shared language which was not English. The shortest and most confident of them acted as their spokesperson and interlocutor. The girls were slowly and desultorily lifting fishing lines out of the water and checking them. They had the air of teenagers who are pretending to be busy in order to prevent 10 adults from giving them something more demanding to do.

"I'm Mara," the woman said, as she kept plucking the seagull. "I'm married to him." She pointed across to a man who was moving towards us, the same age as her, also wiry, also tough, his beard scissors-clipped and orderly. The floating people had their own 15 technique for crossing the ropes and nets between the rafts: instead of slowing down and picking their way carefully, they sped up and put their feet so precisely on the knots and firmer planks that they seemed to skip over the water. This man was so confident on the tricky passage between rafts that he was brisk and 20 delicate, like a goat on a steep hillside. Once he was on the big raft he had a few words with the teenagers, then a few words with the children, and then he came to Mara and me and squatted down in front of us.

"I'm Kellan," he said. He had the same up-and-down, not-quite 25 English lilt as his partner. Kellan didn't say he was in charge; he didn't have to. I knew already that there were people here who knew a lot about how to live at sea, and it was clear that I had now met two of them. I got the story later. Kellan and Mara had been raised by two sets of parents who were keen sailors before the 30 Change; they met at sea, across on the far side of the Atlantic; they more or less grew up on boats. You felt that the closer you stayed to them, the better your chances of keeping alive.

"I'm Kavanagh," I said. He nodded and looked at me. Not friendly and not unfriendly, but assessing. "I'm grateful to you for taking 35 us in," I said, partly because it was true and partly because I felt the need to say something.

"We voted," he said. It wasn't clear which way he'd voted, but Mara was smiling at me.

"OK," I said. "Well, thank you for that. Thank you for what you 40 did." It didn't seem close to adequate, but then what can you say to people who have taken you in and saved you from certain death? "Thank you for what you did." We had not told them who we were, that we were Defenders who had been put to sea. It seemed certain that it would not improve our chances of being 45

given sanctuary if they knew that our entire life's purpose had
been to stop people like them getting to safety.

sanctuary protection or a safe place

He let the silence lengthen for a moment or two and then Mara
laughed.

5 "Don't let him tease you, we all agreed. We wanted some more
people who can look after themselves."

Kellan was smiling too now. He said, "You look like a swimmer."

I said, I was, a bit. Swimming wasn't especially popular in the
world after the Change, but it had been my best sport at school.
10 Nobody swam in the sea any more.

"The water here isn't deep," he said. "Not hard to see why, the sea
floor underneath us used to be part of this island. The one we can
look at but can't touch."

We stood for a moment and looked at the island and I imagined
15 what it had once been like – beaches, gentle slopes, maybe a few
houses down near the water. In living memory the sea floor below us was dry land. All drowned now. Part of the old drowned
world.

"When the water isn't turbulent we can see the sea bed. It's only
20 a few metres down. Less in some places. We reckon there's probably things down there we can eat. Sea vegetables, shellfish, who
knows. Perhaps there are techniques we could use to catch fish
further down, not just lines off the side of the rafts. A person with
good lungs could dive to the sea bottom. Strong boy like you,
25 maybe you can go down and take a look. Not all at once, have a
few goes, build your fitness up. As long as you can see down
there?"

to reckon (*infml.*) think or believe

He made a gesture in the direction of my eyes, or rather my
glasses.
30 "No, that's fine," I said. "It's different under water. I can see OK.
Swimming makes you hungry, though. I could easily end up
burning and eating more calories than I find."

He shrugged.

"The only way we'll work it out is by giving it a try. I'm more
35 worried about the cold. Worried on your behalf. That's why I
want to do it now. Later in the year, when the season turns, it'll be
too late. Too much of a risk to try it. Now, if you keep it short and
sweet, the chance is worth it. Or at least I think so, but it's you
going into the water. So you must think it through for yourself."
40 "I'll try it," I said. It would of course have been difficult to say no
to the person responsible for giving us sanctuary; Kellan was well
aware of that. His way of leading was different from the Captain's, but it was effective.

short and sweet (*infml.*) *kurz und bündig*

"Good," he said. Then he looked at Mara tearing up her gull and
45 said, "I think I'll leave you two to it."

Get stuffed! (sl.) *Du kannst mich mal!*

"Get stuffed, old man," said Mara. Kellan laughed and went over to the children, who made play-fighting moves as he approached, and then went to talk to the teenagers. I noticed that when they realised he was coming over to them they became much more busy around the fishing lines. ⁵

That was how I got the job of being the community's diver. I was glad of having something specific to do. Hifa was given the job of experimenting with bird traps, Hughes was to join me in trying to dive, James and the Captain were put on a mixture of watch and fishing duties. Nobody was **idle**. There were always things to do ¹⁰ concerning traps and nets and food preparation. I could see the talent Kellan and Mara had for the work of survival, not just because diving was an idea worth trying but because it gave my days a sense of purpose and structure and something to do other than just exist and wait for … for … it wasn't clear what. If we were to ¹⁵ leave, the sensible thing would be to get on with it. The sun still had some warmth, but the days were getting shorter and the year would soon turn. Winter would be a difficult time to travel, so if we were going to head south, we would need to leave before long. To gather our strength and head off. I tried to think about that and ²⁰ found that I couldn't bear to. Winter would also be a difficult time to stay on the water, on the rafts, but the community had already survived a winter and knew how to do it. I could almost hear a voice whispering 'stay, stay …' The truth was, it was hard to imagine ever getting away from here. But it might be that we would ²⁵ never need to. Perhaps we weren't waiting for anything, but this was just life, life in its new form. There had been floating communities before, in the world before the Change. So maybe that is what we now were and would always be. It was better not to **brood** on it, so I tried not to. I tried to stick to the daily **necessities**. ³⁰

My diving work started that same day, as soon as Kellan left us. I took a long look over the side of the raft at the spot where Mara was plucking her seagull. It was unpromising. I couldn't see the sea bed. I walked around the rafts looking for places where the water seemed **shallowest**. I hadn't even begun mastering the art ³⁵ of moving around on the rafts. On a boat, everything moves in a coordinated way, so even when you are bucking and dropping and swaying on the waves, there's a kind of logic and coherence to the fact that you're on a single platform. The boat dips and swings left, you dip and swing with it. The dancing of the rafts ⁴⁰ was much more complicated and involved many moving parts **jigging** to **subtly** different rhythms. I found myself staggering and tripping even when the water was relatively still. My frequent trips and falls were painful and **disconcerting** and they were made more irritating by the sight of Hifa moving light-footedly and ⁴⁵

idle ['aɪdəl] not working

to brood on sth. to think for a long time about things that make you sad, worried or angry
necessity *Notwendigkeit*

shallow *niedrig*

to jig to dance/move quickly up and down
subtle ['sʌtəl] not obvious
disconcerting making sb. feel uncertain, uncomfortable and worried

rapidly across the rafts as she checked the fishing lines. She had got the hang of it straight away.

Hughes joined me and we kept walking around the community trying to find a place for our first dive. We took turns: one of us
5 would hold onto the other as he leant as far as possible over the side, face just above the water. We could always have started by diving in and seeing the underwater conditions first-hand and for ourselves, but the water was cold and I thought our stamina would give out. We'd manage one or two dives and then have to
10 stop. Better to do some research first. The sea was a little turbulent that day and although the anchors gave evidence that the water was only a few metres deep, we couldn't see the bottom, which was discouraging. Neither of us liked the idea of making our first plunge down into murk where we had no visibility. It's a
15 primal fear, the idea of the thing lurking below you in the deep. We wanted to dive where we could see. The trouble was there didn't seem to be any clear water anywhere around the rafts. I started to think we would have no choice but to go to wherever was shallowest, according to the anchors, and dive to the bottom
20 to take a chance on what was down there. But then our luck changed. We found a spot which looked as if it might be viable. It was on the innermost, island side of the rafts. The water was slightly shallower, and clear enough to see the bottom, which had patches of bare brown and patches of green. It might not have
25 been more than ten or twelve feet, easily diveable.

I didn't relish the thought of the cold, but the water, at this point where it was clear, looked cleansing and elemental and inviting. I wanted to have the first try at diving and said so.

"Be my guest," said Hughes. We got some spare cloth to use as a
30 towel and borrowed a metallic space blanket; I knew that once I got out of the water I would be desperate to dry off and warm up as quickly as I could. With no external sources of heat, I would be using my own body warmth, what was left of it. Fine. But best be prepared. I stripped off and put my foot in the water and then
35 realised that this was one of those times when there's no point taking too long to get yourself ready, so I let myself go all the way in. The cold was shocking and, for a moment, obliterating: I had no thoughts, only the sensation of complete, stinging, icy cold. I came back up to the surface spluttering and coughing. Hughes,
40 leaning down close to the side of the raft, looked worried. No doubt that was partly concern for me and partly the thought that it was going to be his turn next.

"Five minutes," I said when I had got my breath. "Tell me." He nodded, I emptied my lungs, breathed deeply, exhaled completely,
45 refilled them, and dived.

---

to get the hang of sth. (*infml.*) to learn how to do sth.

stamina staying power

to give out (*phr. v.*) to stop working

murk darkness or thick cloud

primal fear [ˈpraɪməl] *Urangst*
to lurk *lauern*

viable able to succeed

to relish to like or enjoy sth.

obliterating *vernichtend*
stinging *stechend*
to splutter *prusten*

The cold was stinging but it was thrilling to be in the water, that sensation of flying downwards. I felt free, unburdened. In a few seconds I was at the bottom. The sea bed was covered in a thick mat of what appeared to be grass from the surface, but up close you could see it was two different kinds of seaweed, one long and 5 frond-like, the other mossy and dense. I took a handful of each, having to pull a little harder than I expected, and once I felt my breath starting to give out, went back to the top. I gave the sea-weed to Hughes, caught my breath and dived again. It would be a good idea to take a knife down next time, because the frond-like 10 grass grew two or three feet tall and it was easy to imagine it wrapping around your legs when you tried to head back to the air. I brought up several more handfuls of the different seaweeds. On my fourth and final dive, I found something hidden in between the moss and the grass, a shell, and snatched at it, again pulling 15 harder than I thought I'd have to. A scallop. I pushed back up to the surface with a sense of elation but when I got there, I was too weak to pull myself out of the water. Hughes had to help me. He wrapped me first in the improvised towels, then in the space blan-ket. After a minute, as I warmed up, I started shivering. That 20 made me realise I had pushed my body temperature dangerously low: when you are too cold to shiver, you're on the edge of full-blown hypothermia. That was a lesson I had learned during type 2 cold on the Wall. Out here that degree of cold would almost certainly kill you. 25

Kellan came over while I was recovering and Hughes was psych-ing himself up for his turn. He picked over the seaweed and tapped the scallop. He looked pleased.

"I don't know if any of this is edible," I said.

"All seaweed is edible," said Kellan. This is good, very good. Vita- 30 mins are not easy here. So this is a real help. Also where there's one scallop there will be others and they're just over a calorie per gram."

"I don't know how many turns we can do at a time. It's just too cold." 35

"We'll get a rota going once we work out what's down there and where it is. You should only do one set of dives each per day. You can be in charge. Good, well done, Kavanagh." He reached out and, a paternal gesture that seems strange to describe but at the time felt right, ruffled my hair. 40

Hughes did only three dives and at the end of them he was shivering – cold, but not as cold as I had been. We set three dives as a daily maximum. Over the next week or so Hughes and I mapped the sea bed around the community and, where it was safe, underneath the rafts. Once we grew more confident 45

frond-like *wedelartig*
mossy *moosing*
dense *dicht*

feet (foot) a unit of measurement; 1 foot is about 31 cm

scallop *Muschel*

elation state of extreme happiness or excitement

full-blown full developed
hypothermia [ˌhaɪpəˈθɜːmiə]
Unterkühlung

paternal typical of a kind father
to ruffle *strubbeln*

to map sth. to make a plan of sth.

we started exploring the areas where we couldn't see the bottom from the raft. It was anxious work the first couple of times, diving where you couldn't see. My particular fear was that while I was under water I would drift sideways and get below the floating structures and be trapped. I realised though that while you couldn't see clearly to the surface, there was always light, so you always knew which way was up. It was not hard to detect where the rafts were. It was dangerous but not complicated. We found a great deal of seaweed, enough to make it clear that there was what amounted to an infinite supply. That was good news, not least because the seaweed tasted pretty good, once you gave it a quick rinse in rainwater to get the salt off: it was fresh and sharp and green and I found I could visualise it doing me good on the inside, charging up my supply of nutrients and vitamins.

to amount to add up in number or quantity
infinite without limits
supply *Vorrat*

to charge sth. up *here*: to increase
nutrient *Nährstoff*
vitamin ['vɪtəmɪn]

In addition to all the seaweed we found three areas with a good quantity of scallops. These were frustrating, because the shells were beautiful and big, broader than an outstretched palm, but then when you opened them the shellfish was nothing but a dab of red coral and coin-sized blob of meat. The rule sometimes seemed that the bigger and more promising the shell, the smaller the yield of edible scallop. The fact that they were delicious, tangy and sweet and subtle, was a cruel trick; such hard work to get them, but so small, but so good … They were excellent for morale, though, especially with the new supply of seaweed to vary the diet of seabirds and mackerel.

dab small amount
blob fat round drop

yield *Ertrag*

morale the amount of confidence felt by a person or group of people, especially when in a dangerous or difficult situation
mackerel *Makrele*

Kellan had been waiting for a while to investigate the sea bed, but hadn't done so because there was nobody able to do it. We could tell that there had once been more people in the floating community. The subject was never discussed. If enough time went passed, I was planning to ask what had happened to the rest of them; to ask in detail, I mean, because I could guess the rough outline. They had sailed away looking for some solid ground and had not come back. Perhaps some of them had succeeded in getting to land in the south. It wasn't impossible. It was also possible some of them had died trying to get over the Wall. I didn't want to think about that too much.

James did some diving too, but he was a poor swimmer and wasn't fit, so he didn't bring up much of anything. Hifa was better but she got cold quickly and she was doing such good work with the fishing that it was a more effective use of her time. As for the Captain, he wasn't well enough yet to swim let alone to dive, so he spent most of the day working on the nets, repairing them. He sat on a plastic crate on the side of the raft and picked over the lines and nets. When he saw a weak spot he set to the task of

let alone *geschweige denn*

crate *Kasten*

to sew [səʊ] *nähen*
incongruous strange

to leap (leapt, leapt) to make a large jump

to utter (*fml.*) to say sth.

to mend to repair

subtext hidden or less obvious meaning
deception *Täuschung*
remorse feeling of sadness and being sorry
deceit *Betrug*

to have the measure of sb. to have a way of judging sb.

stitching and sewing it back together: an incongruous sight but somehow an ancient one too, the fisherman fixing his tools. The children were frightened of him at the start but after a few days began going over to sit beside him and watch him work. They were fascinated by his facial scars. I once saw him sitting on his 5 plastic crate while two of them standing in front of him, reached out and touched them, very carefully, as if he might suddenly change his mind and leap up at them. It occurred to me that he was the only one of us who had left children behind. I had no feelings about that: his choices were what they were. The teenage 10 girls sometimes went over too and sat with him; he had a language in common with one of them. I could occasionally hear the two of them laugh together. He gave them small jobs testing the repaired lines or feeling over the nets to look for weak spots for him to inspect. 15

In general I avoided the Captain. Since we had been put to sea, since the time he had said why he had done what he did, I don't think I had heard him utter twenty sentences. He was as quiet in the community as he had been on the lifeboat, and it was hard to know what he thought. I found it difficult to believe that he 20 would prefer being on the open sea to being here, though. One day we went diving near the section of raft where he was mending his nets, and when I came up I was only a few feet away from him. I dried myself and wrapped myself in the space blanket and shivered myself back to warmth. Hughes went to get 25 some dried fish from Mara's big raft. I stood hopping and jiggling. He was passing a net through his hands, looking for holes and damage. He did not look at me. But I had something I wanted to know.

"Do you ever think about it? What they would do if they knew 30 who we are?" I said to him. I think the subtext of that was: do you, an expert in deception for many years, feel any remorse about this new deceit?"

"They do know. I told them," he said.

I should have been used to being surprised by what the Captain 35 did, but that proved I still didn't have the measure of him. I stopped still.

"You could have got us all killed. More likely than not."

He shrugged. "No more lies."

"Your lies." 40

"Everybody's lies."

I thought about it for a moment.

"What did they say?"

"They told me that they have a saying here: nothing before the sea was real." 45

This conversation with the Captain was one I replayed over and over afterwards. I thought about it for all the time we were on the rafts; I especially brooded on what the Captain had said, no more lies. I couldn't stop thinking about it. I eventually realised that
5 was the closest he would ever get to an apology. He wouldn't say he was sorry for his lies. He didn't feel it. But he would say, no more lies. His life of lies on the Wall had used him up. Nothing before the sea was real. Nothing before this, here and now, was real. I could understand why they might say that, if they had
10 reconciled themselves to life out here. To me, it felt the other way around: life before this was real, but the sea was a dream or delirium. An afterlife.

I noticed that the Captain stayed well clear of Kellan and made no attempt to be in charge or to lead. The only adult he regularly
15 spoke to was Hifa, because she was doing most of the work of setting up and checking the nets and lines.

"What do you talk about?" I asked her one night. By tacit agreement, the rest of the community let us use the back of the lifeboat as our place to sleep when it wasn't raining. When it rained they
20 needed the cover. So although there was no privacy by day, we were able to be intimate in the evening. That meant that the days had a shape, company and work by light and just the two of us by night.

"Nets. Ropes. Fishing. He knows about it, he used to fish back
25 where he came from."

I thought about that.

"Does he ever talk about it?"

I felt Hifa shake her head in the dark.

"He never talks about his past, or the Wall, or anything. Just nets
30 and rope and fish."

We lay there listening to the creaking and slapping of the rafts and the water, the faint high note of the wind, which in the lee of the island, we could hear but not feel. You had to take the good moments where you found them, and since memories were pain-
35 ful, and hopes were elusive and tormenting – what if we could sail to here, what of there were no Wall there, what if what if what if – you tried to make the most of the good moments you could find in the present tense. We had some, there in the back of the lifeboat, floating, amniotic, in the fuggy air under the awning.
40 When I fell asleep, I always had the same dream, of fire: of looking at a fire in a grate, or a cooking fire, or a bonfire; watching the flames flicker and change shape and feeling their warmth and their glow and thinking, that was funny, it was such a long time since I saw fire that I'd forgotten what it was like, I really missed
45 fire, I'm so glad it's back in my life, I must never take it for granted

---

apology saying that you are sorry

to reconcile in Einklang bringen

delirium the state of being unable to think because of mental confusion
afterlife life after death
to stay clear of sb. to avoid interacting with sb.

tacit unspoken

elusive trügerisch
tormenting quälend

amniotic relating to the amnion (= Fruchthöhle)
fuggy stickig
grate Kaminrost
bonfire a large fire that is made outside to burn unwanted things, or for pleasure

again, there's really nothing in the world as lovely as a fire, as giving and generous, as sure to make you feel safe, I'm so glad about the fire. When I woke from that dream there were always a few moments when I felt as if the fire were still real, as if I could still feel its glow, still see the flicker, still feel warm and secure, 5 and those moments were the best times I had on the sea.

21

The prevailing wind towards and around the island was very consistent, and came from the south-west with variations in intensity
but not much change in terms of direction. It was this which gave
us safety in the lee shore and made it possible for the floating
community to exist. That's not to say the wind was always completely identical. From the south-west, broadly speaking, yes, but
there were many small shifts of a few degrees here, a few degrees
there, like someone changing position in their sleep, and they all
had a different effect on the rafts, changing the sway and shift of
the planking. Some of the rhythms were gentle and regular and
easy to get used to, but some of them were jarring and dissonant,
making the rafts buck and move out of sync with each other. The
member of the community all seemed to have got used to this a
long time ago, but I found there were times when I could hardly
stand let alone move, let alone do anything difficult or fiddlesome. I hadn't ever felt sick on the boat, but there were moments
on the rafts when I was queasy; it was the chaotic nature of the
motion that did it. Hifa noticed but she could tell that I was trying
to keep it to myself and she was sympathetic. She had been seasick on the lifeboat but was fine on the rafts.

I stopped counting the days but I think it was a few weeks after
we joined the community that the weather took its first proper
turn for the worse. There had been bursts of rain, just enough to
give a feel for what the winter might be like, but nothing really
bad. The night before the storm was completely still and clear.
According to Kellan that was a warning sign of bad weather
ahead. In the morning we saw thick banked black clouds at the
horizon, moving not in the usual direction, straight towards us
from the south-west, where we would be protected by the island,
but at an angle, directly from the south. That was bad news, because it meant the weather would be coming at us more laterally
than it ever had before. We started to prepare by pulling in lines
and ropes and nets, fastening down the tops of the water contain-
ers so they wouldn't spill or be contaminated by salt spray. People
worked quickly and knew what they were doing; this wasn't their
first time. The girls went round the rafts picking up any loose
objects and putting them away. I went to the far end of the rafts
where Kellan was looking at the sky. Above us the clouds were
slate grey, then a little further they were dark grey, then black. He
saw my expression and put his hand on my arm.

"It'll be fine," he said. I wanted to believe him but the fact that he'd
felt the need to say it meant that I didn't. My worry, the obvious
worry, was that the weather's change in the direction, combined

prevailing dominant
consistent always being in a
similar, esp. positive, way

jarring shaking or moving
violently

fiddlesome needing delicate use
of the fingers

sympathetic *mitleidend*

laterally towards the side

to contaminate to make sth.
less pure

anchorage a place where a boat is firmly fastened

sheet a large quantity

slanted *geneigt*
to drench to make sb./sth. extremely wet
to soar to rise quickly to a high level

intent giving all one's attention to sth.
to squint *blinzeln*

to hold sb./sth. at bay (*idm.*) *jdn./ etw. in Schach halten*

thrash *Schlag*

squall a sudden strong wind and rain
to brace for sth. to prepare for sth.; *sich wappnen gegen*
lull a short period of calm
gust a sudden strong wind
to deflect sth. to prevent sth. from being directed at you
to throw up (*infml.*) to vomit; *sich übergeben*

with the strength of the wind and waves, would be so strong that the rafts were torn from their anchorage and broken apart. Realistically, that was likely to happen one day, so why not today? I stood and watched for a while. The storm came closer and the swell began to move differently. The rafts started to float and 5 dance. The teenagers looked like I felt, apprehensive, but the younger children thought it was fun and funny; they giggled and ran about and flicked bits of water at each other, and ignored the adults who tried to grab them and get them to calm down. They only stopped messing around when the bad weather hit, which it 10 did suddenly and frighteningly. The storm began with a sheet of wind and rain racing sideways at us, visible from at least a kilometre away. The slanted stinging rain drenched us at a forty-five-degree angle, and the ocean hit the rafts with a giant rolling punch from below. The rafts soared and buckled and were pulled 15 apart from each other, but held. I was still standing next to Kellan. He was calm but intent, looking in the direction from where the weather was coming, squinting a little against the rain and wind. That first impact made me think we could not survive the storm – that the community would be ripped apart. I walked as fast as I 20 could over the kicking, plunging rafts back to our lifeboat. I climbed aboard and got in under the awning in the back of the boat, where Hifa and Hughes were already sitting. I wondered for the moment where James and the Captain were riding out the storm. I did not think it would sink us, sink the lifeboat, but I did 25 think it would mean we couldn't stay together as a collective; the rafts and boats would be scattered over the seas and we would have to look for each other or for a different place of temporary safety. The sensation of despair, which I had been holding at bay ever since we had been put to sea – I suppose because we had 30 been so busy with the work of survival – came back in full force. I was sure the rafts would be forced apart.

I was wrong. The storm never built from that first great thrash. The wind and rain came again and again, but did not grow in intensity and was never more than a series of frightening but brief 35 squalls. We braced ourselves for the weather to build to a crisis, but it didn't happen. The squalls came at irregular intervals, sometimes no more than two minutes apart, sometimes with lulls of fifteen or twenty minutes, followed by a longer and more violent but still manageable gust. I think the island deflected just enough 40 of the storm's force, changed its nature just enough, to save us. I felt sick but didn't actually throw up and was helped (I'm not proud of this) by the fact that Hifa began to look a little green too. Three small squalls came together, each a little longer than the last, the waves rocking us so little now that no new water was 45

being splashed in. There was a pause of more than twenty minutes and then the shortest, smallest burst of wind and rain so far. The storm was passing. We had survived. The rafts would not be torn apart. The community would keep going. I could have cried
5 with relief. Hifa was still looking green but I reached out and squeezed her arm and got up and left the awning and then left the lifeboat to go and look around.

Kellan was still standing on the side of the rafts closest to the island, closest to the storm. He couldn't have been there the whole
10 time, I thought, that would be superhuman; he must have kept coming in and out as the squalls moved on. Elsewhere on the rafts people were coming out of shelters, stretching, beginning to tidy up and straighten up. In the distance the skies moved from a much lighter grey than before to, at the horizon, a paint-roller
15 swipe of bright blue. He turned to me and smiled.

"Told you," he said.

"I was worried," I said.

"Sure," he said. "But look." He held out his hand and pointed at the horizon as if he owned it, still smiling, then slowly swung his
20 extended arm from one side of the horizon to the other, and then kept turning and pointing, a single broad swipe, doing a full 360-degree tour of the sea and sky, as if he were revealing his handiwork, the world he had made. When he got to the seaward side of the boat, in the direction where the storm had gone, his
25 face changed, and because I was looking at him and laughing, it was as if what happened began there, with his expression changing, looking, for the first time since I had known him, not just frightened but more than frightened, aghast, blanching, horrified. I turned to look too and I saw, coming in our direction into the
30 weather and the wind, battering against the waves, a big ship, heading straight at us. A gust of wind and rain, the final one of that storm, came and went, and I stood there and got soaked while it passed, wishing that when the sky cleared, the impossible boat would have gone and we would laugh about the shared hallucina-
35 tion. My heart was beating so fast that my chest hurt. It was a ghost boat, something from a dream or nightmare, a phantasm of the rain and mist. We were seeing things. But the squall moved past us and when it did the ship was still there, still coming, still pointed towards us like a knife. It had lights on the mast and rig-
40 ging; the same five lights in a triangular pattern that I had seen weeks before, at night in the open sea. This was the same ship.

swipe Pinselstrich

handiwork work done skilfully with the hands

aghast suddenly filled with strong feelings like shock and worry
blanching turning pale with shock
to batter against to hit violently

to soak to make sb./sth. very wet

phantasm sth. that is seen but not real

rigging Takelage

22

My first thought was: maybe it'll be OK. Maybe they'll just want to join us ... but that didn't make sense. There could be any number of people on a ship that size, and at the fewest there wouldn't be fewer than say fifteen or twenty, and fifteen adults was too many. Maybe they were coming in peace? But there was, even at 5 first sight, a feeling that they weren't coming in peace. If that ship had been a person they would have been staring at us as they approached, bristling with aggression, looking for any excuse to start a fight.

Kellan did not move and did not speak. He just kept looking at the 10 ship. The rest of the community was now seeing what we were seeing. Everybody stopped what they were doing to stare. Even the children stopped what they were doing. There wasn't a face that didn't seem racked with apprehension. I had sometimes imagined that other arrivals might come to the rafts, but had pic- 15 tured them arriving the same way we came in the lifeboat, desperate and barely surviving and grateful for any respite from the sea. We had been even more grateful when we found we could be useful and had skills and manpower to contribute. I could imagine a repeat of that. I hadn't imagined this, though. What this ship 20 looked like, more than anything else, was a warship.

The Captain came out from one of the shacks in the middle of the raft and took in what was happening. He went to the end of the community closest to the approaching ship. It was now about two kilometres away. Visibility had been poor during the storm. This 25 ship could only have come across us by chance, just as it had only been by chance that our lifeboat had come to that place. Unless they had naval charts and were looking for the island; in which case they might be professionals, might be even Guards. Perhaps they were looking for us? Our case had been debated, somebody 30 in authority had decided we had been treated unfairly, and the Guards had been sent to look for us and bring us home? This wild thought came to me from nowhere and I suddenly felt sick with hope. Guards sent to save us, Guards sent to save us. I told myself, my mouth dry with fear and longing, I wanted to tell Hifa but 35 knew that I couldn't because I was probably wrong and if I was I would have done a bad thing, given her the hope and then given her the despair. So I stood and stared, speechless, with the rest of them, my feelings strobing between fear and hope. We had no way of defending ourselves, there was nothing we could do. 40

The Captain was the only one of us who seemed to have a plan or any sense of what to do. He moved down the rafts. He was even more heavy-footed and off-balance than I was on the moving

to bristle with sth. (*phr. v.*) to be full of sth.

to rack to cause physical or mental pain

poor bad

to strobe to flash (a light) quickly on and off

surface. He got to the very far end and stood with his hands on his hips. Hifa had come over to me and Kellan and she asked a question with her expression. I had no answer. We waited. The ship came closer, plunging up and down, the spray over its bows grey-
5 green-white as it smacked into the waves. James and Hughes came over to us too and we all stood together. The squall which had hit us a minute or so before now hit the boat and again I had the childish wish that when it cleared, the ship would have vanished. A magic trick, here one second and gone the next. But
10 when the rain and wind passed, there it still was.

"Let's go over to that end," said Hifa. So that's what we did, picking our way over the rocking rafts, in between members of the community, towards the Captain. I can't explain the instinct to go and stand with him, other than that it had been ingrained on the Wall,
15 the idea that we were Defenders and that's what Defenders do, you stand there and wait to see what comes. The community looked at us as we walked past. They were standing still and staring; nobody else had moved since they saw the ship. We got to the Captain when it was only a couple of hundred metres away. At closer range,
20 it looked smaller: not a huge ocean-going ship but a practical working boat about the size of a fishing trawler. There were men on deck; fifteen or so. There was no flag or insignia or writing or identification of any kind. I felt something inside me curdle. My heart, already racing, sped up and was now beating as fast as I had
25 ever known it. These were not Guards. These were not our people. The ship closed as it got closer to us and came to a halt, with engines running to hold it in place, no more than fifty metres away. At that range the deck loomed far above us and I could only see four men standing at the bow. Three of them had rifles slung over
30 their shoulders. Even with the noise of the wind and waves and the engines, they were well within calling distance, but they didn't say anything. The Captain, at the very end of the rafts, spread his arms to their full width. You could see that the gesture meant: we have no weapons. We are at your bidding. He held the
35 pose for all of ten seconds.

One thing you learn in combat is that when people are shot in the head, they are there one moment, and then they cease to exist. They drop in a way that no living thing drops; they fall to earth like inanimate objects, because that is what they now are. The
40 transition from life to death is instantaneous. That is what happened to the Captain. He seemed to fall before the noise of the shot. He had hit the deck of the raft before I understood what had happened. They had killed him just to make a point. Just like that – gone. I heard Hifa make a noise between a gasp and a cry
45 and heard someone else swearing and realised that it was me.

to ingrain to establish something such as a belief so firmly that it is not likely to change

insignia an object or mark which shows that a person belongs to a particular organization or has a particular rank
to curdle *stocken, gerinnen*

to loom above *drohend näher rücken*

at sb.'s bidding (*idm., old use*) under sb.'s orders

to cease to stop

inanimate *leblos, unbeseelt*
instantaneous immediate

gasp *Keuchen*
to swear *fluchen*

The ship, what we now understood was a pirate ship, manoeuvred until it was sideways on to the rafts. There were the four men at the bow of the ship and about ten or a dozen armed men standing at the side, pointing weapons at us. They lowered their anchor and a ladder and an inflatable boat and eight of them got ⁵ in it and crossed over to us. Hifa and I bent down to the Captain's body, lying on the floor of the raft in one of the positions that only the dead adopt, his arms bent under him, his legs folded backwards under his hips, his head, what was left of it, bent down over his chest. 10

I say 'his' – was he a he any more? Probably not. But it is difficult to think of a dead body, a body so recently dead, as an 'it'. For a few seconds I thought of all the things the Captain had been to me, the different selves he had incarnated, from my first minutes on the Wall through the weeks of duty to fighting together to his 15 betrayal to the time at sea; and through all of that the side of his life I never seen and did not know, the place he had come from, his family, his people, his overt treachery and secret loyalty and the terrible consistency of his courage and his betrayal. The bravest man I would ever know, and the most loyal, and the biggest 20 traitor. He had at one point been the person I admired most; he had saved my life; he had done me more harm than anyone else; if he hadn't directly murdered me, he had come very close. For a moment I felt the force of all those things he had been, ebbing out on the floor of a raft on the open sea. And then the pirates ar- 25 rived. We were still crouched over him when the first of them got onto the raft and came over to us. He pointed his gun, a semi-automatic rifle, at us and wiggled it from side to side. The gesture clearly meant: step away. Hifa and I got up and moved back a couple of paces. The pirate raised his head and two of the other 30 pirates came over. All three of them slung their guns over their shoulders and they stooped and picked up the Captain's body and pushed it over the side of the raft. It floated for five seconds and then slowly sank.

The first pirate pointed his rifle at us again and jabbed it back- 35 wards. We turned and saw that all the other members of the community had gathered in the middle section of the rafts, at the demand of the five others pirates who were walking around the rafts, looking into shelters, opening boxes and water catchments. It was clear that they were taking a rough inventory of every- 40 thing we had. The thing they looked at longest was our water. They took a long hard look at the stores of firewood and the community's fuel tank, opening it, tapping it on the side and listening to the echo. That made sense. Water and fuel, the two most valuable commodities out on the sea. The pirates who were taking the 45

---

to incarnate to embody; *verkörpern*

overt done or shown publicly
treachery deceit; *Verrat, Heimtücke*
consistency *Stetigkeit*

to ebb *verebben*

to crouch *(hin-)hocken*

to stoop to bend the top half of your body down

demand order, command

to take an inventory to list/find out what goods are in a place

to tap sth. to hit sth. gently,

commodity a substance or good

inventory called the first pirate over in a language I did not recognise. He went across to them and they talked and pointed. I could see that our supply of water was big news to them. Three of them tried our drying fish and gulls and passed them back and for-
5 wards between them, with commentary.

After they had taken this quick look around four more pirates joined them and they began a more thorough search. Two of them stood guard over us in the middle of the rafts. They held their rifles pointed directly at us. I read their body language to mean that
10 they thought they would find things; and that when that happened, people would often do something stupid. The other pirates went into every shelter, opened every box, searched every crevice and cranny. It took a long time and while they were doing it we had nothing to do but sit on the floor of the rafts. James
15 started to whisper to me, but the nearest pirate hit him on the shoulder with the butt of his rifle, and the meaning was very clear, so after that we sat in silence. Physical discomfort did nothing to alleviate the fear. I found myself trying to work out not what the pirates would do, because that was obvious: they were
20 going to take everything they wanted. The question I was thinking about instead was, what would they leave? What would we have to help us survive?

The more I thought about it, the more obvious the answer became. The pirates would leave us with nothing. Why would they
25 do anything else? They were people who killed on sight, just to make a point. The benefit to them of leaving us with enough water and food to sustain ourselves was exactly zero. As I was thinking that, two of them came past, carrying the two remaining boxes of supplies of our lifeboat. There was a dummy compart-
30 ment in the boat with other boxes hidden behind it, which we had tacitly agreed not to tell the community about, not yet anyway. It was our insurance policy and also our guilty little secret. I had been starting to feel ashamed about that, but now it seemed an astute thing to have done. It could be the only food we had left.
35 Enough for what remained of the community for two or three days. Longer, on starvation rations. A week, say. So, not enough. Not by any standards.

I watched the pirates work, systematically stripping the rafts of everything they could carry. There would be rustling and a stifled
40 cry, not from the pirates but from the community, when they came across something precious among people's personal possessions – a jewelled flask, an empty silver picture frame, a ceremonial dagger. When people murmured or cried out, the guards raised their rifles and the community went quiet again. Once the pirates had
45 taken the valuables, they took the food. All of it. They stacked the

thorough detailed and careful

crevice Spalte, Ritze
cranny Versteck, Winkel

butt Kolben

discomfort a feeling of being uncomfortable
to alleviate to make sth. less severe

to sustain to allow sth. to continue for a period of time

dummy hidden

tacitly stillschweigend

astute wise, clever

to strip sth. of sth. (phr. v.) to take sth. away; etw. ausplündern
rustling Rascheln
to stifle [ˈstaɪfəl] unterdrücken, zurückhalten

flask bottle; Fläschchen
dagger Dolch

to stack to arrange things in an orderly pile; stapeln

to winch sth. up *etw. hochwinden*

drying fish and birds onto two racks and four of them carried them over to their boat and then winched them up the side. There was a moment when I thought it was all going to tip over and be lost and I felt panic at the thought and then realised that was stupid because as far as we were concerned it was all lost anyway. 5 After they had taken the food they took the water. There was enough of it that they called for help, and some of their crewmates who had been standing watching from the bow of their ship came over and joined them in the hard work of stealing our water. That went on for a long time: the catchments were heavy. The pirates 10 cursed and sweated as they carried them across the raft and winched them on their ship. Dark was beginning to fall by the time they had finished.

When they had taken everything, the pirates came back, this time towards the community where we sat in the middle of the rafts, 15

to barge in *(phr. v.)* to force a way into a space

ten pirates this time, their guns raised, and they barged their way in among us and grabbed the three teenage girls, It happened fast and because it was hard to believe or understand it was also hard to react in time. Hughes, who was standing next to the tallest and oldest of them, stepped in front of them as they dragged her away 20 and was smashed to the ground by a pirate behind him. He hit

stock *Gewehrkolben*

Hughes on the back of his head with the stock of his gun. I think Hughes was unconscious before he hit the floor of the rafts. As the pirates pulled the girls away from the group Kellan and Mara ran after them and took hold of the girls, both of them shouting, 25 "No, no," and the pirate nearest them stepped backwards and swung the rifle to the left, hitting Kellan in the head, and then to the right, hitting Mara too. Both of them fell to their knees. It took a second at most. The pirate then raised his gun and pointed at the rest of us, as if asking, who's next? No one was next.   30 They dragged the girls to the far end of the rafts, where their inflatable boat was waiting to take them the fifty or so metres to their ship. All three of the girls were screaming and fighting. The pirates who had been on the rafts started to get on the inflatable, pulling the girls with them; once again, it was so full it looked as 35 if it might tip over. There was a lot of noise from the pirate ship, raised voices, voices in a new tone. I think they were celebrating; some of the voices from the ship sounded drunk, or on the way to drunk.

"No no no no no," said Hifa. I looked at her and realised some- 40 thing: they would have taken her if they had realised she was a woman. But just like the first time I'd seen her, she was wrapped in multiple thick layers of clothing and had her cap pulled down and you could hardly see her face. They hadn't seen her for who

nausea the feeling that you are going to vomit

she was. Nausea, and I'm ashamed to say relief, hit me. I can't 45 remember what I said, but James stepped forwards, his hand inside his clothing, and for the first time during the attack, I remembered his grenade.

"I have to stop them," he said.

5 I could think of nothing that would stop the pirates except setting off the grenade, which would kill them and anyone near them, including the girls. Then I saw that was what he meant. I could tell Hifa had the same train of thought. We stood looking at each other. Kellan and Mara were hopping and skipping over the rafts
10 towards the pirates, moving, as always, as if they had been born on the water. I remember that clearly: how elegant, even dainty, they were as they danced quickly over the rafts that last time. I remember how at ease they were here in their home on the water. They were calling out "stop" and "wait" and "please". Their voices
15 were frantic, beseeching. The first pirate onto our boat, who had dragged one of the girls away himself, was standing next to the inflatable, still holding her by the arm. He now turned and looked at us. For a second I thought, wait, he's changing his mind. He handed the girl to another pirate, passed her over like a parcel,
20 and then he took his gun down off his shoulder and pointed it at Kellan and Mara, who were running towards him and the inflatable and the ship.

Kelan and Mara did not stop shouting and did not stop running and got to the last section of raft, the one closest to the pirates.
25 Just as they set foot on it, the pirate shot them, Kellan first, then Mara, in the chest. It wasn't like the Captain; they didn't die instantly. Instead they fell and were lying twitching and thrashing and bleeding and coughing blood on the floor of the raft. Several of the pirates laughed and one of them did a little mime of how
30 they had flailed and fallen. The shooter laughed at that, then he braced the rifle against his shoulder and took careful aim and shot them in the head, first Mara, then Kellan. He turned with the gun still at his shoulder and looked over to the rest of us, sitting in the middle of the rafts. Again the look spoke: it was saying, any
35 more? Nobody moved. The pirates got into the inflatable and crossed to their ship and half carried, half forced the girls up the ladder. There was more cheering and whooping.

"I have to," said James. I think, looking back, he was wanting us to say something or do something that would either change his
40 mind or give him a different idea. I didn't know what to say. I was thinking: Hughes might know what to say or do. The Captain might know. Kellan or Mara might know. But Hughes was unconscious and the others were dead and I didn't know what to do. James reached inside his clothes and wriggled around under them
45 and took out the grenade. I realised that the explosion would be

to skip over sth. to move with quick steps and little jumps

dainty small, delicate, and moving in a careful way

at ease relaxed

frantic extremely upset, esp. because of anxiety and fear
to beseech (*lit.*) *anflehen*

to flail to wave violently and aimlessly about; *mit den Armen rudern*

to whoop to give a loud, excited shout, especially to show your enjoyment of or agreement with sth.

to wriggle *herumsuchen*

unpredictable *unvorhersehbar*

unpredictable and dangerous for the rafts so I began moving people down towards the back of the community and told them to get
into shelter where they could find it, and keep their heads down.
I went over to Hughes. He was out cold but breathing regularly;

to be out cold *(infml.)* to be
unconscious
to clot *gerinnen*

the cut on his head was bleeding but it would clot and he was 5
probably going to be OK. He was too heavy to drag away and in
any case there was some cover from a nearby shelter so I put him

recovery position *stabile
Seitenlage*

in the recovery position and left him there. I would have covered
him with a space blanket if the pirates hadn't taken them all.
James walked slowly across to the pirate ship. There was a gap 10
between our rafts and their vessel. They had taken the inflatable
back but their ladder was still down. There was nobody standing
guard or looking over at us. The pirates had clearly decided we
were no threat to them. He lowered his legs over the side of the
raft, then got into the water, holding the grenade in his left arm, 15

to side-stroke *auf einer Seite
schwimmen*

above the water. He side-stroked over to the ship, got his right
arm on the ladder and stayed there for a few moments. He was
gathering his strength or making sure he was certain, or both.
Then he started to climb.
Everyone in the community who could move had gone to shelter. 20
Five people apart from the two of us. Before the pirates came we

strong *having the stated number
of people*

had been fifteen strong. Most of them didn't know exactly what
was happening but they had done what Hifa and I told them
to do.
"We need to get to cover," I said to her. She nodded and we both 25
crossed to our lifeboat. A gust of wind came and the rafts rocked
and we stumbled into each other. That was how we got into the
lifeboat, holding onto each other. We sat on the floor of the boat,
the back of our heads against the side. For the first time since the
pirates had come I was conscious of the movement of the sea, still 30
unquiet after the storm.
"How long?" she said.

fuse *Zünder*

"Not long. He'll run towards them. The fuse time is five seconds,

to prime sth. *to make a bomb
ready to explode*

yes? He'll probably climb up then prime it, pull the pin, then run
at them. They'll kill him as soon as they can but they probably 35
aren't carrying their guns any more, so ..."
"The girls might be at the other end of the ship. We'll have a
chance to rescue them. We wait for the big bang then we go and
see."
"Yes," I said, knowing that was unlikely, and that even if we could 40
make it work, the surviving pirates would kill us. But with James
having done what he was about to do, we would have to do our
part as well. Our odds were so bad without food and water that
almost nothing we could do would make them worse. I started
counting to ten, then realised there was no point, that it would 45

happen when it happened. The silence – I mean apart from the noise of the wind and water and the creaking rafts – went on for longer than I had thought possible. Maybe James had given up and was coming back towards us. I felt a cowardly twinge of relief
5 at the idea. That was when there was an explosion, a reverberating concussive pulse through the air. I felt my breath catch and could see the same look on Hifa's face. A few seconds later there was another, much bigger explosion. This was truly huge, a physical sensation more than a noise. It couldn't be the grenade, it was
10 a far bigger bang. I felt the whole structure of the community give a violent jolt, an energy that went through all the rafts and hit our lifeboat in the side. I started to put my head up but Hifa grabbed me and I knew she was in the right: if we'd had our heads above deck when the second bang happened we could easily have been
15 killed. There could be more to come. I kept my head down and waited. I could hear things, but I wasn't sure what: noises which were neither human nor aquatic, not the wind, not the sea. Tearing noises and hissing noises. I waited and waited and eventually said, "Yes?" Hifa nodded. We both put our heads over the side of
20 the lifeboat.

The rafts had broken up and were on fire. Acrid smoke was pouring up from the tar-soaked ropes that had bound the community together. The pirate ship was on fire too, what was left of it, but the top half of the ship had disappeared. The grenade must have
25 ignited a big supply of either fuel or ammunition or both. The first explosion was the grenade, the second was whatever the first one had set off. There could be no survivors on the ship and not many on the rafts either and the fire was coming towards the lifeboat. The section of raft nearest us had detached from the rest
30 of the community. We were already five or ten metres away from the other rafts, which had broken into three big pieces. 'Our' raft, the one we were tied to, was on fire. The fire was getting closer. I could see no survivors on the other boats, but it was getting dark and in the fire and smoke I might not have been able to see them
35 even if they had been there.

I thought: Hughes. He would still be unconscious, still lying in the recovery position. If the fire hadn't got him yet. But there was nothing I could do – no way to help my shift twin. The rafts were already torn apart. If I tried to swim to them I would never make
40 it back. There was no choice.

"We have to cut loose," I said to Hifa, "or we'll burn." She looked around and I could see her running the same calculations that I had. Then she nodded and began untying the set of ropes at the stern of the boat while I went to the bow and did the same. The
45 toxic smoke stank and stung. We worked as fast as we could but

cowardly *feige*
twinge a sudden short feeling of pain
reverberating repeated, echoing
concussive *erschütternd*
pulse *Schlag*

jolt sudden, violent movement

aquatic living or growing in the water
to tear (tore, torn) to pull or break apart
to hiss *zischen*

acrid *beißend, ätzend*
tar *Teer*

to ignite sth. to start burning or explode

to detach from to separate or remove sth. from sth. else

to run a calculation *eine Berechnung durchführen*
stern the back part of a ship or boat

the soaked, cold, thickly interwoven ropes were almost impossible to untie. It occurred to me that Kellan had tied them like that on purpose, to stop us making a secret getaway. As we struggled with the ropes we drifted further away from the flaming rafts, which we could now see only through the light of their own fire. 5 I realised that the other rafts were anchored, whereas we weren't. We would drift away and there was nothing I could do to stop it.

to undo a knot *einen Knoten lösen* I tried harder to undo the knots but my fingers were tired and numb and shaking with cold. I could see that Hifa was doing no better. The fire on our raft was coming closer and within minutes 10 was going to be at our boat.

to reek to smell strongly
to choke to block normal breathing
thread [θred] *Faden*

Finally, with the bitter, reeking smoke from the fire stinging our eyes and choking our lungs, I worked my rope down to its last threads and was able to tear them apart. I threw the far end of the rope away and went to Hifa and helped her do the same thing. By 15 now we were both frantic. We were starting to feel gusts of heat

to suffocate *ersticken*
to cough *husten*
to gasp *keuchen*

from the flames and the smoke was suffocating. We picked and tore the rope and, coughing and gasping, threw it over the side. I pushed at the side of the burning, sinking raft to get it away from us. Our lifeboat swung in the current as we moved away from it. 20 The fire and smoke had blocked our view and I now looked for the other rafts We might have turned around as we floated free, so they could now be behind us; I scanned the sea in all directions, then turned and did it again. I grew more desperate as I realised I couldn't see them. We had drifted too far away. Night had fallen 25 and we were alone on the sea.

23

That night we did nothing except hold each other and let the boat drift. Both of us had inhaled smoke and we both had racking coughs. We were too tired and distraught even to feel frightened. The Captain and Kellan and Mara all dead, James and the girls
5 blown to pieces, the rafts broken up and on fire, the burning hulk of what was left of the pirate ship – they cycled through my mind, one image after the other. I kept thinking about Hughes and how we had left him unconscious. I slept for a little, woke to replay the previous day, then slept again.
10 When I woke it was just starting to be light and Hifa was still sleeping. I had realised, during the hours of darkness, that there would be one moment to hope for, one moment of possible salva- tion, and it would come when the sun rose and we could look for the island. There was no way of knowing how far and fast we
15 were drifting. We might be hardly moving. We might be moving at a walking pace, say three miles an hour, so that by daylight we could be more than twenty miles away. I just couldn't tell. If we could see the island, we could row towards it and find what was left of the community. I didn't think that everyone could have
20 survived, but half of them might still be alive, and half of the rafts still workable, and with that we could try to start again. On this lifeboat we had some food and water, but the community, what was left of it, had none. Unless we weren't the only ones with a secret cache that the pirates hadn't found. But where we had once
25 built up reserves of food and water, with luck we could do it again. Maybe. We'd just have to get through the first few days with the supplies we had on the lifeboat and hope we were lucky with fresh rainwater.
A sign that day had fully broken was when a bar of light came
30 over the side of the lifeboat and illuminated the edge of the awn- ing. I lay where I was for a few minutes, putting off the moment when I would, one way or another, know.
Hifa turned over in semi-sleep. That meant she would be waking up soon. For reasons I can't explain, I wanted to face the facts of
35 our situation for a little while on my own: I wanted to know first. I carefully got up and crawled out from beneath the awning. The day was calm and clear. I took a long slow scan of the horizon, then another, then a third one to be sure. There was a patch of cloud on one point of the horizon that could, just possibly, have
40 been a bank of weather gathering over the island where we had sheltered. I stood and watched it for a few minutes, then looked away, and looked back, and there was no mistaking that the clouds were changing shape and dissipating. They had not

racking very bad and very painful

distraught extremely worried, nervous and upset

hulk the body of an old ship; *Rumpf*

pace the speed at which sb./sth. moves

cache a hidden store of things

to put sth. off (*phr. v.*) *etw. verschieben*

bank mass

to dissipate to gradually disappear

gathered over the island. There was nothing else to be seen, at any point of the compass. We had drifted away from the island and the community and were now on the open sea.

A few minutes later, Hifa joined me. By that point we had spent so much time together on the Wall and on the water that the first 5 seven-eighths of any conversation were had in silence. She did the same tour of the horizon I had done, then looked at me. I nodded to say, yes, you're right, I've looked too and there's nothing there.

"I'll set up the water catchments and the lines, you do the inven- 10 tory. Or the other way around," said Hifa. I could see in her face the same thoughts I'd been having, not of fear – there would be time for that later – but sadness and loss. The people who weren't with us any more were still there in her eyes. No doubt she could see the same thing in me. 15

"Inventory," I said.

So that's what I did. The secret compartment was under a false panel at the back of the boat. Even though I knew it was there, it still took me a moment to find, and I had a wild second of panic when I thought I'd been imagining the hidden cache – but no, it 20 **seamless** *nahtlos* was just a very clever design, a false plank fitting seamlessly with the real planks around it. Thank God, because otherwise the pirates would have found it, and we would have been as good as dead already. I opened the compartment and started sorting through what we had. The news was good. My rough calculation 25 was four weeks' food, more if we were very careful and didn't do too much manual work. There was only about a week's water, but my hunch was that with only two of us, given how much rain there was, we could probably make it to four weeks with water too. Lack of food kills you in three weeks, lack of water in three 30 days. We would be OK for a little while. No sooner had Hifa finished putting out the lines than she was pulling two of them in again, mackerel wriggling on the end. I tried to take that as a good omen. She killed them and put the lines out again. Then she wiped her hands on herself and came and sat next to me where I 35 was putting the food stores back in the hidden compartment.

"Plan?" she said.

I shook my head. I said: "We're drifting south-west, I think. Away from the Wall. But I'm guessing. I don't really know where we are." 40

"The Captain's plan was to head south. He said there were places where people would help us."

"He said he knew places – we don't. Big difference."

Hifa shrugged. I shrugged too. I can't remember who spoke first and who agreed, but what we settled on was, south. Towards the 45 places where the Others came from. It made sense: we were Others now.

For the next week we did a mixture of drifting and gentle rowing to correct our course. We had no compass so the navigation
5 wasn't rough and ready so much as rough and rougher. There were sharp ups and downs to our emotions, not just hour by hour but minute by minute. There were times when I could imagine finding settleable land, finding food, finding somewhere we could live peaceably for the rest of our lives, be happy, even live a kind
10 of idyll, and other times when I came close to thinking the best thing would be just to get over the side of the lifeboat and swim away from it until my strength gave out and the end came. Hifa at times was affectionate, at times irritable, at times silent, and there were even times when we joked and laughed as much as when we
15 were back in our private room in barracks on the Wall. We cuddled to keep warm and even had sex once or twice. Death and sex – close companions. We didn't talk much about what had happened, and when we did, we were quick to absolve ourselves. There wasn't much that we could have done that was any differ-
20 ent, or would have made any difference. There were a lot of ways we could have got ourselves killed too.

We caught a few fish. We collected some rainwater. I think those supplies extended our probable survival time by a week to ten days. I told Hifa I was trying not to think about it, but in truth I
25 was running calculations all the time: how long we had left, how far we could drift or row, what were our odds. I thought we would be unlucky to head roughly south for a month and not come across land at any point, but I also had no illusions about just unlucky it was possible to be. As Sarge would have pointed out, if
30 we weren't freakishly unlucky, we wouldn't be here in the first place.

On the afternoon of the eighth day, I saw something on the horizon. I went through that usual sea-sequence of thinking something is a cloud, then suspecting/hoping it might not be, then the
35 hope growing, then ecstatically letting yourself accept that hope is justified. The thing I could see was too square, too abrupt in its angles, to be a natural object. We were past caution, so we adjusted our direction and started rowing towards it, hard shifts of thirty minutes each. We were desperate to get there while it was
40 light, because we knew that once darkness had fallen, we might never find it again, whatever it was. We could drift away from it in the night as we had drifted away from the island. So it was now or never. My hands had grown unused to rowing when we were on the rafts, but the diving had helped me to get reasonably fit,
45 and having a destination in sight made it easier too. We rowed for

rough and ready simple but good enough

to give out (*phr. v.*) to stop working

affectionate showing feelings of love

irritable *reizbar*

to cuddle *kuscheln*

to absolve to free sb. from guilt or responsibility

to be past sth. *sich nicht mehr um etw. kümmern*

caution great care and attention

to adjust *anpassen*

apparent easy to see, clear

about three hours. As we came closer it became apparent that it was an oil or gas installation. From a distance there was no way of telling if it was inhabited or not. At closer and closer range, that was still true. There was nobody to be seen on deck and no sign of activity.　　　　　　　　　　　　　　　　　　　　　　　5

"What if we can't get up it?" Hifa asked, while I was rowing. She was standing at the front of the boat, not looking at me but at the platform. She had read my mind, because once I realised what the platform was, I had begun to worry that there would be no means of getting off the lifeboat and onto the structure; that we would 10 bump up against it as we almost had against the island, and find no way of climbing aboard. The disappointment of that could kill me. "It's some sort of installation, there must be ways on and off it," I said, sounding, to my own ears anyway, a lot more confident than I felt. The platform was close now, so I rowed and kept rowing, 15

adverse difficult

but the currents here were adverse, and it was harder work than I had thought possible to close the last few hundred metres. At this

rig a large structure that is used for removing oil or gas from the ground or the bottom of the sea

range you couldn't see how it worked. It was an oil or gas rig; I couldn't tell, and wouldn't have known how to tell, the difference. The main deck was high, seventy metres or so above the water. 20 There was a tower on the main deck. The whole structure was supported on four legs, which as we got closer could be seen to

pillar Säule
to attach to connect to sth.

each have one thick main pillar and another smaller one attached to it.

Since the attack on the Wall, I had learnt to accept the worst. That 25 was proving to be a useful habit. We came to the structure and manoeuvred alongside the nearest leg so that the currents would press us against it and it would take less work at the oars to hold us in place. There was no ladder there, but I didn't panic. There were four main legs, each with an inner leg, so there were eight 30 places where we might find a ladder. Eight chances. One down, seven to go. Hifa held the lifeboat in place with small movements of the oars, while I took a break to recover some strength. My arms were shaking and weak from the rowing. Once we moved from that spot, we would need enough muscular strength to row 35 back to the structure against the currents. I took fifteen minutes

to brace to prepare oneself physically or mentally for sth. unpleasant

to rest, then braced myself for the next thing. I guessed that we had half an hour of light left at the most and I had by now convinced myself that this was our last chance; if we didn't find a ladder now it would be too dark and we would be too weak, and 40 we wouldn't be able to hold ourselves in place all night. We pushed off and I rowed while Hifa looked. It didn't take long to check the inside legs. Then we took a turn around the outside, fighting hard not to drift too far from the platform and then fighting harder to row back to it.　　　　　　　　　　　　　　　45

No luck. There was no ladder, no handhold, no dangling ropes, nothing. No hope. Hifa didn't say anything and nor did I. I rowed back to our starting position, panting, my arms burning, the taste of blood in the back of my throat. At that point, it might have
5 made as much sense to let the current pull us away from the platform, to give up on the hope of it and let it go, but the sea was so big and we were so alone that it was impossible to leave a site where people had been, where human activity had made its mark, even if it offered nothing for us. The light was starting to fade
10 now, I thought we might have enough rope to loop around one of the inner legs of the platform and tie us in place until the morning. Then we could decide what to do next.

"Hang on a minute," said Hifa. She pointed across the platform to one of the inner legs on the far side. "I don't remember that being
15 there ten minutes ago."

I looked. I blinked, rubbed my eyes, and looked again. A ladder was clearly visible. For a moment I doubted what I was seeing, then realised that it must be a retractable ladder and that somebody had extended it for us. That meant two things, two very
20 important things, two things so important and so wonderful that I could hardly believe them: that we were not alone, and that somebody was making us welcome.

I was suddenly feeling a lot less tired. I pushed off and rowed across underneath the platform and we tied ourselves up to the
25 ladder and looked at each other to see who should go up first. Hifa nodded and took off her cap and shook out her hair and set off. There was a small stage halfway up and I let her get to it before following her. I'm not great with heights and that thirty-five metres of ladder felt like a hell of a lot of ladder. My arms were
30 jelly when I got to her.

"I don't know what to wish for," she said.

"I know. Best just to wait and see."

Hifa set off up the next stretch of ladder. This went all the way to the main deck. She passed through a circular hole at the top and I
35 started up after her. I should have been boiling with thoughts about what was up there and what would happen next, but all I could think about was how I hated being so high up with nothing but a ladder to cling to. I told myself not to look down, but told myself so insistently that it turned into a mantra, (don't) look
40 down look down look down. I got to the top and pulled myself through and lay on the metal main deck, trembling all over and gasping for breath. I don't think I could have pulled myself up a single further rung of the ladder. But I didn't have to. We had made it.

to dangle baumeln

to make your/a mark on sth. (idm.) to have an important effect on something
to loop to tie

retractable able to be drawn or pulled up/in
to extend here: to lower

stage here: Plattform

circular shaped like a circle

insistent beharrlich
mantra Mantra, Motto

rung Sprosse, Stufe

24

alcove *Nische*

We were in a small alcove or entrance hallway at the top of the ladder. Hifa was sitting ten feet away, cross-legged, waiting for me. One third of the platform was open to the elements. At the edge, you could look down and see the sea. From where I collapsed on the floor, all I could see was cloud and the gathering dark. The other two thirds of the platform were taken up by the tower, with this alcove as the only entrance. The sides of the walls facing us were lined with sheet metal. The only way through the alcove into the tower was via a metal door.

sheet metal *Metallblech*

When I got my breath back, I said, "No reception committee?" She shook her head. "Just me. But we can't go further. We're locked out." I walked over to the door and tried the handle. It didn't move. I tried to rattle the frame, but it stayed as still as concrete. The door wasn't just locked but bolted. It had the solidity of an industrial piece of architecture; not the kind of door you can kick in, and from the outside, there was no lock to pick. There was no way through unless someone allowed us through. But it wasn't all bad news. On the floor of the platform, next to the immovable door, were a plastic jug of water and a small paper bag. I opened the bag and did a double take at the contents: six power bars of the kind we had been given when we were on the Wall. I looked at Hifa, and she shrugged back at me.

to bolt sth. *etw. verriegeln*

to pick a lock to open a lock by using sth. that is not the key

jug *Krug*

"Somebody making us welcome," she said. "Or sort-of-welcome. We're being watched."

"You'd have thought so. Not sure who by, though."

"So, now what?"

"Let's just sit here for a bit."

So we did. It wasn't as if we had much choice, that evening, after the day we had had. We sat on the platform and waited to get our strength back. The sun was right on the horizon now and the sky had cleared for dusk. They grey metal platform was flooded by incongruously beautiful evening light. It was good to feel that this night at least we would be dry and safe. When I stopped shaking, Hifa and I ate the power bars, slowly and deliberately. The very first bite was of dried red fruits, the same as the first one I had had on my first morning on the Wall. It gave me an overwhelming flashback: I was suddenly back there between Hifa and Shoona, aching with longing for the twelve hours to go past. It felt as if that was ten minutes ago; it felt as if that was two lifetimes ago.

incongruous unusual, uncharacteristic

to ache to feel a continuous pain
to long for sb./sth. *sich sehnen nach*

When we had finished the power bars, it was dark. In the alcove next to the locked door, we were sheltered from the wind, and it wasn't cold. We lay back against the corner of the metal walls.

Line numbers in right margin: 5, 10, 15, 20, 25, 30, 35, 40

Hifa snuggled against me and we settled down for the night. "This is weird," she said.

"Yes," I said, and I was so tired I could hear myself slurring. "But good weird. Tomorrow we'll find out." I didn't say what we'd find
5 out, because I didn't know. But I felt sure we'd find something out. I fell asleep with Hifa's head on my shoulder.

The next time I opened my eyes, we were lying the other way around, with my head on her shoulder, and it was bright day. The night had passed in a state more like unconsciousness than sleep.
10 We must have been out cold for at least eight hours. Hifa was still out; I was so stiff I felt as if my bones would crack before my muscles would bend. My neck was cricked, my arms were both heavy and stinging, my right leg was cramping and my left leg had gone dead. Despite all that, I felt good. We were up here
15 rather than down there. My intuition told me that we were safe; at a minimum, safer than we had been, and maybe much better than that. As slowly as I could, trying not to wake Hifa, I leant over and stated to stretch and as I did do, turning my head, I saw something which made me feel even better: a fresh jug of water
20 had been left out and, better still, in fact the best news ever, the door that had been bolted shut the night before was now ajar.

I got up and went to the edge of the ladder and looked down. I could see the end of our lifeboat, which meant it was still there tied up; good. For a few minutes I looked around the horizon. It
25 was a clear day with little cloud and not much wind, and I could see a very long way; blue sky and blue-green sea and not a sign of boats or planes anywhere. Good. I shook Hifa awake, gently at first, and then more firmly.

She blinked, opened her eyes, took a moment to focus. I could see
30 her putting together what had happened, where we were.

"Ouch," she said. "Wow. What?"

I pointed at the door. Hifa jumped up, going from groggy and just-woken to fully alert in a split second. Then she exhaled and slowed herself down for a moment, and we looked at each other.
35 And then we went through the alcove door into the tower.

The inside of the tower was, at first sight, hard to take in. The only light came in through slit-like windows high in the walls and, as we entered from the bright outdoors, it was initially difficult to see anything at all. I gradually took in an impression of
40 what seemed to be complete chaos. The floor was covered in pipes and cables and metal boxes and wooden crates, many of them partly smashed. On the side of the room closest to the door, where we were standing, the debris was piled so high it was almost impassable. I didn't trust myself to clamber over the obsta-
45 cle course until I could see properly, so we stood there for a few

to snuggle *sich anschmiegen*

to slur *lallen*

unconsciousness *Bewusstlosigkeit*

to bend to curve
cricked *verrenkt*

ajar slightly open

to take in to appreciate
or understand
slit *Schlitz*

debris *Trümmer*

to clamber *kraxeln*
obstacle course *Hindernisparcours*

minutes and tried to understand what we were seeing. Then we began pushing through the mess. We stepped over and between pipes and cables and metal boxes as we went. This, the ground floor of the installation's tower, had evidently been some kind of control centre. The far side of the room had seven or eight com- 5 puter monitors, all of them black and silent. There were stacks of computer equipment on the floor of the room's far half. The sense of mess and abandon was absolute.

There was a metal ladder in the corner of the room, the same kind that we'd used to get up onto the platform, passing through a 10 circular hole in the floor above. We slowly and carefully climbed up it, Hifa going first. On this upper floor, the second of the tower's three storeys, the windows were bigger and it was much easier to see. And that is where we met our host. A pale, very thin man, wearing nothing but black drawstring trousers, was squat- 15 ting in the far corner of the room. He was just this side of emaciated; you could see his ribs, which were heaving in and out; he was panting with what must have been excitement or fear. His face was covered in thick dark beard and the only part of it easily visible was his eyes, which were wide and startled. He could have 20 been any age from thirty to sixty. He was sitting next to one of the windows. Beside him, resting with the end down on the floor, was a metre-long telescope. That was clearly how he had spotted us and monitored our approach. In front of him was a cardboard box. The box was resting on a small low table, like a footstool. The 25 bottom of the box had been removed and it had been placed on its side so the cardboard looked like a proscenium arch. On the floor also were small torn fragments of paper, folded over so they could stand up.

"Hello," said Hifa. She walked across to him and squatted down so 30 that she was the same level as he was. I followed her and did the same. "My name is Hifa and this is Kavanagh. Thank you very much for lowering the ladder for us. You saved our lives."

The man said nothing but moved some of the pieces of paper around while looking at them through the box. My first thought: 35 he's lost his mind, he doesn't know who he is or where he is or what he's doing. But there was something about the game he was playing which seemed orderly and full of intent. The pieces of paper were just that, pieces of paper in different colours, but they had been carefully folded, and he now took all of them out of the 40 box apart from one tall piece and a small flatter piece. He moved them around and then he picked other pieces of paper up and put them in the box and moved them around too. I watched him for a little while but there was no evident pattern to what he was doing. Hifa and I gave each other a quick look. 45

---

evidently obviously

abandon (lit.) Aufgeben

host [həʊst] sb. who has guests

drawstring Kordel

just this side of not quite, almost
emaciated very thin and weak
to heave in and out to move in and out

startled surprised and slightly frightened

proscenium arch an arch that is over the front of a stage; Vorbühne

intent meaning

"Do you mind if we take a little tour?" said Hifa. The man made no reply but his head twitched. It must have been an involuntary movement but we decided to take it as a yes. We straightened up from our squatting and, like the pirates on the floating commu-
5 nity, set out to take an inventory. As on the lower floor, the whole of this level was one big room. It was divided into two halves; our new friend was in the tidier section, where there were a number of chairs and a table covered in papers, as well as his cardboard box and telescope.

10 The other half of the room was as chaotic as I had been down-stairs: an obstacle course of boxes and crates and huge circular cans. Hifa and I moved over to check what was in them, giving frequent looks back at the man, who didn't seem at all bothered by what we were doing – he had gone back to shuffling his bits of
15 paper around inside the cardboard box. Some of the crates I rec-ognized as food crates, of the same type that we had on the life-boat. I tapped the sides of them as I passed; about half were emp-ty, about a quarter were part full, about a quarter were completely full. I felt a surge of hope, of joy. One of the full crates
20 had a partially open lid; I lifted it and looked inside. There was a lot of food there, really a lot. It didn't matter how old the tins in-side were, this stuff lasted forever. As for the big storage cans, they might be water or they might be oil, but it was hard to think of anything else they could be, and whether they were water or
25 oil, it was the best imaginable news. Hifa and I looked a question at each other and decided that we would wait a little before we opened them to find out. We didn't want to seem as if we were launching a hostile takeover. We had just got here and who knew what our host might be thinking.

30 We went up the ladder to the next and last storey of the tower. Here again the windows were even bigger, so there was gradually more light as you went further up inside the tower. It was full morning now and blazingly bright. The layout on this floor was different. These had been, it seemed, the living quarters, divided
35 into rooms off a central corridor, with huge windows at each end, so it was as if you were looking straight out into the sky. It was noticeably warm, not just sunlight-warm, but central-heated warm – the first time I had felt external heat since we had been put to sea. I hadn't really expected to feel warm ever again. Hifa
40 and I turned to each other. Her eyes were huge.

We went to the first room. It seemed to be where the tower's sole occupant lived. There was a mattress on the floor and a chair with some bedding folded over it. On the bedding there was a thick paperback book with a torn cover. I picked it up to find the title
45 page. It was the complete works of Shakespeare. When I put it

to twitch zucken

to launch sth. to begin sth.
hostile takeover feindliche Übernahme

blazingly extremely

occupant a person who lives or works in a building
bedding Bettzeug

then after a while it did. Sometimes you can take strength from the thought that you have no choice. I got up and without delaying any further, stated down the ladder. I stared straight ahead and counted the rungs in tens and tried to go not too fast and not too slow. Hifa waited at the top, probably because she thought I 5 might freak out and start climbing back up and she didn't want to be in the way. I counted ten rungs, then another ten, and ten more, and lost count of how many sets I had done, and suddenly I was at the halfway resting stage. The sea was much closer from here. I knew I would be able to do it. Hifa came down the ladder 10 much more quickly than I had and gave me a hug.

"It's going to be OK from here," she said. And it was, at first – though it was very hard physical work, as hard as any I had ever done. We decided to empty the storage compartment of the lifeboat. There was a security-blanket feeling to keeping our secret 15 supplies of food and water, but we couldn't guarantee that somebody wouldn't come and take our boat. If they came to the installation, which somebody at some stage was likely to do, and couldn't get up it, which was also likely – in fact was certain, since we knew from experience that the only way up was the lad- 20 der, and the only way up the ladder was if the occupants chose to let you use it – then the only thing for them to take would be our lifeboat and its contents.

The decision was simple, but the work of carrying everything up to the platform was not. The tinned food was in boxes and we 25 couldn't think of any way to get those up the ladder. The only possible course of action was to take everything out of the boxes and carry it up in our pockets and in a single small heavy-duty bag which would go over the shoulders and leave our arms free. It would be three trips each to take care of the food, and another 30 five each to move the water. We decided to do it in stages, first carrying our load to the halfway resting point. The formula was, drag self up the ladder, dump what we were hefting, collapse onto the platform and wait until our arms had stopped burning, then go back down the ladder, rest again for a few moments, repeat. As 35 the day went on the rest grew gradually longer and less effective. By the time we had each taken eight trips, the halfway platform was full of boxes and cans and bottles and my whole body was burning and shaking.

I was lying on the floor of the halfway platform when Hifa came 40 up, threw the last contents of the lifeboat beside me and dropped to the metal deck, gasping with effort. By now we had each climbed nearly a thousand feet of vertical ladder and the sun was low in the afternoon sky. We must have lain there without speaking for the best part of half an hour. I didn't feel much better for the rest. 45

heavy-duty made of very strong material

to dump to drop
to heft to lift heavy loads

"This isn't going to happen," I said. "Not today."

"No," said Hifa, still lying on her back.

"I don't even know how I'm going to make it up from here."

"Me neither."

5 "Let alone carry anything."

We lay for a little while longer. It was oddly peaceful. The resting stage had a low metal ledge around the outside, and when we were lying down, we were below the lip, so we were sheltered from the wind but could still feel the effect of the sun. I felt no

10 impulse to move or be anywhere else.

"We have to go down one more time, to check the ropes. And then we're done," said Hifa.

"OK. But not today."

"No, not today."

15 She took two power bars out of a trouser pocket and slid one over to me. I unwrapped it and started eating. It was mainly nuts, pleasantly complicated in flavour but very drying in the mouth. I raided the supply of water, took several swigs, then passed the flagon to Hifa. She had already finished her bar.

20 "We leave all this stuff here tonight," she said. "Tomorrow we finish. Then we can retract the ladder, and we're safe."

"Safe." I could feel myself tearing up at the word, my eyes swimming; a sign of how exhausted I was. Safe. We lay there on the platform, barely moving or speaking, for a long time. The sun had

25 lost its warmth, and was starting to head for the horizon, when Hifa sat up and said that it was time for us to get going.

"We don't want to be on the ladder in the dark," she said. "We don't want the hermit to forget that we're here."

I was a little groggy and stiff and still felt weak from the earlier

30 exertions. That's why I made my mistake. I said, "Fine. You go first." She nodded, stretched, bent to give me a kiss on the cheek, and started up the ladder: I gradually stood, rolled my neck, looked around the empty horizon, yawned and looked up. Hifa had gone; she had climbed the ladder in record time and was no-

35 where to be seen.

"Hello?" I yelled up. She either was in the alcove at the top of the ladder and couldn't hear me, or had gone inside.

I put my hands on the ladder and started up. At first I felt all right but quickly, within a few sets of ten rungs, realised I was in trou-

40 ble. It didn't feel like fear, not at first, just that my body would not do what my mind told it to. I was too weak. I could plant my feet on the rungs well enough, but the strength in my hands and arms simply wasn't there. It was a little like the old days on the Wall, of type 1 and type 2 cold. This was type 2 fatigue. It wasn't going to

45 get better after a few minutes' rest. It was getting worse, and I was

oddly in a strange and surprising way

lip Rand

swig kräftiger Schluck

flagon Karaffe

to tear up [tɪər] to get tears in your eyes

getting weaker, and the ladder was seeming longer and steeper with every second I spent on it. I looked up and the platform was as distant as the sky. Hifa wasn't there. I took the risk of looking down. That too was far, much too far to drop. If I tried to slip down the ladder and recover on the platform I would certainly 5 fall. I was trapped.

On the Wall, the closest thing you ever got to loneliness was when you were standing at your post for a twelve-hour shift; but even then you could see the other Defenders, you could hear chatter on your communicator. On the sea I had never been on 10 my own. I hadn't spent a second entirely on my own for months. Now I felt completely alone and abandoned as I never had before. It was me and this ladder, alone in the universe. I was hyperventilating and failing fast. I realised, after everything I had gone through, that I could die here. I could slip and fall and be gone. 15 I pulled myself up one rung. It was the thought of dying which made me do it – my revulsion at the idea of dying here and now, after everything. Then one more rung. Then another. Not here, not now, I thought. I stopped counting in tens. I just allowed the sense of wrongness and injustice to drive me. Wrong, no, can't 20 die here, one rung. Unfair, unlucky, unjust, wrong, another step. No hope, no future, no chance, no luck, wrong, unfair. That's how I drove myself upwards, after I had nothing else left.

I was at the platform. I pushed through the hole at the top of the ladder and lay on the metal floor. I was so weak and gasping so 25 hard I didn't even feel relief. I had never been so spent. I felt sick, then knew I was going to be sick, then was. I don't know how long I lay there, half conscious. I felt movement and Hifa was standing there beside the doorway.

"I don't know how I made it," she said. "I threw up." 30
I nodded. I couldn't speak yet. She handed me a water bottle and sat down next to me. I swallowed a few mouthfuls, and immediately felt sweat blossom on my forehead. I was so exhausted that even drinking water made me feel a little out of breath. We sat there for a while longer. The sun was going down and the light 35 was beginning to fade: it was around the time of day we had arrived at the platform twenty-four hours ago.

"We're going to sleep on a mattress tonight," I said. Hifa's face lit up.
"I know," she said. "Let's go in. If you're ready."
I made a gesture which meant, I'm ready to try. She unfolded 40 herself to her feet and held out a hand. I waved it away and tried to get directly up but wasn't strong enough. I reached for her hand again and with Hifa's help was able to get to my feet. My legs were sore but functioning. It was the upper half of my body which felt useless. 45

---

abandoned left behind

revulsion Abscheu, Widerwille

to be spent verausgabt sein

to blossom to develop

"I thought I wasn't going to make it," I said. I'm not sure if it was clear whether I meant up the ladder or up onto my feet, but Hifa nodded as if she understood. She held the door open for me and we went through into the chaotic lower level of the tower. We picked our way through the debris. I shook my head at the wall of blank monitors, the control centre for activities which would never happen here again.

Another ladder, up to the hermit's level. This one felt very different from the long ladder down to the sea. Hifa went up first and I followed. This room too was the same as it had been in the morning, the hermit in the same place, on the far side of the room, with his pieces of paper and his cardboard box. It seemed perfectly possible that he hadn't moved all day. One difference was that this time he looked up as we came in, not a flinching or covert glance but a definite sustained look, then went back to his compulsive game. I walked across the room and stood over him for a moment. He didn't look up and he kept shuffling his bits of paper around.

"Thank you again," said Hifa. "We would have been lost without you."

"Why?" I asked. "Why did you let us on?" He looked up at me. I felt he was really seeing me, connecting with the reality of my presence in front of him, for the first time. Maybe he saw my exhaustion, and maybe also he saw in my face the trace of what I had been through that day, how close I had come to being defeated by the climb up the ladder. He very deliberately reached out and picked up all the pieces of paper on the floor of the cardboard box. He put them down next to him. Then he picked one of them back up, looked at it, looked at me and Hifa, and replaced the folded piece of paper in the middle of the box. He looked at us again. Then he put all the other pieces of paper back in the box, left them there for a moment, and removed them all so that the same piece, the first one, was the only one left. I suddenly saw what this was, what the box meant: he had created a version of theatre or television for himself and he moved the pieces around to tell stories. He was putting on a show. So what did this mean? He went through the same sequence again: leaving the central piece in place, he filled the floor of the box, then emptied it. He looked through the cardboard box at the central piece in the middle of the table – in the centre of the stage, occupying the whole of the screen, in his mind. Then, slowly and deliberately, he looked up at me and Hifa.

"He's lonely," I said. And then to the man: "There used to be people here, but they all went away, and now you're on your own, and you got tired of it."

to flinch to make a sudden, quick movement
covert hidden or secret
compulsive feeling the need to do sth. repeatedly

deliberately slowly and carefully

to flare *aufflackern*

I saw something flare in his eyes: the first moment I'd really felt contact with what was in the mind of our hermit.

"That must have been hard," said Hifa. He looked at her: yes. His expression did not change. He brought some more pieces of paper to the box and moved them around and watched them. Now that 5 I knew he was trying to tell a story his actions made much more sense. I felt as if I understood: the pieces of paper were other people, other sea-going vessels, coming to the platform. He moved them in circles around the central piece, one by one, and then put them to one side. The central piece, the one representing our her- 10 mit himself, stayed where it was. Other boats had come to the platform but he had not lowered the ladder. He repeated this sequence six or seven times. I could tell they were separate actions because he didn't reuse the pieces but put them to one side once he had finished with them. At one stage three different pieces of 15 paper were brought to the platform and he moved them round it in circles, then put them down, then moved them around again. Three ships had come to the platform and had stayed there for several days, looking for a way onto it. That must have been terrifying. If they had got onto the installation and found him and 20 realised that he had been refusing to let them on, they would have killed him. I wondered if they had guessed that he was there, observing them? Like when you hide from a knock on the door, hoping that the person outside will go away, but then they ring the bell, and knock louder and louder, again and again, knocking 25 and ringing together, and you know that they know that you're

to be committed to sth. to promise to oneself to take a course of action
to flinch to move back in fear

hiding, and they're getting angrier and angrier, but you're committed to hiding now so there's nothing you can do except duck down, low and quiet, and wait and flinch and hide and long for them to stop and go away, except a secret part of you fears that 30 they never ever will, that they can wait longer than you, outlast you, that it's a contest to the death … and then they go away and you find you've been holding your breath and it's all fine and you're safe. For now.

He stopped moving the pieces around and took the three ships 35 away. The single piece – the hermit himself – was still in the middle of the box. Then he brought another piece of paper to the edge of the box and left it there for a few seconds. He moved it very slightly and left it again. And again. He kept doing this. I got it: a vessel approaching the installation, but slowly, very slowly. It 40 took at least a couple of minutes for the boat to get to the platform. The boat was moving so slowly that it had to be under sail or oar – and that's when it came to me: this must be the story of how he had seen us coming and what he had decided to do. This was us rowing towards the platform. 45

Our boat got to the middle of the box, right next to the hermit. He
left it there and folded his arms. He had seen us coming, he had
seen us arrive, and then he had thought about what to do next. He
looked at the pieces on the board, then picked them up and put
5 them down beside the box, and then he looked at us, as if to say:
and now here we are.

"Why us?" Hifa asked, her voice soft.

He seemed not to be listening, but after a few seconds, he held up
two fingers. The answer appeared to be, because there were only
10 two of us.

"Thank you," said Hifa. The man gave her a circular movement
of his head which I took to mean something along the lines of
"Don't mention it."

"Thank you," I said. It was nowhere near a large enough state-
15 ment for what I felt, but what else was there to say?

"We're going to go upstairs," I said. "I hope that's OK." Again he
showed no reaction, but there was something about his non-reac-
tion which was a form of "yes". Yes-stillness was different from
no-stillness. This was going to take some getting used to as a form
20 of communication, learning a new non-language.

I went up the ladder first this time. There was just enough light. I
went first to 'our' room to check that it was all as we had left it.
Hifa came in behind me and sat on one of the mattresses. I knew
that I should eat but I felt too tired. I knew what I wanted instead:
25 light. I went to see if there was another one of those oil lanterns.
There didn't seem to be one in any of the other rooms on this
floor, except the hermit's, and I couldn't take that. By now the sun
had gone down. The ladder was the darkest point of the building,
in the centre away from the windows, and I went down very care-
30 fully. The hermit was still in the same corner but looking out the
windows in the direction where the sun had set. Past him I could
see the first stars.

"I'm on the hunt for one of those lanterns," I said, "with your permission. It's been such a long time."

35 There was a pause of a few seconds. I think it was still so
strange to him hearing human speech again that it was taking
him a while to process what he heard. He pointed at a far corner of the room. That was a huge moment, the first gesture he
had made that didn't involve his cardboard stage set. I picked
40 my way through the stacked and teetering supplies and found,
sitting on top of a crate, an oil lantern, identical to the one I had
seen upstairs in his room. Next to it, just as miraculous, was a
box of matches. It occurred to me that the matches were as
valuable as the oil. I turned to look at him and, with the starlight
45 behind him and the moonlight pouring across the windows in

to teeter schwanken

miraculous surprising, difficult
to believe
to occur to sb. (phr. v.) to come
to sb.'s mind

front, he made a double-handed gesture which clearly meant: go, take it.

I went back up to Hifa. She was still sitting on the mattress. I showed her my bounty, my booty, my plunder, my gift. She scooched over on the mattress and I sat next to her. My hand $_5$ shaking – I was nervous, now it had dawned on me how precious the matches were – I opened the window of the lantern, turned the tiny tap for the oil supply, and struck a match. Its flare of light was the most extraordinary thing I had seen in a long time. I touched it to the wick and the lantern came into life. The light $_{10}$ was yellow-blue, gold, the most beautiful thing I had ever seen. I bent forwards and put the lantern down on a chair at the end of the bed. The light was flickering but reliable, the most cinematic and biggest sight. I sat down next to Hifa and we watched the light for many minutes. $_{15}$

"We can bring the supplies up tomorrow," I eventually said.

"I'll set out lines."

"He'll withdraw the ladder. Maybe he already has."

"But we'll leave the boat there. You never know."

"You never know." $_{20}$

We were silent again for a long while.

"I didn't actually want to Breed," said Hifa. "It was more about wanting sex. And wanting to get off the Wall. I got tired of wait-ing, I thought you'd never ask."

Did I believe her? I'm not sure. Jokes ran through my mind: I $_{25}$ thought about saying, I know, or You did the right thing, or Now she tells me. Instead I just squeezed her arm. I thought, I could watch this light forever, I will never tire of watching this light, this light is the best thing I have ever seen. My arms and back hurt, I was tired and hungry, I was, when I thought about it, de- $_{30}$ hydrated, with a dry mouth and a nasty headache, but I didn't care about any of that, all I wanted to do was sit on the bed and watch the lantern.

"Tell me a story," said Hifa.

I tried to think of one. "Everything is going to be all right," I said, $_{35}$ that's what a story is, something where everything turns out all right, but I said that and I could see it wasn't what she wanted to hear. That is another thing a story is, something somebody wants to hear, but my mind was blank and all I could think was, she wants me to tell her a story, a story where something turns out all $_{40}$ right. I said this to myself over and over again, that's what a story is, something that turns out all right, and then it came to me, and what I said out loud began like this:

"It's cold on the Wall."

---

bounty *Gabe, Geschenk*
booty *Beute*
plunder stolen goods
to scooch over (*infml.*) to slide over
to dawn on sb. (*phr. v.*) *jdm. dämmern*

wick *Docht*

cinematic presented as a motion picture

eventually finally

Additional texts

About the Author – John Lanchester

John Lanchester (*1962) was born in Hamburg, Germany. Because of his father's occupation at the Hong Kong and Shanghai Bank, his family travelled a lot, and Lanchester spent his childhood and youth in Hong Kong, Ragoon (Myanmar, also known as
5 Burma), Calcutta (India), Labuan (Malaysia) and England, where he graduated from St John's College, Oxford.
As a journalist, he has worked as a football reporter, obituary writer, restaurant critic, as well as a book editor, including for the *London Review of Books*, and *Penguin* publishers.
10 Lanchester regularly writes for the *Daily Telegraph* (a weekly column), *The Observer* (restaurant reviews), *The Guardian* and the *New Yorker.*
He is married to the historian and author Miranda Carter and they have two children. He currently lives in London.

obituary [əˈbɪtʃʊəri] *Nachruf*

Professional career
Lanchester is a member of the editorial board of the *London Review of Books.* He worked as an investigative journalist, writing about the 2008 global economic crisis and, in 2013, examined the materials from Edward Snowden on behalf of the *Guardian.*
Additionally, he wrote several essays and reports on economic, scientific and global issues, e. g.
- Money Talks: Learning the Language of Finance (2014)
- The Snowden Files (2017)
- The Robots Are Coming (2017)
- You Are the Product (2017)
- Chinese Cyber-Sovereignty (2019)

editorial board *Redaktionsleitung*

investigative journalist *Enthüllungsjournalist*

Edward Snowden (*1983) US American whistleblower and former CIA employee

Literary work
Lanchester's first novel, *The Debt to Pleasure,* was published in 1996 and won several literary prizes, e. g. in the category "literary food writing".
Lanchester has written five novels so far.
- **The Debt to Pleasure** (1996) – a novel about an unorthodox gourmet called Tarquin Winot, who goes on a mysterious journey around France.
- **Mr Phillips** (2000) – a novel about a day in the life of the accountant Victor Phillips, written from the perspective of an interior monologue.

accountant *Buchhalter*

- **Fragrant Harbour** (2002) – a novel about three immigrants to Hong Kong in the 1980s.
- **Capital** (2012) – a satirical novel set in London about the 2008 financial crisis; the novel was made into a TV series for the BBC in 2015.
- **The Wall** (2019)

Among the many **prizes** John Lanchester was either awarded or nominated for are:
- the Whitbread Book Award (1996)
- the Hawthornden First Novel Prize (1996)
- the E.M. Forster Award (2008)
- the Booker Prize (nominated, 2019)

Original contribution by Iris Edelbrock

Abraham Maslow
The Hierarchy of Human Needs

Abraham Maslow (1908–1970) was an American psychologist who created a 'hierarchy of human needs', which illustrates his theory of psychological health and self-actualization. In his scientific work, Maslow stressed the eminent importance of focusing and strengthening the positive qualities in people.
According to his theory, a human being achieves self-actualization after having ascended the levels of the hierarchy, one at a time.

homeostasis tendency towards stable physical condition
excretion the discharging of matter from the body; *Ausscheidung*

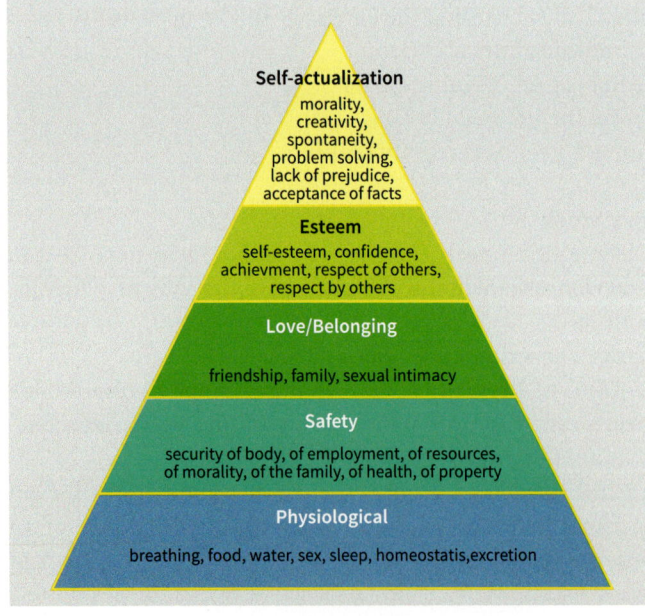

- The **first two levels** are important for the basic needs and the physical survival of a human being.
- The **third and fourth levels** are important for a person's psychological well-being, the feeling of having accomplished something, being accepted, recognized and successful.
- The **cognitive level** is important to stimulate human beings intellectually and make them want to explore.
- The **aesthetic level** refers to a person's need for harmony, order and beauty.

to accomplish sth. to finish sth. successfully
to be recognized to be respected

The need of **self-actualization** occurs when people engage in achieving their full potential and build up feelings of self-confidence.

to occur to happen

By definition, self-actualization is a person's motivation for "achieving the fullest use of one's talents and interests" and "becoming everything that one is capable of becoming" (Abraham Maslow, *The farther reaches of human nature*, The Viking Press, New York 1971, p. 269).

A person's basic needs must be met before self-actualization can be achieved.

Original contribution by Iris Edelbrock

Mark Brown

Author of Dystopian Climate Crisis Is "Deeply Optimistic"

People have a "moral obligation" to be optimistic about the climate crisis because the alternative would be to despair and allow the worst to happen, the novelist John Lanchester has said.

obligation sth. that you must do; *Verpflichtung*

Lanchester's new book is a dystopian vision of a world after a
5 climatic event called 'the Change'.

But he told the Hay festival in Wales that it did not mean he was pessimistic. "I'm deeply optimistic," he said. "My main ambition for the book is to be wrong, and I'll take any form of wrongness ... because we can't bequeath that world, it would be a shameful
10 thing to do.

Hay festival an annual arts festival held in Wales

to bequeath to pass on property to sb. on death

"I think there is a moral obligation to be optimistic, because if we're pessimistic we will despair, and if we despair, this will happen. If we despair we won't act and we morally can't let it happen."

15 Lanchester said the worst did not have to happen, the Intergovernmental Panel on Climate Change (IPCC) was not saying: "We're doomed, it's finished, it's all over."

IPCC a body of the United Nations providing the world with scientific information about climate change
doomed certain to be killed or destroyed

1.5 degrees special report on the impacts of global warming of 1.5 °C above pre-industrial levels

"The IPCC conference last year said it was still possible to keep the temperature of the world to within 1.5 degrees of what it was at the end of the industrial revolution and we've had one degree already," said Lanchester. "That's no paradise. It leaves the oceans still getting warmer for centuries to come." 20

But it is "incomparably better" than two degrees, which is the **Paris target** a 2016 global agreement to fight climate change

Paris target, he said. "It is tens of millions of lives."

Lanchester's book explores intergenerational tensions, with the young blaming the old for the world they now live in, a subject which resonates today. He was asked whether young people should consider not reproducing, a real-world phenomenon known as birth striking. 25

to resonate to continue to have a powerful effect

Lanchester said that would be "heartbreakingly sad", adding: "I think acting as if we have a future is very, very important. Apart from anything else, it does personalise it. Every stake we have in the future is a good thing, every bit of us that is committed to the future is a good thing. It's that future that will make us act in the present." 30

to have a stake in sth. einen Anteil haben an

35

The climate emergency is something we would all like to deny if it was possible, he said, and is a challenging subject because "most of the people who are going to be catastrophically impacted by climate change aren't here. They don't exist. They haven't been born yet. The people who are going to suffer most are the unborn poor close to the equator. They are the ones whose lives are going to be utterly wrecked. 40

utterly totally

"That's why works of the imagination are so important. In effect we are having to imagine these people into being and then act on behalf of their interests. This is a new thing." 45

The Wall is the fifth novel by Lanchester, a writer and essayist who is celebrated for his ability to explain hugely complicated concepts in accessible terms. [...]

accessible easy to understand

to immerse yourself in sth. to become completely involved with sth.

Lanchester, who immersed himself in research for *The Wall*, was asked the big question: what will it take for the world to change in order to prevent the climate catastrophe? 50

catastrophe [kə'tæstrəfi]

hunch Ahnung, Gefühl
momentum Impuls

He said his hunch was that a shift in the political momentum would have to come from a shift in the economic momentum. "You're starting to hear that corporations are panicking, they don't want to be seen as the baddies." 55

baddies = bad guys; die Bösen

Another key factor, he added, would be young people perceiving the climate crisis "as an emergency ... not just an item on the to-do list. Those things are going to shift it."

https://www.theguardian.com/books/2019/may/27/john-lanchester-author-of-dystopian-climate-crisis-novel-says-hes-deeply-optimistic, 27 May 2019. Copyright Guardian News & Media Ltd 2020 [18.01.2020]

Thomas More
Utopia

Thomas More (1478–1535) was an English lawyer, philosopher, author and statesman, who also worked as chancellor in the reign of Henry VIII. His book, *Utopia*, published in 1516, is a narrative about a fictitious island society and its social, economic, political and religious status and structure. Originally written in Latin, it was published in English in 1551.

Many details of More's island society resemble life in monasteries. More's political ideas depicted in *Utopia* are considered to have influenced communism and socialism.

The excerpt below is written in more modern English.

The island of Utopia is in the middle two hundred miles broad, and holds almost at the same breadth over a great part of it, but it grows narrower towards both ends. Its figure is not unlike a crescent. Between its horns the sea comes in eleven miles broad, and

5 spreads itself into a great bay, which is environed with land to the compass of about five hundred miles, and is well secured from winds. In this bay there is no great current; the whole coast is, as it were, one continued harbour, which gives all that live in the island great convenience for mutual commerce. But the entry

10 into the bay, occasioned by rocks on the one hand and shallows on the other, is very dangerous. In the middle of it there is one single rock which appears above water, and may, therefore, easily be avoided; and on the top of it there is a tower, in which a garrison is kept; the other rocks lie under water, and are very danger-

15 ous. The channel is known only to the natives; so that if any stranger should enter into the bay without one of their pilots he would run great danger of shipwreck. For even they themselves could not pass it safe if some marks that are on the coast did not direct their way; and if these should be but a little shifted, any

20 fleet that might come against them, how great soever it were, would be certainly lost.

On the other side of the island there are likewise many harbours; and the coast is so fortified, both by nature and art, that a small number of men can hinder the descent of a great army. [...]

25 Utopus, that conquered it [...], brought the rude and uncivilised inhabitants into such a good government, and to that measure of politeness, that they now far excel all the rest of mankind. Having soon subdued them, he designed to separate them from the continent, and to bring the sea quite round them. To accomplish this

30 he ordered a deep channel to be dug, fifteen miles long; and that the natives might not think he treated them like slaves, he not

breadth [bredθ] the distance from one side to the other
crescent ['kresənt] *Sichel*

compass length, area

current *Strömung*

convenience *Annehmlichkeit*
mutual *gegenseitig*

descent attack, movement

to subdue sb. *jdn. unterwerfen*
to accomplish sth. to achieve sth.

only forced the inhabitants, but also his own soldiers, to labour in carrying it on. As he set a vast number of men to work, he, beyond all men's expectations, brought it to a speedy conclusion. And his neighbours, who at first laughed at the folly of the undertaking, no sooner saw it brought to perfection than they were struck with admiration and terror.

There are fifty-four cities in the island, all large and well built, the manners, customs, and laws of which are the same, and they are all contrived as near in the same manner as the ground on which they stand will allow. The nearest lie at least twenty-four miles' distance from one another, and the most remote are not so far distant but that a man can go on foot in one day from it to that which lies next it. [...]

They have built, over all the country, farmhouses for husbandmen, which are well contrived, and furnished with all things necessary for country labour. Inhabitants are sent, by turns, from the cities to dwell in them; no country family has fewer than forty men and women in it, besides two slaves. There is a master and a mistress set over every family, and over thirty families there is a magistrate. Every year twenty of this family come back to the town after they have stayed two years in the country, and in their stead there are another twenty sent from the town, that they may learn country work from those that have been already one year in the country, as they must teach those that come to them the next from the town. By this means such as dwell in those country farms are never ignorant of agriculture, and so commit no errors which might otherwise be fatal and bring them under a scarcity of corn. But though there is every year such a shifting of the husbandmen to prevent any man being forced against his will to follow that hard course of life too long, yet many among them take such pleasure in it that they desire leave to continue in it many years.

These husbandmen till the ground, breed cattle, hew wood, and convey it to the towns either by land or water, as is most convenient. They breed an infinite multitude of chickens in a very curious manner; for the hens do not sit and hatch them, but a vast number of eggs are laid in a gentle and equal heat in order to be hatched, and they are no sooner out of the shell, and able to stir about, but they seem to consider those that feed them as their mothers, and follow them as other chickens do the hen that hatched them. [...]

They sow no corn but that which is to be their bread; for they drink either wine, cider or perry, and often water, sometimes boiled with honey or liquorice, with which they abound; and though they know exactly how much corn will serve every town

---

to contrive to make in a clever way

husbandman (*old use*) the man of the house
contrived *here*: ausgestattet
to furnish to provide

to dwell (*fml.*) to live in a particular place

scarcity *Knappheit*

to till to prepare and use land for growing crops
to hew to cut down

to hatch *brüten*

to stir about to move around

perry cider made from pears
liquorice *Lakritz*
to abound with sth. to have a great quantity of sth.

and all that tract of country which belongs to it, yet they sow much more and breed more cattle than are necessary for their consumption, and they give that surplus of which they make no
80 use to their neighbours. When they want anything in the country which it does not produce, they fetch that from the town, without carrying anything in exchange for it. And the magistrates of the town take care to see it given them; for they meet generally in the town once a month, upon a festival day. When the time of harvest
85 comes, the magistrates in the country send to those in the towns and let them know how many hands they will need for reaping the harvest; and the number they call for being sent to them, they commonly dispatch it all in one day.

Their cities [...]

90 He that knows one of their towns knows them all – they are so like one another, except where the situation makes some difference. [...]
The inhabitants have fortified the fountain-head of this river, which springs a little without the towns; that so, if they should
95 happen to be besieged, the enemy might not be able to stop or divert the course of the water, nor poison it; from thence it is carried, in earthen pipes, to the lower streets. And for those places of the town to which the water of that small river cannot be conveyed, they have great cisterns for receiving the rain-water, which
100 supplies the want of the other. The town is compassed with a high and thick wall, in which there are many towers and forts; there is also a broad and deep dry ditch, set thick with thorns, cast round three sides of the town, and the river is instead of a ditch on the fourth side. The streets are very convenient for all carriage,
105 and are well sheltered from the winds. Their buildings are good, and are so uniform that a whole side of a street looks like one house. The streets are twenty feet broad; there lie gardens behind all their houses. These are large, but enclosed with buildings, that on all hands face the streets, so that every house has both a door
110 to the street and a back door to the garden. Their doors have all two leaves, which, as they are easily opened, so they shut of their own accord; and, there being no property among them, every man may freely enter into any house whatsoever. At every ten years' end they shift their houses by lots.
115 They cultivate their gardens with great care, so that they have both vines, fruits, herbs, and flowers in them; and all is so well ordered and so finely kept that I never saw gardens anywhere that were both so fruitful and so beautiful as theirs. [...]
But now their houses are three stories high, the fronts of them are
120 faced either with stone, plastering, or brick, and between the

tract an area of land

surplus more than is needed

to dispatch to finish quickly

to fortify to strengthen sth., esp. in order to protect it
fountain-head a spring that is the source of a river; *Quelle*
to besiege *belagern*
to divert [daɪˈvɜːt] to cause sb./ sth. to change direction
earthen *Ton*

to compass *here*: to surround

ditch *Graben*

on all hands on all sides

door leaves *Türblätter, Türflügel*
of your own accord to do sth. without being asked to

by lot *nach dem Zufallsprinzip*

plastering *Putz*

facing an outer layer covering the wall; *Verblendung*

lead [led] *Blei*

to glaze *glasieren*

gummed *gummiert*

facings of their walls they throw in their rubbish. Their roofs are flat, and on them they lay a sort of plaster, which costs very little, and yet is so tempered that it is not apt to take fire, and yet resists the weather more than lead. They have great quantities of glass among them, with which they glaze their windows; they use also in their windows a thin linen cloth, that is so oiled or gummed that it both keeps out the wind and gives free admission to the light. 125

Their magistrates

to take an oath to give a formal promise

to proceed to continue with a course of action

suffrage ['sʌfrɪdʒ] right to vote in an election

Thirty families choose every year a magistrate, who was anciently 130 called the Syphogrant [...]. All the Syphogrants, who are in number two hundred, choose the Prince out of a list of four who are named by the people of the four divisions of the city; but they take an oath, before they proceed to an election, that they will choose him whom they think most fit for the office: they give him 135 their voices secretly, so that it is not known for whom every one gives his suffrage. The Prince is for life, unless he is removed upon suspicion of some design to enslave the people. [...]

public till *öffentliche Kasse*

There are always two Syphogrants called into the council chamber, and these are changed every day. It is a fundamental rule of 140 their government, that no conclusion can be made in anything that relates to the public till it has been first debated three days in their council. It is death for any to meet and consult concerning the State, unless it be either in their ordinary council, or in

body group

the assembly of the whole body of the people. [...] 145

Their occupations

occupation a person's job

Agriculture is that which is so universally understood among them that no person, either man or woman, is ignorant of it; they are instructed in it from their childhood, partly by what they learn at school, and partly by practice, they being led out often 150 into the fields about the town, where they not only see others at work but are likewise exercised in it themselves.

peculiar particular, special

to apply oneself to sth. to work hard at sth.

flax plant used to make textile fibre; *Flachs*

masonry the skill of building with brick and stone

smith *Schmied*

carpenter *Zimmermann*

esteem respect, admiration

to alter to change

Besides agriculture, which is so common to them all, every man has some peculiar trade to which he applies himself; such as the manufacture of wool or flax, masonry, smith's work, or carpen- 155 ter's work; for there is no sort of trade that is in great esteem among them.

Throughout the island they wear the same sort of clothes, without any other distinction except what is necessary to distinguish the two sexes and the married and unmarried. The fashion never 160 alters, and as it is neither disagreeable nor uneasy, so it is suited to the climate, and calculated both for their summers and winters. Every family makes their own clothes.

All among them, women as well as men, learn one or other of the
trades formerly mentioned. Women, for the most part, deal in
wool and flax, which suit best with their weakness, leaving the
ruder trades to the men. The same trade generally passes down
from father to son, inclinations often following descent: but if any
man's genius lies another way he is, by adoption, translated into
a family that deals in the trade to which he is inclined; and when
that is to be done, care is taken, not only by his father, but by the
magistrate, that he may be put to a discreet and good man: and if,
after a person has learned one trade, he desires to acquire another,
that is also allowed, and is managed in the same manner as the
former. [...]
The rest of their time, besides that taken up in work, eating, and
sleeping, is left to every man's discretion; yet they are not to
abuse that interval to luxury and idleness, but must employ it in
some proper exercise, according to their various inclinations,
which is, for the most part, reading. It is ordinary to have public
lectures every morning before daybreak, at which none are
obliged to appear but those who are marked out for literature; [...]
After supper they spend an hour in some diversion, in summer in
their gardens, and in winter in the halls where they eat, where
they entertain each other either with music or discourse. They do
not so much as know dice, or any such foolish and mischievous
games. [...]
And thus, since they are all employed in some useful labour, and
since they content themselves with fewer things, it falls out that
there is a great abundance of all things among them; so that it
frequently happens that, for want of other work, vast numbers
are sent out to mend the highways; but when no public undertaking is to be performed, the hours of working are lessened. The
magistrates never engage the people in unnecessary labour, since
the chief end of the constitution is to regulate labour by the necessities of the public, and to allow the people as much time as is
necessary for the improvement of their minds, in which they
think the happiness of life consists.

Their social relations

But it is now time to explain to you the mutual intercourse of this
people, their commerce, and the rules by which all things are
distributed among them.
As their cities are composed of families, so their families are made
up of those that are nearly related to one another. [...] No family
may have less than ten and more than sixteen persons in it, but
there can be no determined number for the children under age;
this rule is easily observed by removing some of the children of a

rude *here:* rough

inclination a feeling that you want
to do a particular thing; *Neigung*
descent [dɪˈsent] *Abstammung*

discreet careful

to acquire sth. to get/learn sth.

discretion [dɪˈskreʃən] personal
choice
to abuse to use to bad effect,
to misuse
idleness [ˈaɪdəlnəs] the act of not
working and being inactive

to be obliged *verpflichtet sein*

diversion (*fml.*) [daɪˈvɜːʃən]
an activity you do for your
entertainment
discourse (*fml.*) communication
dice *das Würfelspiel, Würfeln*
mischievous [ˈmɪstʃɪvəs] *bösartig*

to content oneself with sth. (*phr.
v.*) *sich mit etw. zufrieden geben*
abundance the state of having more
than you need
to mend to repair

determined *festgelegt*

fruitful having a lot of children

plague [pleɪg] *die Pest*
to supply to provide sth. that is needed
to abandon to leave, to give up

pretence *Vorwand*

stew bathhouse, commonly doubled as a brothel (= *Bordell*)

spare hour free time

more fruitful couple to any other family that does not abound so much in them. [...]

If an accident has so lessened the number of the inhabitants of any of their towns that it cannot be made up from the other towns of the island without diminishing them too much (which is said to have fallen out but twice since they were first a people, when great numbers were carried off by the plague), the loss is then supplied by recalling as many as are wanted from their colonies, for they will abandon these rather than suffer the towns in the island to sink too low.

But to return to their manner of living in society: the oldest man of every family, as has been already said, is its governor; wives serve their husbands, and children their parents, and always the younger serves the elder. [...]

Thus you see that there are no idle persons among them, nor pretences of excusing any from labour. There are no taverns, no ale-houses, nor stews among them, nor any other occasions of corrupting each other, of getting into corners, or forming themselves into parties; all men live in full view, so that all are obliged both to perform their ordinary task and to employ themselves well in their spare hours; and it is certain that a people thus ordered must live in great abundance of all things, and these being equally distributed among them, no man can want or be obliged to beg [...]. ... so that indeed the whole island is, as it were, one family.

http://theopenutopia.org/wp-content/uploads/2012/09/UtopiaComplete.txt [18.01.2020]

Coloured woodcut of the island of Utopia; cover of the 1516 edition

John Constable

Weymouth Bay (1816–17)

John Constable (1776–1837) was an English landscape painter in the Romantic tradition.

Romanticism – as a counter-reaction to the Industrial Revolution – glorified the past and idealized nature and individualism.

The movement emphasized intense emotion and developed new aesthetic categories experiencing and praising the beauty of nature.

Constable's painting *Weymouth Bay* is believed to have been inspired by John and Martha Constable's honeymoon in October 1816, which they spent on a tour of the south west of England.

honeymoon *Flitterwochen*

Benjamin Williams Leader

The Valley of the Llugwy (1883)

Benjamin Williams Leader (1831–1923) was an English landscape painter and a friend of John Constable.
The river and valley depicted in the painting are located in the north-west of Wales and have become a popular tourist destination.

William Shakespeare
This Scepter'd Isle

The text below is taken from William Shakespeare's play *Richard II*, (act II, scene I, lines 40-66), written ca. 1595, and is a celebration of the English nation and its achievements and superiority, but also of its separateness.

The patriotic monologue, spoken by John of Gaunt, the Duke of Lancaster, on his death bed, prophesies the downfall of an idealized England under the rule of Richard II.

This royal throne of kings, this scepter'd isle,

seat of Mars home to the Roman god of war
This earth of majesty, this seat of Mars,

demi-paradise a place like paradise, only smaller
This other Eden, demi-paradise,

This fortress built by nature for herself,

Against infection and the hand of war,   5

happy breed a blessed (*gesegnet*) population
This happy breed of men, this little world,

This precious stone set in a silver sea

Which serves it in the office of a wall,

moat *Festungsgraben*
Or as a moat defensive to a house,

Against the envy of less happier lands,   10

This blessed plot, this earth, this realm, this England,

teeming fruitful, pregnant
womb [wuːm] *Gebärmutter, Schoß*
This nurse, this teeming womb of royal kings,

Fear'd by their breed and famous by their birth,

renowned famous
Renowned for their deeds as far from home, –

chivalry [ˈʃɪvəlri] *Ritterlichkeit*
For Christian service and true chivalry, –   15

sepulchre (*old use*) *Grabkammer*
stubborn Jewry reference to the Middle Ages, when Jews resisted Christian conversion by medieval crusaders (*Kreuzritter*)
As is the sepulchre in stubborn Jewry

Of the world's ransom, blessed Mary's son:

the world's ransom metaphorical reference to Jesus Christ
This land of such dear souls, this dear, dear land,

Dear for her reputation through the world,

leased out sold out
pelting useless, worthless, miserable
Is now leas'd out – I die pronouncing it, –   20

Like to a tenement or pelting farm:

England, bound in with the triumphant sea,

Whose rocky shore beats back the envious siege

Neptune Roman god of the sea
Of watery Neptune, is now bound in with shame,

inky blots reference to King Richard's tricks used to exploit the nation's wealth to finance war in Ireland
With inky blots and rotten parchment bonds: 25

That England, that was wont to conquer others,

conquest *Unterwerfung*
Hath made a shameful conquest of itself.

from *Richard II* by William Shakespeare. University of Toronto Libraries, Toronto 2012, https://rpo.library.utoronto.ca/poems/richard-ii-excerpts-royal-throne-kings-sceptred-isle [13.07.2020]

Jonathan Franzen
What If We Stopped Pretending?

Jonathan Franzen (*1959) is a highly acclaimed American novelist and essayist. He has been awarded several literary prizes and was also a finalist for the Pulitzer Prize in Fiction.

The climate apocalypse is coming. To prepare for it, we need to admit that we can't prevent it.

There is infinite hope," Kafka tells us, "only not for us." This is a fittingly mystical epigram from a writer whose characters strive
5 for ostensibly reachable goals and, tragically or amusingly, never manage to get any closer to them. But it seems to me, in our rapidly darkening world, that the converse of Kafka's quip is equally true: *There is no hope, except for us.*

I'm talking, of course, about climate change. The struggle to rein
10 in global carbon emissions and keep the planet from melting down has the feel of Kafka's fiction. The goal has been clear for thirty years, and despite earnest efforts we've made essentially no progress toward reaching it. Today, the scientific evidence verges on irrefutable. If you're younger than sixty, you have a good
15 chance of witnessing the radical destabilization of life on earth – massive crop failures, apocalyptic fires, imploding economies, epic flooding, hundreds of millions of refugees fleeing regions made uninhabitable by extreme heat or permanent drought. If you're under thirty, you're all but guaranteed to witness it. If you
20 care about the planet, and about the people and animals who live on it, there are two ways to think about this. You can keep on hoping that catastrophe is preventable, and feel ever more frustrated or enraged by the world's inaction. Or you can accept that disaster is coming, and begin to rethink what it means to have hope.
25 Even at this late date, expressions of unrealistic hope continue to abound. Hardly a day seems to pass without my reading that it's time to "roll up our sleeves" and "save the planet"; that the problem of climate change can be "solved" if we summon the collective will. Although this message was probably still true in 1988,
30 when the science became fully clear, we've emitted as much atmospheric carbon in the past thirty years as we did in the previous two centuries of industrialization. The facts have changed, but somehow the message stays the same.

Psychologically, this denial makes sense. Despite the outrageous
35 fact that I'll soon be dead forever, I live in the present, not the future. Given a choice between an alarming abstraction (death) and the reassuring evidence of my senses (breakfast!), my mind prefers to focus on the latter. The planet, too, is still marvelously

epigram *Sinnspruch*
ostensibly *scheinbar*

converse the opposite
quip a humorous and clever remark

to rein in *sich zügeln*

to verge on sth *(phr. v.) grenzen an*
irrefutable impossible to prove wrong

to enrage to cause sb. to become very angry

to summon *herbeizitieren*
collective will *Gemeinwille*

denial *Leugnung*

to reassure *zusichern, beschwichtigen*

impending *drohend*

asteroidal *stemartig*
binary consisting of two parts

to compound to make a problem
or difficult situation worse
to fray *ausfransen*

severity seriousness

a host of a large number of sth.

constraint *Beschränkung*
relentless continue in an extreme
way

to offset *gegenrechnen*

to avert sth. to prevent sth. bad
from happening

draconian extremely severe

intact, still basically normal – seasons changing, another election
year coming, new comedies on Netflix – and its impending col- 40
lapse is even harder to wrap my mind around than death. Other
kinds of apocalypse, whether religious or thermonuclear or asteroidal, at least have the binary neatness of dying: one moment the
world is there, the next moment it's gone forever. Climate apocalypse, by contrast, is messy. It will take the form of increasingly 45
severe crises compounding chaotically until civilization begins to
fray. Things will get very bad, but maybe not too soon, and maybe
not for everyone. Maybe not for me. [...]

Our atmosphere and oceans can absorb only so much heat before
climate change, intensified by various feedback loops, spins com- 50
pletely out of control. The consensus among scientists and policymakers is that we'll pass this point of no return if the global
mean temperature rises by more than two degrees Celsius (maybe
a little more, but also maybe less). The I.P.C.C. – the Intergovernmental Panel on Climate Change – tells us that, to limit the rise to 55
less than two degrees, we not only need to reverse the trend of the
past three decades. We need to approach zero net emissions, globally, in the *next* three decades.

This is, to say the least, a tall order. It also assumes that you trust
the I.P.C.C.'s calculations. New research, described last month in 60
Scientific American, demonstrates that climate scientists, far from
exaggerating the threat of climate change, have underestimated
its pace and severity. To project the rise in the global mean temperature, scientists rely on complicated atmospheric modelling.
They take a host of variables and run them through supercom- 65
puters to generate, say, ten thousand different simulations for the
coming century, in order to make a "best" prediction of the rise in
temperature. When a scientist predicts a rise of two degrees Celsius, she's merely naming a number about which she's very confident: the rise will be *at least* two degrees. The rise might, in fact, 70
be far higher.

As a non-scientist, I do my own kind of modelling. I run various
future scenarios through my brain, apply the constraints of human psychology and political reality, take note of the relentless
rise in global energy consumption (thus far, the carbon savings 75
provided by renewable energy have been more than offset by
consumer demand), and count the scenarios in which collective
action averts catastrophe. The scenarios, which I draw from the
prescriptions of policymakers and activists, share certain necessary conditions.   80

The first condition is that every one of the world's major pollut-
ing countries institute draconian conservation measures, shut
down much of its energy and transportation infrastructure, and

completely retool its economy. According to a recent paper in
85 *Nature*, the carbon emissions from existing global infrastructure,
if operated through its normal lifetime, will exceed our entire
emissions "allowance" – the further gigatons of carbon that can
be released without crossing the threshold of catastrophe. [...]
Making New York City a green utopia will not avail if Texans
90 keep pumping oil and driving pickup trucks.
[...]
Finally, overwhelming numbers of human beings, including millions of government-hating Americans, need to accept high taxes
and severe curtailment of their familiar lifestyles without revolt-
95 ing. They must accept the reality of climate change and have faith
in the extreme measures taken to combat it. They can't dismiss
news they dislike as fake. They have to set aside nationalism and
class and racial resentments. They have to make sacrifices for
distant threatened nations and distant future generations. They
100 have to be permanently terrified by hotter summers and more
frequent natural disasters, rather than just getting used to them.
Every day, instead of thinking about breakfast, they have to think
about death. Call me a pessimist or call me a humanist, but I don't
see human nature fundamentally changing anytime soon. I can
105 run ten thousand scenarios through my model, and in not one of
them do I see the two-degree target being met.
To judge from recent opinion polls, which show that a majority of
Americans (many of them Republican) are pessimistic about the
planet's future, and from the success of a book like David Wal-
110 lace-Wells's harrowing "The Uninhabitable Earth", which was
released this year, I'm not alone in having reached this conclusion. But there continues to be a reluctance to broadcast it. Some
climate activists argue that if we publicly admit that the problem
can't be solved, it will discourage people from taking any amelio-
115 rative action at all. This seems to me not only a patronizing calculation but an ineffectual one, given how little progress we have
to show for it to date. The activists who make it remind me of the
religious leaders who fear that, without the promise of eternal
salvation, people won't bother to behave well. In my experience,
120 nonbelievers are no less loving of their neighbors than believers.
And so I wonder what might happen if, instead of denying reality,
we told ourselves the truth.
First of all, even if we can no longer hope to be saved from two
degrees of warming, there's still a strong practical and ethical
125 case for reducing carbon emissions. In the long run, it probably
makes no difference how badly we overshoot two degrees; once
the point of no return is passed, the world will become selftrans-
forming. In the shorter term, however, half measures are better

to retool sth. to organize sth. in a
different way in order to improve it

to exceed *übersteigen*

to avail to help or be useful

curtailment *Beschränkung*

harrowing extremely upsetting

reluctance *Widerwille*

ameliorative improving

eternal forever

salvation *Errettung*

to cut to reduce	than no measures. Halfway cutting our emissions would make the immediate effects of warming somewhat less severe, and it ¹³⁰ would somewhat postpone the point of no return. The most terrifying thing about climate change is the speed at which it's advancing, the almost monthly shattering of temperature records. If
devastating causing a lot of damage and destruction	collective action resulted in just one fewer devastating hurricane, just a few extra years of relative stability, it would be a goal worth ¹³⁵ pursuing. [...]

Although the actions of one individual have zero effect on the climate, this doesn't mean that they're meaningless. Each of us has an ethical choice to make. During the Protestant Reformation, when "end times" was merely an idea, not the horribly con- ¹⁴⁰

doctrinal [dɒk'traɪnl] *lehrmäßig* crete thing it is today, a key doctrinal question was whether you should perform good works because it will get you into Heaven, or whether you should perform them simply because they're good – because, while Heaven is a question mark, you know that *this* world would be better if everyone performed them. I can re- ¹⁴⁵ spect the planet, and care about the people with whom I share it, without believing that it will save me.

More than that, a false hope of salvation can be actively harmful.

to persist in sth. *auf etw. bestehen* If you persist in believing that catastrophe can be averted, you commit yourself to tackling a problem so immense that it needs ¹⁵⁰ to be everyone's overriding priority forever. One result, weirdly, is a kind of complacency: by voting for green candidates, riding a bicycle to work, avoiding air travel, you might feel that you've done everything you can for the only thing worth doing. Whereas, if you accept the reality that the planet will soon overheat to ¹⁵⁵ the point of threatening civilization, there's a whole lot more you should be doing. [...]

All-out war on climate change made sense only as long as it was winnable. Once you accept that we've lost it, other kinds of action take on greater meaning. Preparing for fires and floods and refu- ¹⁶⁰

pertinent *(fml.) sachdienlich* gees is a directly pertinent example. But the impending catastrophe heightens the urgency of almost any world-improving action. In times of increasing chaos, people seek protection in

tribalism *Stammessystem* tribalism and armed force, rather than in the rule of law, and our best defense against this kind of dystopia is to maintain function- ¹⁶⁵ ing democracies, functioning legal systems, functioning communities. In this respect, any movement toward a more just and civil society can now be considered a meaningful climate action. Securing fair elections is a climate action. Combatting extreme

to combat to fight wealth inequality is a climate action. Shutting down the hate ma- ¹⁷⁰ chines on social media is a climate action. Instituting humane immigration policy, advocating for racial and gender equality, promoting respect for laws and their enforcement, supporting a free

and independent press, ridding the country of assault weapons –
175 these are all meaningful climate actions. To survive rising temperatures, every system, whether of the natural world or of the
human world, will need to be as strong and healthy as we can
make it.

And then there's the matter of hope. If your hope for the future
180 depends on a wildly optimistic scenario, what will you do ten
years from now, when the scenario becomes unworkable even in
theory? Give up on the planet entirely? [...] Any good thing you
do now is arguably a hedge against the hotter future, but the really meaningful thing is that it's good today. As long as you have
185 something to love, you have something to hope for. [...]

There may come a time, sooner than any of us likes to think,
when the systems of industrial agriculture and global trade break
down and homeless people outnumber people with homes. At
that point, traditional local farming and strong communities will
190 no longer just be liberal buzzwords. Kindness to neighbors and
respect for the land – nurturing healthy soil, wisely managing
water, caring for pollinators – will be essential in a crisis and in
whatever society survives it. A project like the Homeless Garden
offers me the hope that the future, while undoubtedly worse than
195 the present, might also, in some ways, be better. Most of all,
though, it gives me hope for today.

https://www.newyorker.com/culture/cultural-comment/what-if-we-stopped-pretending,
8 September 2019 [26.01.2020]

hedge a way of protecting or controlling sth.

buzzword *Modewort, Phrase*

pollinator *Bestäuber*

Homeless Garden an organization in Santa Cruz, California, which offers gardening as self-employment for homeless people

Aldous Huxley
Brave New World

Aldous Huxley (1894–1963) was an English writer and philosopher and a firm believer in pacifism and humanism.

In his 1932 dystopian novel *Brave New World* Huxley portrays a futuristic world state whose inhabitants are genetically modified and live in an intelligence-based social hierarchy.

squat short and wide
hatchery *Brutanstalt*
conditioning *Konditionierung*

A squat grey building of only thirty-four storeys. Over the main entrance the words, CENTRAL LONDON HATCHERY AND CONDITIONING CENTRE, and, in a shield, the World State's motto, COMMUNITY, IDENTITY, STABILITY.

The enormous room on the ground floor faced towards the north. 5 Cold for all the summer beyond the panes, for all the tropical heat of the room itself, a harsh thin light glared through the windows, hungrily seeking some draped lay figure, some pallid shape of academic goose-flesh, but finding only the glass and nickel and bleakly shining porcelain of a laboratory. Wintriness responded 10 to wintriness. The overalls of the workers were white, their hands gloved with a pale corpse-coloured rubber. The light was frozen, dead, a ghost. Only from the yellow barrels of the microscopes did it borrow a certain rich and living substance, lying along the polished tubes like butter, streak after luscious streak in long reces- 15 sion down the work tables.

harsh unpleasantly bright
pallid very pale, unhealthy
goose-flesh *Gänsehaut*
bleak empty, unattractive

corpse *Leiche*

streak long thin line or mark
luscious *üppig*

to fertilize *befruchten*

"And this," said the Director opening the door, "is the Fertilizing Room."

Bent over their instruments, three hundred Fertilizers were plunged, as the Director of Hatcheries and Conditioning entered 20 the room, in the scarcely breathing silence, the absent-minded, soliloquizing hum or whistle, of absorbed concentration. A troop of newly arrived students, very young, pink and callow, followed nervously, rather abjectly, at the Director's heel. Each of them carried a note-book, in which, whenever the great man spoke, he 25 desperately scribbled. Straight from the horse's mouth. It was a rare privilege. The D.H.C. for Central London always made a point of personally conducting his new students round the various departments. [...]

to plunge in/into sth. (*phr. v.*) to force into an unpleasant situation

to soliloquize to speak to yourself
callow (*lit.*) young and inexperienced
abject very humble; *unterwürfig*

incubator a container in which a premature baby can be kept alive
test-tube *Reagenzglas*
ovum, ova egg produced by a woman
gamete *reife Keimzelle*
ram *Widder*
thermogene sth. that keeps you warm
to beget (*old use*) to be the father of

"These," he waved with his hand, "are the incubators." And open- 30 ing an insulated door he showed them racks upon racks of numbered test-tubes. "The week's supply of ova. Kept," he explained, "at blood heat, whereas the male gametes," and here he opened another door, "They have to be kept at thirty-five instead of thirty-seven. Full blood heat sterilizes." Rams wrapped in thermo- 35 gene beget no lambs.

Still leaning against the incubators he gave them, while the pencils scurried illegibly across the pages, a brief description of the modern fertilizing process; spoke first, of course, of its surgical
40 introduction – "the operation undergone voluntarily for the good of Society, not to mention the fact that is carries a bonus amounting to six months' salary; continued with some account of the technique for preserving the excised ovary alive and actively developing; passed on to a consideration of optimum temperature,
45 salinity, viscosity; referred to the liquor in which the detached and ripened eggs were kept; and, leading his charges to the work tables, actually showed them how this liquor was drawn off from the test-tubes; how it was let out drop by drop on to the specially warmed slides of the microscopes; how the eggs which it con-
50 tained were inspected for abnormalities, counted and transferred to a porous receptacle; how (and he now took them to watch the operation) this receptacle was immersed in a warm bouillon containing free-swimming spermatozoa – at a minimum concentration of one hundred thousand per cubic centimetre, he insisted;
55 and how, after ten minutes, the container was lifted out of the liquor and its contents re-examined; how, if any of the eggs remained unfertilized, it was again immersed, and, if necessary, yet again; how the fertilized ova went back to the incubators; where the Alphas and Betas remained until definitely bottled; while the
60 Gammas, Deltas and Epsilons were brought out again, after only thirty-six hours, to undergo Bokanovsky's Process.
"Bokanovsky's Process," repeated the Director, and the students underlined the words in their little note-books.
One egg, one embryo, one adult – normality. But a bokanovski-
65 fied egg will bud, will proliferate, will divide. From eight to ninety-six buds, and every bud will grow into a perfectly formed embryo, and every embryo into a full-sized adult. Making ninety-six human beings grow where only one grew before. Progress.
"Essentially," the D.H.C. concluded, "bokanovskification consists
70 of a series of arrests of developments. We check the normal growth and, paradoxically enough, the egg responds by budding."
Responds by budding. The pencils were busy.
He pointed. On a very slowly moving band a rack-full of test-tubes was entering a large metal box, another rack-full was
75 emerging.
Machinery faintly purred. It took eight minutes for the tubes to go through, he told them. Eight minutes of hard X-rays being about as much as an egg can stand. A few died; of the rest, the least susceptible divided into two, most put out four buds; some
80 eight; all were returned to the incubators, where the buds began to develop; then, after two days, were suddenly chilled, chilled

to scurry *huschen*
illegibly *unleserlich*
surgical *operativ*

to excise to remove by cutting out
ovary *Eierstock*

salinity salt content
viscosity *Zähflüssigkeit*
detached separated

slide *Objektträger*

porous *porös*

receptacle container
to immerse to place deep into sth.

to bud to produce buds (*Knospen*)
to proliferate grow and increase quickly

to purr to make a quiet, soft sound

susceptible easily harmed by sth.

to chill to make cold but not freeze

to be dosed with sth. *mit etw. vollgepumpt werden*
to burgeon to grow or develop rapidly
fatal very serious and bad

prodigious extremely great
piddling (*infml.*) small, unimportant
viviparous *lebendgebärend*

by scores (*fml.*) in large numbers
largesse donations, gifts

batch *Charge, Menge*

tremulous shaking; *zitternd*

to apply sth. to sth. *etw. anwenden auf etw.*

and checked. Two, four, eight, the buds in their turn budded, and having budded were dosed almost to death with alcohol; consequently burgeoned again and having budded – bud out of bud out of bud – were thereafter – further arrest being generally fatal – left to develop in peace. By which time the original egg was in a fair way to becoming anything from eight to ninety-six embryos – a prodigious improvement, you will agree, on nature. Identical twins – but not in piddling twos and threes as in the old viviparous days, when an egg would sometimes accidentally divide; actually by dozens, by scores at a time.

"Scores," the Director repeated and flung out his arms, as though he were distributing largesse. "Scores."

But one of the students was fool enough to ask where the advantage lay.

"My good boy!" The Director wheeled sharply round on him. "Can't you see? Can't you *see*?" He raised a hand; his expression was solemn. "Bokanovsky's Process is one of the major instruments of social stability!"

Major instruments of social stability.

Standard men and women; in uniform batches. The whole of a small factory staffed with the products of a single bokanovskified egg.

"Ninety-six identical twins working ninety-six identical machines!" The voice was almost tremulous with enthusiasm. "You really know where you are. For the first time in history." He quoted the planetary motto. "Community, Identity, Stability." Grand words. "If we could bokanovskify indefinitely the whole problem would be solved."

Solved by standard Gammas, unvarying Deltas, uniform Epsilons. Millions of identical twins. The principle of mass production at last applied to biology.

from *Brave New World* by Aldous Huxley. Vintage Classics, USA 2004, pp. 5 ff.

Salena Godden
Shade

Shade: Comparative darkness and coolness caused by shelter from direct sunlight.

inferiority *Minderwertigkeit*
obscurity the state of not being known to many people
kinda (*infml.*) kind of, sort of
shady *here*: likely to be dishonest or illegal

The darker part of a picture.

A position of relative inferiority or obscurity.

To publicly criticize or express contempt for someone, to act in a casual or disrespectful manner towards someone, throwing shade, acting kinda shady.

Sometimes I think I am about the same shade as Beyoncé. But it is hard to tell because it depends how much light they give her.
10 Some days I think I'm about the same shade as Rihanna but that's also difficult to say as she switches shade too. Your shade is not skin deep. Your shade is not just about your heart and soul; your religion and spirituality, your elders and your history, your connection to a country, to geography and to a time and place. Your
15 shade is an industry, your shade is a token, shade is a passport, shade is a cage and shade is a status.

token *Gutschein, Wertmarke*

You tick: Other.

[...]

to tick *Häkchen (in einem Formular) machen, ankreuzen*

Wherever you live, wherever you are from, it seems it is all about
20 shade. Universally we are divided and whatever shade you are born it is not right or good enough. We are in a giant brainwash, we are being organized by colour and tone, the natural shade of your skin must be improved, altered and filtered. Your skin is a living organ. Your skin is the casing for your sausage-meat soul.
25 And the armour for your muscles, bones ands flesh. Skin is the protective layer of the interior of you with the exterior world, but it is always wrong. You are too white or too black. Too light is bad? Too dark is bad? I get confused. I am in the middle here. Hang on a minute, what shade am I to you?
30 My mother is the same shade as Oprah or Maya. Some summers I have seen my big brother almost as brown as Idris but closer to Obama in the winter. Bob Marley was mixed, Jamaican and Celtic, same as me, his shade looks pale in some photos, sometimes much darker. You see, it all depends on the filter and the time of
35 year, it all depends on the light, it all depends on the shade. It depends on what point people are trying to make, to advertise things, to sell you things, to make money. That is the point, to get the shade right, to make shade the issue. To give shade, to put someone in the shade, to put someone in their place, to let some-
40 one know they are less, more or less, because of their shade. Advertising companies, big corporations, banks and politicians need to maintain this, to control the division of people through racism and shade, throwing shade of difference and indifference, good immigrant and bad immigrant, refugee and benefit scrounger.
45 This keeps us in our place, humans bickering, focusing on their differences, distracted, and at each other's throats, competing and separating –

to alter *to change*
casing *protective covering*
armour *Rüstung*
protective layer *Schutzschicht*

Oprah Oprah Winfrey (*1954) African American media executive, actress, television host and television producer
Maya Maya Angelou (1928–2014) African American poet and civil rights activist
Idris Idris Elba (*1972) British actor, producer and musician
Obama Barack Obama (*1961) US president (2008–2016)
Bob Marley (1945–1981) Jamaican singer and songwriter
to put sb. in their place to tell sb. that they are not as good or important as they thought

Divide and rule.

[...]

indifference lack of interest in sb./ sth.
benefit scrounger *Sozialschmarotzer*
to bicker to argue about things that are not important
distracted troubled, confused
divide and rule the gaining and maintaining of power by turning one's enemies against each other

50 Do you mind me asking you a question: where do you come from?

You tick: Other.

savvy (*infml.*) practical knowledge and ability, know-how

itinerant [*itin'ərənt*] travelling from place to place

[...]

Welcome aboard my Good Ship. Let us sail to the colourful island of mixed identity. You are free to use your own rules and savvy 55 because they haven't invented a filter for our shade yet. You are a pirate and you're itinerant. You eat from the cooking pot of mixed culture and bathe in the cool shade of being mixed-race. You disembark and hesitate, your pen hovers over your boarding pass.

You tick: Others. 60

[...]

flock a group of sheep or birds
shoal a large number of fish swimming in a group
in unison acting or speaking together

fickle *unbeständig*

Britain is an island surrounded by salt seawater and inhabited by people of every shade. On a whole I do not think of people as flocks of sheep but more as shoals of fish, swimming to find food and heat and migrating to survive. We could protect each other 65 better if we swam together in unison, we could protect each other from great white sharks dominating everything. We could, but we are like fish, as fickle as fish.

[...]

All I can do is keep on keeping on, keep sailing my Good Ship. 70

currency *Währung*

stained-glass window *Buntglasfenster*

to blend to mix or combine together

Human colour is the colour I'm truly interested in, the colour of your humanity. May the size of your heart and the depth of your soul be your currency. Welcome aboard my Good Ship. Let us sail to the colourful island of mixed identity. You can eat from the cooking pot of mixed culture and bathe in the cool shade of 75 being mixed-race. There is no need for a passport. There are no borders. We are all citizens of the world. Whatever shade you are, bring your light, bring your colour, bring your music and your books, your stories and your histories, and climb aboard. United as a people we are a million majestic colours, together we are a 80 glorious stained-glass window. We are building a cathedral of otherness, brick by brick and book by book. Raise your glass of rum, let's toast to the minorities who are the majority. There is no stopping time, nor the blurring of lines or the blending of shades. With a spirit of hope I leave you now. I drink to our sameness and 85 to our unique differences. This is the twenty-first century and we share this, we live here, in the future. It is a beautiful morning, it is first light on the time of being other, so get out from that shade and feel the warmth of being outside.

You tick: Other. 90

from *The Good Immigrant* by Nikesh Shukla (ed.). Unbound, London 2016, pp. 181 ff.

Christina Nuñez
Sea Level Rise, Explained

Oceans are rising around the world, causing dangerous flooding. Why is this happening, and what can we do to stem the tide?

As humans continue to pour greenhouse gases into the atmosphere, oceans have tempered the effect. The world's seas have absorbed more than 90 percent of the heat from these gases, but it's taking a toll on our oceans: 2018 set a new record for ocean heating.

Many people think of global warming and climate change as synonyms, but scientists prefer to use "climate change" when describing the complex shifts now affecting our planet's weather and climate systems.

Rising seas is one of those climate change effects. Average sea levels have swelled over 8 inches (about 23 cm) since 1880, with about three of those inches gained in the last 25 years. Every year, the sea rises another .13 inches (3.2 mm).

The change in sea levels is linked to three primary factors, all induced by ongoing global climate change:

Thermal expansion: When water heats up, it expands. About half of the sea-level rise over the past 25 years is attributable to warmer oceans simply occupying more space.

Melting glaciers: Large ice formations such as mountain glaciers naturally melt a bit each summer. In the winter, snows, primarily from evaporated seawater, are generally sufficient to balance out the melting. Recently, though, persistently higher temperatures caused by global warming have led to greater-than-average summer melting as well as diminished snowfall due to later winters and earlier springs. That creates an imbalance between runoff and ocean evaporation, causing sea levels to rise.

Loss of Greenland and Antarctica's ice sheets: As with mountain glaciers, increased heat is causing the massive ice sheets that cover Greenland and Antarctica to melt more quickly. Scientists also believe that meltwater from above and seawater from below is seeping beneath Greenland's ice sheets, effectively lubricating ice streams and causing them to move more quickly into the sea. While melting in West Antarctica has drawn considerable focus from scientists, especially with the 2017 break in the Larsen C ice shelf, glaciers in East Antarctica are also showing signs of destabilizing.

---

to stem sth. to stop
tide *Gezeiten, Flut*
greenhouse gases *Treibhausgase*

to temper to make sth. less strong/extreme

to take a toll on sb./sth. to cause damage to sb./sth.

to swell to become larger, to rise

to induce to cause sth. to happen

attributable to the result of
to occupy to fill, to use
glacier ['glæsiər]

runoff water that flows away from high areas to low areas
to evaporate *verdampfen*
ice sheet *Eiskappe*

meltwater *Schmelzwasser*
to seep *sickern*
to lubricate *gleitfähig machen*

Consequences

⁴⁰

When sea levels rise as rapidly as they have been, even a small increase can have devastating effects on coastal habitats farther inland, it can cause destructive erosion, wetland flooding, aquifer and agricultural soil contamination with salt, and lost habitat for fish, birds, and plants.

⁴⁵

Higher sea levels are coinciding with more dangerous hurricanes and typhoons that move more slowly and drop more rain, contributing to more powerful storm surges that can strip away everything in their path. One study found that between 1963 and 2012, almost half of all deaths from Atlantic hurricanes were caused by ⁵⁰ storm surges.

Already, flooding in low-lying coastal areas is forcing people to migrate to higher ground, and millions more are vulnerable from flood risk and other climate change effects. The prospect of higher coastal water levels threatens basic services such as Inter- ⁵⁵ net access, since much of the underlying communications infrastructure lies in the path of rising seas.

Adapting to the threat

As a result of these risks, many coastal cities are already planning adaptation measures to cope with the long-term prospects of ⁶⁰ higher sea levels, often at considerable cost. Building seawalls, rethinking roads, and planting mangroves or other vegetation to absorb water are all being undertaken.

In Jakarta, a $40 billion project will aim to protect the city with an 80-foot-high seawall. Rotterdam, home to the Global Center on ⁶⁵ Adaptation, has offered a model to other cities seeking to combat flooding and land loss. The Dutch city has built barriers, drainage, and innovative architectural features such as a "water square" with temporary ponds.

Of course, communities vulnerable to rising seas can only go so ⁷⁰ far in holding back the tide. In the Marshall Islands, where rising sea levels are forcing a choice between relocating or building up the land, residents will need help from other nations if they decide to undertake the expensive latter option.

How high will it go?

⁷⁵

Most predictions say the warming of the planet will continue and is likely to accelerate, causing the oceans to keep rising. This means hundreds of coastal cities face flooding. But forecasting how much and how soon seas will rise remains an area of ongoing research.

⁸⁰

The most recent special report from the Intergovernmental Panel on Climate Change says we can expect the oceans to rise between

---

devastating causing a lot of damage and destruction
aquifer ['ækwɪfər] *Grundwasserspeicher*
contamination *Verunreinigung*
habitat natural environment in which an animal or plant usually lives
typhoon a violent cyclonic storm found in the West Pacific area
surge *here*: sudden and powerful wave

prospect possibility that sth. might happen in the future

threat [θret] *Bedrohung*

mangrove tree that can grow in salt water

to combat to fight
drainage ['dreɪnɪdʒ] *Entwässerung*

to accelerate to go faster

10 and 30 inches (26 to 77 centimeters) by 2100 with temperatures warming 1.5 °C. That's enough to seriously affect many of the
85 cities along the U.S. East Coast. Another analysis based on NASA and European data skewed toward the higher end of that range, predicting a rise of 26 inches (65 centimeters) by the end of this century if the current trajectory continues.

If all the ice that currently exists on Earth in glaciers and sheets
90 melted it would raise sea level by 216 feet. That could cause entire states and even some countries to disappear under the waves, from Florida to Bangladesh. That's not a scenario scientists think is likely, and it would probably take many centuries, but it could eventually happen if the world keeps burning fossil fuels indis-
95 criminately.

In the meantime, scientists keep refining their models of sea-level changes. They also point out that the extent to which countries work together to limit release of more greenhouse gases may have a significant impact on how quickly seas rise, and how
100 much.

https://www.nationalgeographic.com/environment/global-warming/sea-level-rise/,
19 February 2019 [19.01.2020]

to affect sb./sth. to have negative effects on sb./sth.

to skew toward to be biased in a particular direction

trajectory *Entwicklungsverlauf*

indiscriminately without careful choice or planning, usually with harmful results
to refine to improve sth.

release the act of setting free

Die Ozeane früher …

… und heute

McKinsey Global Institute

Global Migration's Impact and Opportunity

flashpoint controversial topic

McKinsey Global Institute
American management consulting
firm and research organization

Migration has become a flashpoint for debate in many countries. But McKinsey Global Institute research finds that it generates significant economic benefits – and more effective integration of immigrants could increase those benefits.

Migration is a key feature of our increasingly interconnected world. It has also become a flashpoint for debate in many countries, which underscores the importance of understanding the patterns of global migration and the economic impact that is created when people move across the world's borders. A new report ₁₀ from the McKinsey Global Institute (MGI), *People on the move: Global migration's impact and opportunity,* aims to fill this need. Refugees might be the face of migration in the media, but 90 percent of the world's 247 million migrants have moved across borders voluntarily, usually for economic reasons. Voluntary migra- ₁₅ tion flows are typically gradual, placing less stress on logistics and on the social fabric of destination countries than refugee flows. Most voluntary migrants are working-age adults, a characteristic that helps raise the share of the population that is economically active in destination countries. ₂₀

By contrast, the remaining 10 percent are refugees and asylum seekers who have fled to another country to escape conflict and persecution. Roughly half of the world's 24 million refugees are in the Middle East and North Africa, reflecting the dominant pattern of flight to a neighboring country. But the recent surge of ₂₅ arrivals in Europe has focused the developed world's attention on this issue. A companion report, *Europe's new refugees: A road map for better integration outcomes,* examines the challenges and opportunities confronting individual countries.

While some migrants travel long distances from their origin ₃₀ countries, most migration still involves people moving to neighboring countries or to countries in the same part of the world. About half of all migrants globally have moved from developing to developed countries – indeed, this is the fastest-growing type of movement. Almost two-thirds of the world's migrants reside in ₃₅ developed countries, where they often fill key occupational shortages. From 2000 to 2014, immigrants contributed 40 to 80 percent of labor-force growth in major destination countries.

Moving more labor to higher-productivity settings boosts global GDP. Migrants of all skill levels contribute to this effect, whether ₄₀

gradual happening or changing
slowly

to flee (fled, fled) to escape

persecution *Verfolgung*

flight escape

to reside to live

occupational relating to your job

GDP [ˌdʒiːdiːˈpiː] (*abbr.*) Gross
Domestic Product; the total value
of goods and services produced by
a country in a year

through innovation and entrepreneurship or through freeing up natives for higher-value work. In fact, migrants make up just 3.4 percent of the world's population, but MGI's research finds that they contribute nearly 10 percent of global GDP. They contrib-
45 uted roughly $6.7 trillion to global GDP in 2015 – some $3 trillion more than they would have produced in their origin countries. Developed nations realize more than 90 percent of this effect.

Employment rates are slightly lower for immigrants than for native workers in top destinations, but this varies by skill level and
50 by region of origin. Extensive academic evidence shows that immigration does not harm native employment or wages, although there can be short-term negative effects if there is a large inflow of migrants to a small region, if migrants are close substitutes for native workers, or if the destination economy is experiencing a
55 downturn.

Realizing the benefits of immigration hinges on how well new arrivals are integrated into their destination country's labor market and into society. Today immigrants tend to earn 20 to 30 percent less than native-born workers. But if countries narrow that
60 wage gap to just 5 to 10 percent by integrating immigrants more effectively across various aspects of education, housing, health, and community engagement, they could generate an additional boost of $800 billion to $1 trillion to worldwide economic output annually. This is a relatively conservative goal, but it can never-
65 theless produce broader positive effects, including lower poverty rates and higher overall productivity in destination economies.

The economic, social, and civic dimensions of integration need to be addressed holistically. MGI looked at how the leading destinations perform on 18 indicators and found that no country has
70 achieved strong integration outcomes across all of these dimensions, though some do better than others. But in destinations around the world, many stakeholders are trying new approaches. We identify more than 180 promising interventions that offer useful models for improving integration. The private sector has a
75 central role to play in this effort – and incentives to do so. When companies participate, they stand to gain access to new markets and pools of new talent.

The stakes are high. The success or failure of integration can reverberate for many years, influencing whether second-genera-
80 tion immigrants become fully participating citizens who reach their full productive potential or remain in a poverty trap.

Jonathan Woetzel, Anu Madgavkar, Khaled Rifai, Frank Mattern, Jacques Bughin, James Manyika, Tarek Elmasry, Amadeo di Lodovico, and Ashwin Hasyagar; https://www.mckinsey.com/featured-insights/employment-and-growth/global-migrations-impact-and-opportunity, 30 November 2016 [18.01.2020]

---

entrepreneurship [ˌɒntrəprəˈnɜːʃɪp] *Unternehmergeist*

trillion a million million

to harm to damage

close *unmittelbar*
substitute *Ersatz*

downturn downward trend
to hinge on sb./sth. (*phr. v.*) to depend on sb./sth.

to generate to produce

annually each year

civic *bürgerlich*
holistically in a way that deals with the whole; *ganzheitlich*

stakeholder *Interessenvertreter*
approach the way of considering or doing sth.
intervention *Eingreifen*
incentive *Anreiz*

pool group
stake *Einsatz*
to reverberate to continue to have effects

Most migration consists of people moving to another country in the same part of the world.

Top 10 regional movements,[1] total migrant population in millions, 2015

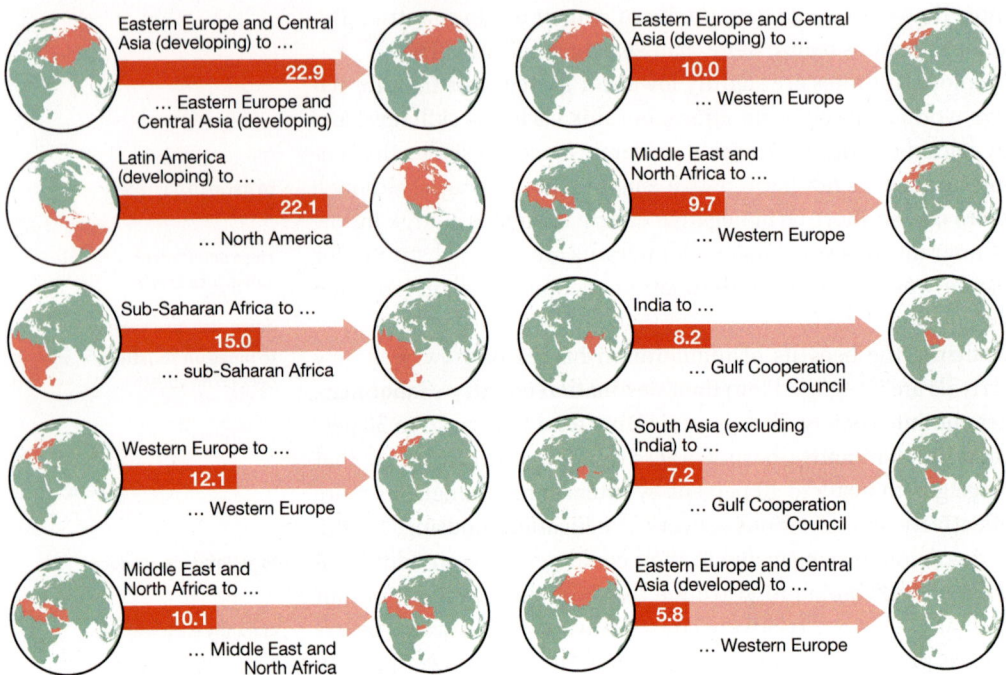

Eastern Europe and Central Asia (developing) to …
22.9
… Eastern Europe and Central Asia (developing)

Eastern Europe and Central Asia (developing) to …
10.0
… Western Europe

Latin America (developing) to …
22.1
… North America

Middle East and North Africa to …
9.7
… Western Europe

Sub-Saharan Africa to …
15.0
… sub-Saharan Africa

India to …
8.2
… Gulf Cooperation Council

Western Europe to …
12.1
… Western Europe

South Asia (excluding India) to …
7.2
… Gulf Cooperation Council

Middle East and North Africa to …
10.1
… Middle East and North Africa

Eastern Europe and Central Asia (developed) to …
5.8
… Western Europe

[1]Includes movement both between and within regions.

Source: United Nations Department of Economic and Social Affairs; World Bank; McKinsey Global Institute analysis

McKinsey&Company

Joachim Scholl

John Lanchester: „Die Mauer" –
Der Klimawandel als dunkle Dystopie

Seit einer furchtbaren Klimakatastrophe schottet eine 10.000 Kilometer lange Mauer Großbritannien vom Rest der Welt ab. Klimaflüchtlinge werden eingeschläfert oder versklavt. Die Idee zu seinem wohl schwärzesten Roman
5 **kam John Lanchester in einem Traum.**

Joachim Scholl: Wir machen jetzt mit dem britischen Schriftsteller John Lanchester einen Gang auf eine Mauer. Für seinen neuen Roman, der genauso heißt, „The Wall", die Mauer, hat er sich eine tiefschwarze Dystopie über eine Zukunft ausgedacht,
10 die vielleicht schon begonnen hat. Willkommen, John Lanchester, welcome!

John Lanchester: Thank you for having me!

Scholl: Bei dem Begriff, Mr. Lanchester, „The Wall", die Mauer, da hagelt es Assoziationen. Man denkt natürlich an die Berliner
15 Mauer, ältere Musikfans vielleicht noch an Pink Floyds depressives „The Wall"-Album, Jüngeren kommt die Mauer in der Fantasy-Serie „Game of Thrones" in den Sinn, und dann gibt es natürlich diesen amerikanischen Präsidenten, der auch unbedingt eine Mauer bauen will. Was hatten Sie im Kopf, John Lanchester? Wie
20 hat sich diese Mauer bei Ihnen aufgebaut?

Lanchester: Es begann mit einem Traum. Ich war eigentlich dabei, ein anderes Buch zu schreiben, als ich einen immer wiederkehrenden Traum hatte von einem Mann, der Wache steht an einer Mauer, ganz alleine, im Dunkeln. Auf der anderen Seite
25 befindet sich das Meer. Und dieser wiederkehrende Traum, der entwickelte seine eigene Welt, die sich dann zu einer eigenen Geschichte entwickelt hat. [...]

Scholl: 10.000 Kilometer lang soll sie sein, Ihre Mauer, ein ganzes Land im Norden umfassen. Wo steht sie denn genau, diese Mauer?
30 Und wozu ist sie da?

Lanchester: Sie haben ja vielleicht schon ganz gut geraten, aber ich wollte diesen Ort und vor allen Dingen auch den Namen Großbritannien hier nicht näher erwähnen, das war mir zu direkt als eine Assoziation. Aber natürlich befindet sich das irgendwie
35 nördlich der irischen Inseln.

Wir leben eben hier in einer Welt, die sich abgeschottet hat, die eine Festung gebaut hat nach einer Klimakatastrophe. Die entwickelte Welt schottet sich hinter einer Festung ab, um diejenigen nicht mehr hereinzulassen, die man einfach nur noch „die
40 anderen" nennt.

abschotten to separate from, to seal off

einschläfern to euthanise

Berliner Mauer Berlin Wall

Pink Floyd (1965–2014) a British rock band, famous for their psychedelic rock and philosophical lyrics

immer wiederkehrend repeated

Festung fortress

Scholl: Ja, und diese anderen, die kommen mit Booten übers Meer, sie sind bewaffnet, sie stürmen die Mauer, werden reihenweise getötet. Wer es dennoch schafft, kommt aber nicht weit, weil inzwischen jeder Mensch einen Körperchip tragen muss in dieser düsteren Zukunft. Und der Flüchtling, der bekommt dann die Wahl: Entweder wird er eingeschläfert oder darf als sogenannter Dienstling, sprich als Sklave arbeiten. 45

Aber „die anderen", „diese anderen", sie kommen trotzdem, so oder so. Ist das Ihre Vision, Mr. Lanchester, für unsere Welt? [...]

Lanchester: Ich glaube nicht, dass das die Zukunft sein wird, aber eine Zukunft, eine mögliche Zukunft, auf die wir uns wirklich zu entwickeln, wenn es dabei bleibt, wie sich diese Gesellschaft verändert und auch wie sich das Klima derzeit verändert. 50

Allerdings glaube ich nicht, dass es schon zu spät ist. Und indem ich mir das so vorstelle, indem ich mir das so ausmale, hoffe ich, vielleicht einen kleinen Teil dazu beitragen zu können, dass die Vision dann doch nicht wahr wird. 55

Scholl: Diese Zeit, die Sie beschreiben in Ihrem Buch, Mr. Lanchester, ist die Zeit nach dem Wandel, nach dem Change. Sie haben schon erwähnt, das ist ein furchtbarer Klimawandel: Es gibt keine Strände mehr auf der Welt, Flugzeuge fliegen nicht mehr, die Zeit des Überflusses ist auch sozusagen vorbei. Und in dieser Zeit lernen wir hier ja jetzt den Helden kennen, Joseph Kavanagh heißt er, ein junger Mann, der sich für zwei Jahre auf der Mauer verpflichtet. 60 65

Und dieser Held, dieser junge Mann, und seine Kameraden, die hegen einen tiefen Groll gegen die ältere Generation, auch gegen die eigenen Eltern, denn diese Generation hat das Land ihrer Meinung nach an die Wand gefahren. „Wer hat die Welt kaputt gemacht?", heißt es an einer Stelle. Sie würden niemals zugeben, dass sie es waren, und doch ist es direkt vor ihren Augen geschehen. 70

Fürchten Sie, Herr Lanchester, dass es so weit kommt, dass unsere Kinder, Ihre Kinder, Ihre Enkel später sagen werden: Du hast versagt, du bist schuld gewesen, dass wir jetzt so leben müssen? [...] 75

Lanchester: Also es war eine mögliche Vorstellung, die ich hatte, als ich darüber nachgedacht habe: Was würde passieren, wenn sich das Klima nur um vier Grad erwärmt? Das wird ja von vielen Klimaforschern durchaus als möglich erachtet. Es hätte ja katastrophale Veränderungen – auf die Weltkarte, auf unsere Gesellschaft –, aber ich habe mir auch gerade ausgemalt, dass es auch ganz starke Veränderungen auf innermenschliche Beziehungen hat: Leute aus unserer Welt und Leute aus einer anderen Welt, wie die sich gegenüberstehen. 80 85

---

bewaffnet armed
reihenweise in large numbers

Dienstling servant

sich etw. ausmalen to envision, to imagine

Überfluss abundance

sich verpflichten to be conscripted

Groll hegen to bear a grudge

etw. an die Wand fahren to run sth. aground

versagen to fail
Schuld haben to be guilty of sth.

innermenschlich intrapersonal

Und das ist eine Frage, die sich jetzt nicht nur Leute stellen, die Kinder haben, das ist nicht nur eine Frage, die sich Eltern stellen, dazu habe ich mich zu sehr auch umgehört. Aber ich bin Vater, und als Vater habe ich mir das ausgemalt, was das auf das Familienleben für einen Einfluss haben könnte, und das könnte zu Brüchen führen innerhalb von Familien.

sich umhören to ask around

Bruch disruption

Die Figur in meinem Roman, Kavanagh, der macht daraus eine persönliche Geschichte, und das kann man sich sehr gut vorstellen, dass das auch so geschieht. [...]

95 **Scholl:** „Es ist kalt auf der Mauer", das ist der erste Satz Ihres Romans, und damit ist der Ton auch gesetzt für das ganze Buch: Es ist kalt, dunkel, trostlos. Wenn man Ihre anderen Romane kennt, dann muss man schon schlucken, Mr. Lanchester, so kein Funken Humor am Ende, auch kaum ein Lichtlein am Ende des
100 Tunnels.

trostlos leak, dismal

schlucken müssen (infml.) to take sth.
ein Funke Humor a spark of humour
Licht am Ende des Tunnels light at the end of the tunnel
Trost comfort

Es ist der schwärzeste Roman, wie ich finde, den Sie je geschrieben haben. Wie hat sich das denn angefühlt beim Schreiben?

Lanchester: Nun, es gibt schon ein bisschen Trost, was die zwischenmenschlichen Beziehungen angeht. Wenn man in so einer
105 Gesellschaft lebt und wenn so eine Dystopie praktisch wahr geworden ist, dann fühlt man sich ja nun nicht jeden Tag so dystopisch. Man begrüßt sich ja nicht gegenseitig und fragt sich, na, wie dystopisch fühlst du dich denn heute? Und es ist auch nicht alles so dunkel und auch nicht alles so schwarz, wie es vielleicht
110 erscheint.

Ich hab es auch mit Humor versucht, als ich das Buch schrieb, hab es dann aber wieder herausgenommen, weil es nicht gepasst hat. Humor schafft immer auch eine gewisse Distanz und eine gewisse Verfremdung, und das funktionierte nicht mit der emotionalen
115 Tonlage vom Rest des Buches. Deswegen hab ich's dann wieder rausgenommen, weil es nicht funktioniert hat.

Verfremdung alienation
emotionale Tonlage emotional pitch

Scholl: Ihr Roman hat schon, bevor er überhaupt gedruckt war, Spekulationen ausgelöst. Seit dem Roman und weltweiten Bestseller „Kapital" plus zwei Sachbüchern über die Finanzkrise sind
120 Sie zu einer Art gesellschaftskritischer Instanz auch geworden. Und jetzt haben natürlich alle vermutet, dass „The Wall" der Brexit-Roman werden wird. Das ist er definitiv nicht, es fallen keine Namen von Ländern oder Politikern, es entsteht für meine Begriffe so eine Art Orwell-1984-Atmosphäre. War das Ihre Ab-
125 sicht? [...]

Sachbuch non-fiction book

George Orwell (1903–1950) English novelist, journalist and critic, famous for dystopian novels like *Animal Farm* and *Nineteen Eighty-Four*

Lanchester: Also ich hatte den Brexit nicht wirklich im Kopf, als ich das Buch geschrieben habe. Der Klimawandel war etwas, was mich sehr viel mehr beschäftigt hat. Und als ich 2016 anfing, mich an dieses Buch zu setzen, da war das eher ein Zufall, dass der
130 Brexit dann plötzlich ein Thema wurde.

Ja, es gibt eine emotionale und auch eine metaphorische Ebene vielleicht in diesem Buch, aber der Brexit – wenn meine Kinder mein Alter haben werden, wird das keine große Rolle mehr spielen, man wird sich arrangiert haben mit der EU. Ich bin wirklich der Meinung, der Brexit ist etwas Vorübergehendes, das werden 135 wir überwinden.

Aber dieser Klimawandel, das ist eben etwas, was sehr viel mehr Einfluss auf uns haben wird und was viel, viel nachhaltiger sein wird.

Scholl: Im zweiten Teil des Buches findet sich der Held Kavanagh 140 auch jenseits der Mauer, denn das ist die finstere Konsequenz. Wenn die anderen es über die Mauer schaffen, werden die verantwortlichen Verteidiger bestraft und auf dem Meer ausgesetzt. Auch da ist man verblüfft über Ihre Grausamkeit, Mr. Lanchester, gegenüber den Figuren, denen ersparen Sie ja wirklich nichts. [...] 145

Lanchester: Nun, Kavanagh ist sozusagen unser Erzähler, und natürlich sympathisieren wir mit ihm, er gehört aber einer Gesellschaft an, die zutiefst verstört ist, zutiefst kaputt und korrupt ist, auch ethisch. Es ist eine Sklavengesellschaft. Das sieht er aber nicht. Dieses ethische Erwachen kommt erst dadurch zustande, 150 dass mit ihm dramatische Dinge geschehen, aber er hat diese Welt eigentlich immer so akzeptiert, wie sie ist, diese düstere Welt, insofern ändert sich nichts an der Düsternis dieser Welt.

Scholl: Im ersten Teil ist Ihr Buch, Mr. Lanchester, ein Action-geladener Silvester-Stallone-Bruce-Willis-Streifen, so hab ich ihn 155 jedenfalls gelesen, später auf dem Wasser eine knallharte Kevin-Costner-„Waterworld". Ich hab sofort einen Film im Kopf gehabt. Es könnte tatsächlich einen Mordsfilm geben oder eine Serie. Hat sich Hollywood oder Netflix schon gemeldet?

Lanchester: Nun, diese Produzenten sind herzlich willkommen 160 sich bei mir zu melden. Sicher gibt es Interesse von Hollywood und auch vom Fernsehen, aber ich sehe das wirklich sehr pragmatisch. Ich glaube erst daran, nachdem es wirklich passiert ist, nachdem es wirklich gedreht worden ist. Weil sie sagen immer, dass sie definitiv Interesse haben, was bedeutet, eigentlich haben 165 sie definitiv kein Interesse.

Scholl: Danke Ihnen, John Lanchester, für den Besuch, thank you for coming!

Lanchester: Thank you very much!

https://www.deutschlandfunkkultur.de/john-lanchester-die-mauer-der-klimawandel-als-dunkle.1270.de.html?dram:article_id=440091, 4 February 2019 [18.01.2020]

---

etwas Vorübergehendes something temporary
überwinden to overcome

nachhaltig sustainable

finster gloomy, sinister

verblüfft stunned
Grausamkeit cruelty
jdm. etw. ersparen to spare sb. sth.
sympathisieren to sympathise
verstört unhinged
kaputt broken

Düsternis gloom

Waterworld a 1995 post-apocalyptic action film starring Kevin Costner and dealing with a world suffering from rising sea levels due to the melting of the polar icecaps
Mordsfilm a terrific, tremendous film
pragmatisch pragmatically, realistically

Skills & vocabulary

Structure and characteristic features of a novel

A novel is an **extended work of fiction** or **prose narrative** which consists of **a connected sequence of events**. It can greatly differ in length and complexity.

Prose (= written or spoken language in its ordinary form, without metrical structure) is the most common form of language, because it applies to the natural flow and the grammatical structure of speech.

Historical development

The word *novel* derives from the Italian word *novella* (= new).

Early examples of this literary genre are Giovanni Boccacio's *Decamerone* (1354), Geoffrey Chaucer's *The Canterbury Tales* (1386–1400), Miguel Cervantes' *Don Quixote* (1605/1615) and Christoffel von Grimmelshausen's *Simplicissimus Teutsch* (1666/68). Particularly Gutenberg's invention of the printing press in 1440, made the printing and publication of books a lot easier and available to a wider public.

In the **19th century**, famous English novelists included Charles Dickens (e. g. *Oliver Twist*, 1839) and Mary Shelley (*Frankenstein*, 1823); Well-known American writers of that time included Herman Melville (*Moby Dick*, 1851), Harriet Beecher-Stowe (*Uncle Tom's Cabin*, 1852) and Mark Twain (*Tom Sawyer and Huckleberry Finn*, 1884).

Famous representatives of **modernism and post modernism** are F. Scott Fitzgerald (*The Great Gatsby*, 1925), Alfred Döblin (*Berlin Alexanderplatz*, 1929), John Steinbeck, (*The Grapes of Wrath*, 1939) and Paul Auster (*New York Trilogy* (1985/86), *Moon Palace*, 1989).

There are many **different types and styles of novels**, for example, romance, horror, mystery, satire, comedy, science fiction, fantasy, coming of age and gothic novels.

Famous and popular **coming-of-age novels** (*Entwicklungsroman*), depicting the development of the protagonist's mind and character, commonly from childhood to maturity – and often through a spiritual crisis – are: J. D. Salinger's *The Catcher in the Rye* (1951), John Irving's *A Prayer for Owen Meany* (1989) and Stephen Chbosky's *The Perks of Being a Wallflower* (1999).

Characteristic features

In general, novels have a **fictitious but largely plausible content**, and tell **one or multiple stories** which usually are a **combination of prose and dialogue**.

As novels are usually quite long, they give room to the development of the plot and the character(s), presented in more or less complex situations and often in intertwined storylines which are connected and resolved in the course of the story.

Narrator/writer/author

The **narrator of a novel often has a third-person omniscient** ("all-knowing", "all-seeing") **point of view**, having insights into the characters' thoughts and emotions. However, other points of view or kinds of narrator are possible.

- The **first-person narrator** is a character of the story and has a limited point of view. He/she only reveals information from his/her perspective and often addresses the reader directly.
- Often, an **interior monologue** or **stream of consciousness** approach is used to express his/her thoughts and feelings. As this type of narrator only has a limited insight into other characters' thoughts, he/she is often subjective and unreliable in his/her way of perceiving the events and characters. The stream of consciousness technique involves an **unbroken current** of feelings, impressions, fantasies, half-formed thoughts and awareness in which the narrator is independent in time.
- The **witness/observer narrator** is a character in a story, but usually takes a rather **objective point of view**.

Narration

There are several ways and techniques of narrating a novel that can be used.

- The narrator can vary the mode of presentation. He/she can use **panoramic presentation** in which the narrator <u>tells</u> the story in a condensed series of events, summarizing in a few sentences what can happen over a long period of time. In the **scenic presentation**, the narrator <u>shows</u> an event in detail as it occurs, using dialogue, depicting thoughts and emotions, describing a scene, etc.
- As a consequence, the **acting time** (*erzählte Zeit*) and **narrating time** (= reading time) can greatly differ and can be used to slow down action (element of **retardation**) or speed it up.
- Novels can be told **in retrospection**, i. e. a narrator talking about or reflecting and contemplating on an event in the past (e. g. in **flashbacks**), or there can be **foreshadowing**, i. e. there are indications about what might or will happen in the future.

to contemplate *betrachten, über etw. nachdenken*

Structure

- Novels are usually rather complex in their structure and development of the **plot** (= the sequence of events), often developing several intertwined storylines.
- The **plot** usually poses a problem which is resolved at the end or

in the course of the novel. There can even be a "story within a story" that can encompass a **long time span** and **different settings**.

- The **setting** (= time + place/social conditions) of novels can vary a great deal; it can be limited to a certain place and time but a novel can also tell a story that takes place at a variety of places and can extend over centuries.
- Usually, novels begin with an **exposition**, which introduces the main character(s), the setting and background of the story, often leaving the reader with certain questions which evoke his/her curiosity and will then be answered in the course of the story.
- Novelists often employ the so-called **"emotional extremes" technique**, i.e. exposing the characters to extreme situations such as happiness, sadness, painful or comic situations, thus making the reader feel empathy with the character's happiness and/or suffering.
- An important element of prose narrative is employing **elements of suspense** to hold on to the interest and anticipation of the reader.

Characters

The characters depicted in novels can have various backgrounds, depending on the plot and setting of the novel. There is no specific type of character that stands out. However, e.g. in a **coming-of-age novel**, the protagonist is typically a teenager or child, often a so-called "loner" or outsider who is suffering from an emotional or spiritual crisis caused by his/her parents, peers, etc. Sometimes, these characters experience extreme isolation or pressure, which makes them look at their environment from a new perspective.

Analysing a novel

When analysing a novel, it is important to pay attention to details. The following is a list of specific features of novels and questions related to them that will help you to examine and analyse central aspects of a novel.

Theme

Generally, a theme expresses the author's ideas and concerns about societal issues, loss, revenge, justice, etc.
- What is the novel's story theme?
- How does the author implement the theme, e.g. through images – characters – action – direct/indirect statements?
- How does the central action and storyline of the novel reveal the theme?

Plot

A novel's storyline, the order of action and incidents, is referred to as the plot.

to evolve to develop gradually

- How does the plot evolve?
- (How) Does the author build suspense? For example by
  - slowly revealing events
  - shifting between the past and present
  - use of memories
  - use of flashbacks or foreshadowing

to blur etw. verschwimmen lassen

  - blurring memory
- How do conflicts help develop the plot? E. g. by
  - unsaid things between characters – dramatic irony

annoyance Verärgerung

  - anger – surprise – annoyance – (interior) monologue
  - dialogue – questions – commands – sentence length

hesitation Zögern

  - hesitation – use of interruptions

Conflict

Conflict can be between two or more characters or simply one character (= **inner conflict**). Conflict can be verbal, physical or non-verbal (psychological).

- Where does the conflict lie?
- Is the conflict
  - between two characters – within one character
  - between a character and his/her surroundings?
- How is the conflict developed?
- (How) Is the conflict resolved?
- Is the central conflict reinforced by other conflicts, e. g. between minor characters or in the setting?

Characters

Authors often use the characters to convey their messages or as a vehicle to convey their thoughts, values and criticism.
Characters bring stories to life.

- Does the character have a major or minor role in the central action of the novel?
- What happens to the character throughout the novel?
- What changes does he/she undergo?
- What is the character's fate, his/her place in society?
- What are the character's strengths and weaknesses?
- How fully developed is/are the character(s)?
- (How) is the reader led to like or dislike the character?
- Do the characters convey their thoughts through monologues/dialogue?

Structure

The structure of a novel reveals a lot about the author's intention and message.

- How is the novel structured?
- What is the effect and purpose of the structure?
- Is there a certain chronology or chain of events?
- How are leitmotif(s), climax, denouement, etc. placed within the novel? What impact do they have?
- Are there flashbacks, foreshadowing, inserted parts or omissions?
- Are there any elements of surprise?

Time

The use (or lack) of time is an important element for structuring a novel and conveying a certain message to the reader.

- When is the novel set (past – present – future)?
- Are there different layers/levels/shifts of time?
- Are the characters preoccupied with time?

Symbolism/imagery

The use of symbols is most common in narrative texts and can be found in various elements:

- objects and setting descriptions
- the characters' appearance, gestures and movement
- the employment of leitmotifs
- the characters themselves
- What images are used?
- How does the imagery help bring out the theme?

Setting

The setting (= time and place/social conditions) helps to give the reader orientation about where and when a certain action takes place.

- Does the setting have any particular significance?
- Does it add to the mood/theme of the novel? How?
- Does the setting change? How?
- What does the setting symbolize?

significance relevance, importance

Key lines

In some texts, certain key lines may reveal and convey the message of the novel.

- Are there specific lines that convey the central message/theme of the story as a whole?
- Are certain lines repeated?
- What leitmotifs do these lines convey?
- What implications does the title of the novel have?

Characterizing a figure in literature

Fictional characters can be presented in a number of ways. In general, a character in a fictional text is developed through action, description, language and ways of speaking.

Types of characters

relevance in the text and characteristics	
• **protagonist** the main character around whom most of the work revolves	• **major characters** main characters who dominate the story
• **antagonist** the person who the protagonist is against; often the villain	• **minor characters** less important characters who interact with the main characters, thus helping to reveal the main characters' personalities, etc.
• **the modern** hero the average man/woman	• **dynamic/round character** three-dimensional, changing and developing personality, unique and different set of traits
• **the anti-hero** often dishonest, graceless or inept person who struggles in life; the loser	• **static/flat character** one-dimensional, unchanging, often stereotypical
• **the tragic hero** e. g. *Macbeth*; person who ends tragically as a result of their personal flaws	
• **romantic** hero a character with a strong will and personality who goes against established norms; often this figure experiences melancholy, isolation and unfulfilled and unhappy love	
• **the Hemingway hero** a character who has been to war, drinks too much, the loner, "cowboy"	

Types of characterization in literature

- In a **direct characterization of a character** the author or one of the other characters **tells** the readers/audience what the character's personality is like.
- In an **indirect characterization** the author **shows/presents** the character through talking and acting, which reveals the character's personality. Indirect characterization can be achieved through:
  a) **Speech** (What does the character say, how does he/she communicate and interact with others?)
  b) **Thoughts** (What is revealed through the person's private thoughts, e. g. in a monologue, soliloquy, etc.?)
  c) **Effect** on others/on the character (How does the person respond to others? Does he/she have many relationships? How do others react to the person?)

d) **Actions** (What does the person do, how does he/she behave?)

e) **Looks** (appearance, body language, gestures, facial expressions, etc.)

Analysing the character of a figure in literature

In your analysis, focus on <u>how</u> a character does or says sth.

- How is the character's mood, feelings and way of thinking, his/her nature and beliefs reflected in his/her manner of speaking, choice of words and use of language in general?
- What additional devices help to flesh out a character to the reader?

Consider the following aspects and what they reveal about a character:

language register	formal, informal, slang, sociolect
choice of words	positive/negative emotive words, metaphorical language
imagery	use of simile, metaphors, personification
sentence structure	long or short sentences, repetition, rhetorical questions, exclamation, climax, antithesis
tone	ironic, sarcastic, upbeat, pessimistic, serious, light, nostalgic, humorous, pompous
sound effects	alliteration, onomatopoeia
action	• How does the character move and act? (standing, moving around, relaxed, hectic, etc.)
objects, clothing	• What are the characters holding and wearing? When?
setting	• Where does the character live? Are there changes? • What does the setting reveal about the character(s) in general (e.g. suburb, megacity, castle, prison, etc.)?
relationships / conversational behaviour	• Who has the most text/lines? • Who has the most turns *(Auftritte)*? • Who has the longest turns? • Who interrupts who? • Who is interrupted? • Who allocates *(zuteilen)* or turns to whom? • Who initiates conversational exchanges and who responds? How? • Who uses speech acts like questioning, commanding, threatening and complaining? • Who uses speech acts like answering, agreeing, acceding *(zustimmen)*, giving in and apologizing? • Who controls/changes the topic of talk? • Who uses "title + surname" terms of address? • Who uses "first name" terms of address?

How to write a literary characterization

Step 1: Collect facts and clues given in the text and move from the outward features and characteristics to the inward nature of the character.

- **personal data** (name, age, sex, nationality)
- **outward appearance** (body, face, clothes, etc.)
- **attitudes/views** (thoughts, dreams, emotions)
- **behaviour** (toward other characters, actions)
- **relationships** (social background, family, friends)

Step 2: Draw your conclusion about the person's character and relate your findings to the text by referring to specific lines. Use the simple present for your characterization.

Step 3: Follow the "introduction – main part – conclusion" pattern in your characterization. Write an introductory sentence that answers the w-questions.

Tip: Do not simply quote what a character says but **first** say what the character's feelings/mood are, **then** quote examples of the text for each separate aspect and explain e. g. what the choice of words suggests or how a certain action shows the character's emotions.

Vary the way you quote from the text, e. g. by

- **referring** to an important part of the text (→ cf., cp.)
- **integrating a quotation** into your sentence, e. g. *Sarge reminds Kavanagh and Hifa to be "back on shift in thirty minutes" (p. 63, ll. 44 f.).*
- **using a full quotation**, e. g. *Hifa says that they "have to go down one more time, to check the ropes" (p. 161, l. 11).*
- **note the abbreviations:**
  - one page or line: p. 8, l. 16
  - two or more pages or lines: pp. 4 – 7, ll. 16 – 22
  - the following page(s), line(s): f./ff. (e. g. pp. 20 f. or ll. 15 ff.)

- **omissions** of any kind are indicated by square brackets and three dots: […]
- **remarks or changes from the original text** are indicated by square brackets: *She [Hifa] told Kavanagh that …*

Vocabulary: Narrative texts and characters

narrative texts	
character	a) a person in a fictional story b) qualities of a person
conflict	a struggle between different forces that produces suspense
internal conflict	a struggle between two opposing views or values that takes place in a character's mind
(leit)motif	a theme/expression/object that recurs throughout the text and represents a certain person, situation or atmosphere
open ending	the conflict remains unsolved → the reader is left to reflect on possible resolutions himself
plot	the author's selection and structure of action as a set of events connected by cause and effect that are meant to create suspense
setting	place/social conditions and time of a story
surprise ending	a sudden and unexpected turn of fortune or events
suspense	a feeling of tension/expectation
tension	the emotional strain caused by a conflict
acting time	the time from the beginning to the end of an episode in a text; this is usually longer than the narrating time because the writer can describe the passing of years in just a sentence; *erzählte Zeit*
interior monologue	a technique used within stream of consciousness; a special kind of scenic presentation, often not in chronological order
mode of presentation	the way the writer narrates events; *Darstellungsart*
panoramic presentation	the narrator <u>tells</u> the story as a condensed series of events, summarizing in a few sentences what happens over a longer period of time
scenic presentation	the narrator <u>shows</u> an event in detail as it occurs, using dialogue, depicting thoughts and emotions, describing a scene, etc.
narrating time	(= reading time) the time it takes to relate an episode in a text; it depends on the mode of presentation; *Erzählzeit*
narrator	person who tells the story (***not*** the author)
omniscient narrator	a narrator who seems to know everything (*allwissender/auktorialer Erzähler*)
point of view	the perspective from which the characters, topics and events are presented (***not*** the author's)
stream of consciousness	the presentation of experience through the mind of one character

characters/character traits			
active	aktiv, tatkräftig	dull	schwerfällig
adventurous	unternehmungsfreudig	easygoing	unbekümmert
affectionate	liebevoll, herzlich	energetic	kraftvoll
alert	munter, aufmerksam	faithful	treu
ambitious	ehrgeizig	fierce	kämpferisch
annoyed	unmutig, verärgert	gentle	leise, sanft, zart
apologetic	bedauernd	generous	großzügig
arrogant	arrogant	glamorous	glanzvoll, mondän
attentive	aufmerksam	gloomy	bedrückt
bold	kühn, gewagt	honest	ehrlich
bossy	rechthaberisch	ignorant	unwissend
brainy	gescheit	industrious	fleißig
calm	sanft	mature	reif
careless	leichtsinnig	mysterious	geheimnisvoll
cautious	zurückhaltend	obnoxious	unausstehlich
charming	entzückend	pleasant	angenehm
cheerful	fröhlich, heiter	reliable	zuverlässig
childish	kindisch, naiv	responsible	verantwortlich
clumsy	tollpatschig	secretive	geheimniskrämerisch
coarse	grob(schlächtig)	skilful	geschickt, gewandt
concerned	besorgt	sly	verschlagen
confident	selbstbewusst	sneaky	heimtückisch
courageous	mutig	(stereo-)typical	stereotyp
cowardly	feige	stubborn	stur
daring	kühn, wagemutig	thoughtful	rücksichtsvoll
decisive	entscheidungsfreudig	trustworthy	vertrauenswürdig
demanding	fordernd	weak	schwach
dependable	verlässlich	wicked	böse, verschlagen
determined	entschlossen	worried	besorgt

Acknowledgements

|Alamy Stock Photo, Abingdon/Oxfordshire: GL Portrait 167; Granger Historical Picture Archive 168; Lebrecht Music & Arts 171; Pictorial Press Ltd 186; The Print Collector 179; WENN Rights Ltd 181; World History Archive 178. |Alamy Stock Photo (RMB), Abingdon/Oxfordshire: Lebrecht Music & Arts 177. |Domke, Franz-Josef, Hannover: 168. |McKinsey & Company: Exhibit from "Global migration's impact and opportunity", November 2016, McKinsey & Company, www.mckinsey.com. Copyright © 2020 McKinsey & Company. All rights reserved. Reprinted by permission. 196. |Stuttmann, Klaus, Berlin: 193.

Wir arbeiten sehr sorgfältig daran, für alle verwendeten Abbildungen die Rechteinhaberinnen und Rechteinhaber zu ermitteln. Sollte uns dies im Einzelfall nicht vollständig gelungen sein, werden berechtigte Ansprüche selbstverständlich im Rahmen der üblichen Vereinbarungen abgegolten.